FAR AND AWAY

A PRIZE EVERY TIME

FAR AND AWAY

A PRIZE EVERY TIME

NEIL PEART

ECW Press

Published by ECW Press
2120 Queen Street East, Suite 200, Toronto, Ontario, Canada M4E 1E2
416-694-3348 / info@ecwpress.com

Library and Archives Canada Cataloguing in Publication

Peart, Neil
Far and away : a prize every time / Neil Peart.

ISBN 978-1-77041-058-9 (bound) — ISBN 978-1-77041-059-6 (pbk.)
Also issued as: 978-1-77090-020-2 (PDF); 978-1-77090-021-9 (EPUB)

1. Peart, Neil—Travel. 2. Motorcycling—North America.
3. Motorcycling—Europe. 4. Drummers (Musicians)—Canada—
Biography. 5. Lyricists—Canada—Biography. 6. Rush (Musical
group). I. Title.

ML419.362A3 2011   786.9'166092   C2011-900515-8

Cover design: Hugh Syme
Text design and typesetting: Tania Craan
Editor: Paul McCarthy
Editor for the press: Jennifer Knoch
Proofreader: Crissy Boylan
Producer: Jack David
Production: Troy Cunningham
Hardcover Printing: 2   3   4   5
Paperback Printing: 1   2   3   4   5

The publication of *Far and Away* has been generously supported by the
Canada Council for the Arts, which last year invested $20.1 million in
writing and publishing throughout Canada, by the Ontario Arts Council,
by the OMDC Book Fund, an initiative of the Ontario Media Development
Corporation, and by the Government of Canada through the Canada Book Fund.

PRINTED AND BOUND IN CANADA BY FRIESENS

To Olivia

Who makes my heart three sizes bigger

Table of Contents

INTRO: **A PRIZE EVERY TIME** ix

1 **THAT'S THE WAY WE ROLL** 1
JULY 2007

2 **EVERY ROAD HAS ITS TOLL** 9
AUGUST 2007

3 **SHUNPIKIN' IT OLD SKOOL** 20
SEPTEMBER 2007

4 **HASTE YE BACK** 28
NOVEMBER 2007

5 **THE HOUR OF ARRIVING** 41
DECEMBER 2007

6 **THE BEST FEBRUARY EVER** 52
MARCH 2008

7 **SOUTH BY SOUTHWEST** 61
MAY 2008

8 **WHEN THE ROAD ENDS** 73
JUNE 2008

9 **INDEPENDENCE DAY** 84
JULY 2008

10 **THE DRUMS OF OCTOBER** 97
NOVEMBER 2008

11 **DECEMBER IN DEATH VALLEY** 110
DECEMBER 2008

12 **A WINTER'S TALE OF SUMMERS PAST** 125
FEBRUARY 2009

13 **THE QUEST FOR THE PHANTOM TOWER** 139
MARCH 2009

14 **UNDER THE MARINE LAYER** 155
JUNE 2009

15 **A LITTLE YELLOW CABIN ON YELLOWSTONE LAKE** 168
AUGUST 2009

16 **THE BALLAD OF LARRY AND SUZY** 192
SEPTEMBER 2009

17 **AUTUMN SERENADE** 202
NOVEMBER 2009

18 **FIRE ON ICE** 212
FEBRUARY 2010

19 **TIME MACHINES** 227
MAY 2010

20 **THEME AND VARIATIONS** 238
AUGUST 2010

21 **CRUEL SUMMER** 252
SEPTEMBER 2010

22 **THE POWER OF MAGICAL THINKING** 272
NOVEMBER 2010

OUTRO: **THE PRIZE** 293

A PRIZE EVERY TIME

Once upon a time, around the nineteenth century, authors like Charles Dickens and Thomas Hardy serialized their novels in monthly magazines, and they were hugely popular. Another celebrated author of the time, Wilkie Collins (*The Woman in White*, *The Moonstone*), outlined the preferred design for audience response: "Make 'em cry, make 'em laugh, make 'em wait—exactly in that order." (Scheherazade may actually have pioneered the technique.)

In 1841, when the serialization of Dickens' *The Old Curiosity Shop* was nearing its tragic finale, New Yorkers were said to have lined up at the docks to ask arriving British sailors, "Is Little Nell dead?"

Oscar Wilde famously remarked, "One would have to have a heart of stone to read the death of Little Nell without dissolving into tears— of laughter." In that case, the order of events would be "Make 'em wait, make 'em cry, make 'em laugh." That works, too.

The old-time serialized novel occurred to me as one way to describe the nature of these stories—a serialized autobiography, perhaps, though not recollected in one's dusty old age, but captured

along the way. By design, these stories are not an attempt to list the facts and incidents of my life, like diary entries. My inspiration always comes from the world around me, driven by the recurring thought, "How can I put this into *words?*" I am more interested in describing what I do and see, how it makes me feel, and sharing it with the reader—almost like a personal letter, with more time spent on the craft. So it's a book of letters, and a serial memoir, and a travel book that includes motorcycling, drumming, snowshoeing, cross-country skiing, natural history, human history, birdwatching, hiking, driving, church signs, amateur philosophy, and . . . pretty much everything.

This collection of wide-ranging stories began more or less accidentally and did not follow old paths—of mine, or anyone else's. I made it up as I went along, not knowing where that road would lead.

The acorn began to sprout in 2005 with the creation of a website, at the urging of my tech-savvy friend and frequent riding partner, Michael Mosbach. I didn't have any idea what I was going to do with a website, but it seemed like the thing to do, and I could see *possibilities*, all right. However, I didn't know if I would be inspired by those possibilities—if I would want to write regular updates on what was going on in my life and work, for the uncertain interest of strangers.

One happy coincidence in the beginning was that Michael's research into claiming domain names found NeilPeart.net to be held by a gifted young multi-media artist ("Master of All Things Creative," he modestly proclaims), Greg Russell. Greg would become the site's designer and engineer, as well as a good friend, fellow motorcyclist, drummer, hiker, and artful conspirator. As the site grew over time, Greg's increasingly creative presentation of the stories, and the entire site, helped inspire me to raise my aim.

The first piece I wrote for the site, in early 2005, was tentative and insubstantial—promising nothing, and delivering little more. In an update for July of that year, I first used the title "News, Weather, and Sports," under which all subsequent stories would appear. I announced that I had finished the first draft of a book, *Roadshow*, and was about to start work on a new instructional DVD, *Anatomy of a Drum Solo*.

I ended the news with some jokes about weather and sports—

> Some guy took some performance-enhancing drugs and hit a triple into the end zone during the fourth quarter with a four under par, but was whistled down for interference.
> Then there was a fight.

The next installment did not appear until April 2006, but was a proper story this time, describing me hosting my bandmates at my house in Quebec, where we discussed the launch of a new project that would become our *Snakes and Arrows* album. Then followed a description of attending a jazz performance featuring eighty-one-year-old drummer Roy Haynes, and relaying the inspiration I felt from Roy and other great drummers.

Inspiration was taking root in the writing, too, along with its usual partner, ambition, and the next story arrived quicker, in June of that year. This one also aimed higher—describing the collaboration of working with my bandmates, and with my friend Matt Scannell, recording three songs for his band, Vertical Horizon. A passage on Canadian hockey foreshadowed the events recounted in "Fire on Ice," three years later.

That June 2006 "News, Weather, and Sports" story also featured the first use of photographs—a device that was to grow into a major feature in these stories. (It's noteworthy that only the previous year, while writing *Roadshow*, a book about a concert tour, I had deliberately avoided using any photographs, aspiring to capture the experience in words alone.)

A few more stories that year crystallized the approach—photos were used as illustrations, but also as narrative touchstones, to introduce episodes, conclude them, move the story along, or change direction entirely.

By 2007, I was more committed to getting those photographs, assisted early on by a friend, Rick Foster, who rode with Michael and me that summer. Rick captured the first images of Michael and me riding together—the perfect complement to the next story, "That's the Way We Roll," which introduces this collection. Late in 2006, the stories had finally gained titles, like "At the Gate of the Year" and "The Count of Words," but it wasn't until "That's the Way We Roll," after two years of experimentation, that I arrived at the template I would follow from then on. The combination of words and photographs was similar to a magazine story, perhaps, but the photos were chosen by the writer to be *part of the story*, and the scope was unfettered by any limitations of space or time.

Publishing online was so *immediate*—I could spend the time to make a story just how I wanted it to be, then Greg would post it within days, sometimes *hours*. A book could take a year or more to emerge in print, and I had always been way too impatient for that.

With the aim of getting closer to "just how I wanted it to be," I began submitting the stories to my esteemed prose editor, Paul McCarthy, with whom I had worked exclusively since 2001, starting with *Ghost Rider*. Paul also brought his "critical enthusiasm" to help guide and improve the increasingly ambitious book reviews that appeared in another department on the site, "Bubba's Book Club." (I remarked to my friend Brutus recently, as I set to work on an overdue issue for the Book Club, "It's the hardest kind of writing there is— 'being smart about books.'")

Along the way, I was heartened to learn of an online art movement called Slow Blogging. Inspired by the Slow Food artisans who rebelled against fast food, Slow Bloggers spent time crafting their words or images before displaying them in front of all the online world. That was how I had been approaching the "News, Weather, and Sports" stories: truly as a labor of love, along with the book reviews in Bubba's Book Club, and a food department Brutus and I "cooked up" for the site, "Bubba's Bar 'n' Grill"—a beginner's guide to cooking "Good Simple Food." (We hope to see that in print one day, too.)

When selecting the shape of this collection, I decided to leave out the early, experimental work and start with "That's the Way We Roll"— the one that established the pattern all the others would follow.

In Ernest Hemingway's introduction to a collection of his short stories, he mentioned a few of them that he particularly liked, then admitted there were others, too: "Because if you did not like them you would not publish them."

Exactly.

"That's the Way We Roll" (the title being both comment and segue, in this case) begins in the summer of 2007, on the road with the band on the *Snakes and Arrows* tour, which also provided the next two stories. There was a winter sojourn in Quebec, "The Best February Ever," with cross-country skiing and snowshoeing described and depicted— employing a photographic innovation called the "Ski-Cam™," giving the viewer more of a skier's-eye view.

Around that time I added the subtitle "Tales from the Trails" to supplement the "News, Weather, and Sports" title for the story department. The May 2008 edition, "South by Southwest," continued the *Snakes and Arrows* tour into that summer, and the photography was becoming more ambitious. I made myself pause to capture the scenic beauty of my two-wheeled travels on American roads, and coached Michael in framing portraits of me motorcycling through the Big Bend country of Texas, or the Everglades, so I could use them in upcoming stories. (I take many photos of Michael riding, but it's clear that having a photograph of me in the middle of the landscape I'm describing makes a more powerful statement. See Greg's photo on this book's cover, for example—it wouldn't be the same if it wasn't of *me*.)

I refined another new technique I called the "Action Self-Portrait," in which I motorcycled along a straight, empty road and held the camera out beside me in my left hand, to frame my helmeted head in front of the passing landscape. (Don't try that at home, kids.) There were many failures, but occasionally I got lucky and captured the kinetic moment I wanted to describe.

From then until the November 2010 story that ends this collection, "The Power of Magical Thinking," I continued writing about . . . what I could not help writing about, really. Many times the writing itself was a welcome relief from month-long runs of a concert tour, a chance to sit in one place, reflect, and craft something *peacefully*—without the violence and sweat of drumming. And while I rode the back roads of North America, Europe, or South America, I would be thinking about what I wanted to write—what I wanted to try to share with others.

Seeing the stories posted so artfully by Greg, illuminated on the backlit screen, and knowing there were tens of thousands of people reading them (in November 2010, we attracted a new record of 63,000 visitors) truly made for "a prize every time."

That phrase dates from my teenage years, a couple of summers working on a carnival midway ("Lakeside Park," for the Rush archivists). The first year, at about age fourteen, I stood under the raised flaps of the Bubble Game kiosk all day and called out, "Catch a bubble—prize every time!" In 2007, for the essay to introduce our *Snakes and Arrows* album, I recollected that phrase and used it to describe making music, listening to music, or playing the game of life—"a prize every time." Now that description seems to embrace the making of these stories—and an attitude toward life, too.

As a lyricist and prose writer, it is a rare thrill when I produce a line that not only endures, but continues to gather resonance over time. One example I often cite is from our song "Presto," from 1989— a line that each year seems to pulse with more depth and truth: "What a fool I used to be."

(Oh, man.)

Likewise, I believe these stories continue to celebrate the refrain of "A Prize Every Time." No matter where I travel, or what I choose to write about, there is the joy of doing, and the joy of sharing.

In the foreword to the story collection mentioned earlier, Hemingway described some places that had been good for writing, like Madrid, Paris, or Havana, but added, "Some other places were not so good but maybe we were not so good when we were in them."

I know that feeling, too. Many good places are described in these stories, carrying this happy traveler over mountain roads, desert highways, and snowy trails to fine meals and cozy accommodations. Other days and nights were not so good, but maybe I was not so good when I was in them.

Still, there was a prize every time . . .

THAT'S THE
WAY WE ROLL

With only a few days at home after the first leg of the *Snakes and Arrows* tour (sixteen shows, 7,257 miles of motorcycling), this will definitely be the "short version." Still, I wanted to try to put up *something* new.

Photographs of the performances are plentifully available elsewhere (my view of the audience this tour is studded with innumerable cell-phone cameras, sticking up like periscopes), so I thought I might just display a couple of motorcycling photos. On this tour Michael and I haven't even carried cameras with us on the bikes, let alone bothered to ease our steady pace to take photos, but recently we had a camera-happy "guest rider," Richard S. Foster. The name might ring a bell to dedicated readers of album credits—our song "Red Barchetta" had a note on the lyric sheet: "Inspired by 'A Nice Morning Drive' by Richard S. Foster."

Rick (as he is known to his friends, among whom I now number myself) tells our long story in another forum, and it's quite an amazing sequence of coincidences and synchronicities. (See photo credits for details.)

The short version (I keep saying that) is that despite my attempts back in 1980 to contact the author of the short story that had inspired "Red Barchetta"—a story I had read in a 1973 issue of *Road & Track*—we only recently managed to actually make contact.

Rick rode with Michael and me through the back roads (the very back roads) of West Virginia for a couple of days between shows in near-D.C. and near-Pittsburgh (so many of those amphitheaters are in the exurbs), and then he attended his first Rush concert in (or *near*) Boston.

But that's his story, and I'll leave it to him to tell. Michael only left Rick with one request, from the movie *Almost Famous*, when the singer says to the young journalist, "Just make us look cool."

(How well Rick succeeded with that challenge, the reader may judge by his story.)

For Michael and me, it was great just to have some photographs of us riding—something we do every day, after all, so it is nice to have it documented like that. After last tour, when I was constantly so intent on note-gathering for the book that became *Roadshow*, this time I have been feeling a real sense of freedom—the freedom of not having to document anything. I can simply experience it, think about it or not, and let the day flow by me as it will.

That being said, so far this tour has certainly been worthy of a book, too, in its way. I kind of wish someone else was writing one about it, but I don't think it will be me. My journal notes consist only of our daily mileages—though I couldn't resist noting a couple of church signs: "GIVE SATAN AN INCH, SOON HE'LL BE A RULER," and one I just love: "TO ERR IS HUMAN, BUT IT CAN BE OVERDONE." So good. And I admire it not only for the worthy sentiment, but for the perfect phrasing, too.

Another church sign caught my eye because of the word "faithless," as in our song on *Snakes and Arrows*. This one seemed kind of mean, though: "AND JESUS REPLIED, SAYING, 'YOU ARE A FAITHLESS AND PERVERSE GENERATION.'"

I assured Michael that he was the only one of us who was *both*.

Also, we now know that "VBS" stands for "Vacation Bible School," as the back roads and small towns of America are full of signs for that exciting-sounding activity. We were once bemused at passing a yellow school bus full of kids, the side of the bus displaying a banner reading

"Soccer With Jesus." (What position do you suppose the Son of God would play? He'd have to be the coach, I suppose. And would that make Mary, the Mother of God, a soccer mom?)

(And if that's sacrilegious, it's certainly not more so than the banner on that bus.)

One Sunday morning in southern Pennsylvania, Michael commented on the Amish carriages we had been passing, with the little boys in their blue shirts and straw hats waving shyly at us from the back. Michael said he wanted to "save" those kids—by buying each of them a BMW R1200GS motorcycle.

Different prophets have different ideas about saving others—but I guess even "motorcycling with Michael" might be more fun than "soccer with Jesus."

But let's talk about the weather.

"Weather-wise, it's such a lovely day" would be an appropriate line from Big Frank's "Come Fly With Me," as Michael and I have had fairly unbelievable weather on our travels up the East Coast. It was often very hot, mostly in the 90s, but—even in an armored leather suit, boots, gloves, and full-face helmet—you adapt to that, basically by facing the fact that "it's hot," and carrying on. It's the same onstage, where I was also often working in very hot conditions—you just play the song, wipe away the sweat, drink some water, and carry on.

In all those thousands of miles, and dozens of days, Michael and I had exactly *one* day of rain—on a country-road ramble from Tupper Lake, New York, to a show near Buffalo. Riding in the rain is not bad when you're not in traffic and you're not in a hurry. You can relax into a smooth, cautious pace (though Michael thinks I ride too fast in the rain—but I think he rides too fast in freeway traffic). I enjoyed those damp, quiet roads through the Adirondacks and the farming country of Western New York.

We often saw deer in our travels around the East, and once a black bear cub in the Delaware Water Gap area of Pennsylvania—and I almost forgot the *huge* alligator we encountered on a flooded dirt road through the Everglades. Later we agreed it had stretched the entire width of the single-lane road, so maybe twelve feet long, and so thick it looked as though it had swallowed a cow. As I had experienced in Africa before, it's always a thrill seeing animals in the wild, but quite a different experience getting close to wildlife that can *eat* you.

However, early that morning in the Adirondacks, we saw something even rarer than deer, bear, or alligator—an animal called a fisher, a large, dark member of the weasel family, darting across the road ahead of us.

The Smithsonian website offers an enlightening entry about the fisher. (I'm a member, so presume I'm allowed to use it.)

(A warning to the squeamish, who might want to skip this paragraph—the fisher is a pretty badass little beast, ripping the faces off porcupines and such.)

Fisher *Martes pennanti*
Order: *Carnivora*
Family: *Mustelidae*

The fisher is a forest-loving predator that eats anything it can catch, usually small-to-medium-sized rodents, rabbits, hares, and birds. It also eats carrion. Fishers are among the few predators able to kill porcupines. They do it by biting the face, where there are no quills, until the animal is too weak to prevent being rolled over and attacked in the soft underbelly. Fishers are active by day or night. They tend to be solitary and defend territories. They were once hunted for their lustrous, chocolate-brown fur, and the range of this species has been reduced greatly in the United States. They are still hunted in some places, but some states and provinces of Canada list the fisher as endangered, and the population has recovered from extreme lows in the last century.

Also known as: Pekan, Fisher Cat, Black Cat, Wejack, American Sable

I have written before that every tour's itinerary varies greatly, and how on previous tours I have found myself riding often through, say, Virginia, and falling in love with it. So far this tour's East Coast revelation has been Pennsylvania, where I have enjoyed riding before, but never had so much of either riding or enjoyment as this tour's itinerary occasioned.

From the Delaware to the Susquehanna to the Three Rivers, the long-ridged mountains and dense woodlands, the old mining and factory towns, and the fantastically beautiful farms of Lancaster County, all have been delightful when seen from the little gray roads (as they are depicted on the Rand McNally maps). Our GPS units have evolved since those I wrote about in *Roadshow*, and though still called Doofus II and Dingus II, I must say they have learned a lot since the *R30* tour. (We sent them to VBS.)

Despite my usual apprehension before embarking on another long concert tour, I have been enjoying this one so far. (Don't tell our manager, Ray—he'll immediately start pitching more shows to me!) Each show is a little shorter this time and doesn't drain me quite so much, so I have a little energy left over to enjoy life offstage. We're also having a few more days off this time, because Geddy found that last tour's schedule, where we often had pairs of shows with a single day off between them, was too hard on his voice. So we're playing fewer shows per week, and though they remain tiring, of course, they're not quite so *draining*. So that's all good.

Here's an excerpt from today's letter to my friend Mendelson Joe:

> I'm home for a few days after the first run of sixteen shows, and about 7,000 miles of motorcycling, and have enjoyed both somewhat more than I expected. The band is playing really well; I like the selection of songs we're playing, and I feel good about my drumming lately. I seem to have reached a new "plateau" that I don't even understand yet. I guess it started with the making of *Snakes and Arrows*, and the inevitable experimenting that goes on during that process, but there's also been an apparent growth in live performance this time—in my timekeeping, my time *sense*, and even in my technique. Call it maturity.
>
> I don't like to analyze it too much, but I'm glad it is so. I listened to

a recording of one of our shows last week, and was pleased to note that I was playing as well as I *thought* I was playing, if you know what I mean. Not *perfect*, you understand, but certainly better than ever. Listening to that show, with almost three hours of music and so many songs, there was only *one* song that I wanted to pull back the tempo on—and that just a little.

Otherwise, at age fifty-four, it's great to feel that I have all the speed, stamina, and power that I ever had, if not more, and at the same time have matured musically in all the ways I would have *wanted* to ten or twenty years ago—better tempo control, and a richer feel that is deeply rooted to the bass drum, and that is always the foundation for the show-off "pyrotechnics," rather than the other way around.

It is also interesting that after making the instructional DVD on drum soloing after the last tour, where I talked so much about how I go about *composing* a solo, and having written recently in other places that as a drummer I considered myself more of a composer than an improviser—I decided to start improvising.

It's like I had finally resigned myself to a personal limitation, then told it to **** off!

Nothing wrong with that, obviously. So this tour the first half of my solo is improvised over a simple foundation of single bass-drum beats and alternating high-hat clicks, as I experiment widely over it every night. It's been taking me some interesting places, while still giving me the consistency of the orchestrated second half, so I know the customers will always be properly satisfied.

I've also been exploring new territory on the bike. GPS has evolved a lot in the past few years, and even though riding partner Michael and I still call our units Doofus and Dingus, I must say I'm much more inclined to *trust* the thing now. On the day before a ride, I look over the maps of the area of the upcoming jobsite, and highlight a route along the smallest roads on the Rand McNally maps. Then Michael puts them in the computer and downloads them to Doofus and Dingus. The next day we simply follow their instructions, clearly (usually) and accurately (usually) displayed in front of us.

In that way, we have been able to ride on roads that I'm sure no one but locals have ever traveled, sometimes one-lane paved or un-paved roads through deep forest. Much more fun to putter along those, past woodlands and occasional farms, than the busier roads, of course. It can even be *relaxing*, in a way that riding in traffic can never be.

Finally, here's another photo of Michael and me on a little one-lane West Virginia road—this one paved.

Our next big ride will carry us through Montana, Idaho, and Washington state, as our western swing begins in Calgary and proceeds to Seattle. I will try to report on that wonderful part of the country next time.

Meanwhile, those of you attending the shows, enjoy them, and those of you riding motorcycles, remember something I learned from bicycling, and try to keep reminding myself, "YOU ARE INVISIBLE."

My new motto (so new I just made it up), "Be as safe as you can while still having fun."

That is deep advice, and, as number-one soul brother Michael likes to say, snapping his middle fingers, "That's the way we *roll*."

EVERY ROAD HAS ITS TOLL

Standing backstage while the opening movie played the other night, poised to run on, sticks in hand, ear-monitors in, I found myself excited by two thoughts. I was idly pondering how I might start my solo that night (since I have been improvising the first part of it this tour, I always try to open with a different figure straight off), and I also felt an unaccustomed eagerness—a curiosity to get out there to *see* the audience.

Not to *hear* the audience, note—not to bask in their cheers and appreciation—but just to look at them. Their number, their faces, their reactions, their dances, their T-shirts, the signs they hold up. Even while I'm supposed to be up there entertaining people, they can be so entertaining for me.

Occasionally signs are scattered among the crowd, like two I saw in the audience at Red Rocks: one quite far back on the stage-right side read, "IF I LOVED A WOMAN LIKE I LOVE THIS BAND, I'D STILL BE MARRIED!" Near the front, on the stage-left side, was another, "I SUPPORT MY HUSBAND'S RUSH ADDICTION!" Two very different stories there, obviously.

One night in Texas I saw a truly great sign from far back in the house, "VBS FIELD TRIP." It was a sly reference to a joke in my previous story on this site (glad to know some people get my lame jokes!). At intermission, Michael and I laughed about that one, and its maker was unanimously declared the night's lucky winner of a pair of drumsticks. That doesn't happen every night, you understand—let's not make this some kind of *competition*—but some nights, a sign or a T-shirt slogan makes me smile, or I see a cute little kid, or sometimes recognize a familiar face from many shows, and send them out a pair of sticks.

One night on the first run I was won over by a professional-looking sign along the barricade that read, "MY 60TH SHOW AND STILL NO DRUMSTICKS. I'M JUST SAYING . . ."

The phrasing alone was irresistible, and Geddy said later that if I hadn't sent the guy out a pair of sticks, he was going to ask his tech, Russ, to get some from Gump and send them out.

One offer, "WILL TRADE MACALLAN FOR 747S" seemed promising, but I doubted anyone had managed to bring a bottle of whisky into the venue. Following our plan, Michael took a pair of sticks out, but asked for the Macallan first. When the guy said he hadn't been able to bring it in, but it was in his car, Michael pretended to turn away—then gave him the sticks.

A few of the signs with requests are inspired in some such fashion, but a scrap of paper scrawled with "STICK?" does not impress so much (though, to be fair, I do appreciate *any* amount of trouble people go to), nor the one I saw the other night, "SPARE STYX?"

At intermission, I told Michael about it, and asked if maybe we could send the sign-holder Michael's beloved 8-track of *The Grand Illusion*. He said no, because all those childhood favorites were on his iPod now.

Ba-da-boom.

But seriously, folks . . . I can report that the *Snakes and Arrows* tour continues to go pretty well. The audiences have been wonderfully large and unbelievably appreciative (adjectives interchangeable), and the shows themselves have been going smoothly for us and our crew.

But . . . just now counting up what we've done, and what we still have to do, I must admit to feeling a little apprehension at the realization that we are only now at the halfway point of the tour. We've done thirty-two shows, and have exactly that many to go. It seems a lot—in both directions.

Getting to those first thirty-two shows, Michael and I have already ridden 13,211 motorcycles miles. At that rate, we'll likely top last tour's total of 21,000—especially by the time Brutus comes into the picture, in Europe, with his mad route-planning. (Though whether he and I will be able to ride to the last few shows, Oslo, Stockholm, and Helsinki, in late October, will depend on a selfish good fortune with climate change. We ought to increase our carbon footprint right away. Maybe by riding faster . . .)

I spent a lot of time and energy on the R30 tour in 2004 taking notes, mental and written, trying to record each day's events, then researching and writing about it so copiously. Thus, this time I have been powerfully aware of how different this tour is from that one—as they all are from each other, I realize. No two tours are alike, just as no two shows are alike—and certainly no two audiences. In each case, there are many similarities, but so many variables and daily occurrences remain unique.

After all the ink I spilled about "magic shows" in *Roadshow*, it is strange to report that this tour has been different in that way, too. I don't think there have been any particularly "magic" shows, in my estimation—though they've all been pretty satisfying in their own ways. My best theory is that each of this tour's shows has been performed at a slightly higher level than ever before, and thus they've all had their bit of magic.

The explanation for that may be partly due to how well prepared we were—how much rehearsing we did before the tour—and to a pleasing variety of songs in the two sets, but it does seem that we have all reached a certain plateau of consistency and competency that is really shining on this tour. As I wrote about my own playing in that context, "Call it maturity."

Many friends have commented to me how well Geddy is singing, and it's true—I've listened to a few recorded shows on days off, and his voice sounds unbelievably good. (It's a simple stark fact illuminating the importance of that voice that if *he* couldn't do it anymore, *we* couldn't do it anymore.) Plus, as I said to Geddy after listening to one of the shows, "You're not just *performing*—you're really *singing out*."

Still, performing at that level takes its toll on Geddy, for he has to treat his voice with such care, even avoiding *talking* on days off, and warming it up methodically before a show. Likewise, performing at that level, and for so *long* (both in the number of hours in the show, and the number of years we've been doing it), takes its toll on us all. The other night Alex was telling me that even the knuckles on his fretting hand were sore after two shows in a row.

The drumming part of my touring life is certainly athletic, though few athletes are expected to surpass their peak at fifty-four years of age. I sure don't take it for granted that I have felt able to do that—I'm very gratified. But . . . it takes its toll.

Taking into consideration that Michael's and my motorcycle rides between shows *average* about 275 miles a day, I actually spend far more time in the saddle than I do on the drum throne. That takes its toll, too—in the sore spots that Michael and I call "saddle tats"; in the tired mind from making a million decisions about traffic and road surfaces as you ride hour after hour; and in a body beaten by wind, vibration, and the physical activity of motorcycling, especially in the mountains, with so much braking, shifting, accelerating, and moving your body on the bike for more effective cornering.

Then there was the heat—in the 100s for many days, especially in the Southwest. Desert heat is one thing, but when the humidity is also high, as in South Texas, and you're wearing the armored suit, helmet, gloves, and boots, you get to feel like you're covered in a coat of slime, riding past a small-town bank clock showing 105°.

We have seen some fantastically scenic parts of the country, though. This western swing carried us through the Rockies, the Cascades, the Sierra Nevada, Northern and Southern California, the Great Basin, a broad swath of northern Arizona, across Colorado (or "Cop-orado," as I have christened the state, for its overzealous enforcement of artificially low speed limits), and some of Texas's prettiest landscapes, the Hill Country and Gulf Coast.

Michael and I spent a very enjoyable couple of days crossing the wonderfully wide-open spaces of Nevada. We sped down long, straight stretches of empty road, both paved and dirt, across the Great Basin of sage, juniper, stunted pines, and occasional twisty bits through the mountains—classic basin and range country. In South Texas we saw the ravages of the flooding from earlier this summer, with scoured riverbeds and rebuilt bridges and runoff areas that had been swept away.

(I am glad to report that rural Texas continues to boast the most courteous drivers in the country, perhaps the world. When you come up behind a pickup or sedan on a two-lane backroad, they not only move over willingly, right onto the shoulder, but wave you by cheerfully.)

We had a few more guest riders on the West Coast run, too, sometimes filling in for Michael when other duties called him away. John Wesley rode through Northern California with me, all the way down to the Hollywood Bowl (sorry about the ticket, Wes—and the hellish traffic around Lake Tahoe); Greg Russell (designer of my website, maker of *Swingin' Serpents*, a film that goes behind this tour's drum solo, and, in general, self-described "Master of All Things Creative") rode with Michael and me from Yuma, Arizona, up to old Route 66 and a classic motel in Seligman, Arizona.

Seligman clings to a tenuous existence on the tourist trade that haunts that old road, but there are so many small towns across America that are still dying—not so much because of being bypassed by interstates these days, as the old Route 66 towns were, but because of being bypassed by *people*. The decline of these small towns, sadly, is measured in the death of dreams—every time I see a shuttered restaurant, a boarded-up gas station, or an abandoned Main Street store, I imagine it is someone's dream that failed. Someone who always dreamed of having their own restaurant, their own gas station, their own little shop. Thus it always feels good to stop at a small-town diner, or stay at a Mom-and-Pop motel. Keep those dreams alive.

Leaving Seligman on our way to the next show in Phoenix, I had planned a route through the pine forests southeast of Flagstaff, on some red dirt back roads to Mormon Lake, then two-lane highways bracketed in woods that swung down through Payson, Pine, and Strawberry.

I had ridden and enjoyed those roads a few times before, but this time I added one new detour—to Roosevelt Dam. Having long been fascinated by the great waterworks of the West, I had visited many of the biggest ones, like Hoover, Grand Coulee, and Bonneville, so I thought I'd like to see the one that was built 100 years ago to feed Phoenix's growth, damming the Salt River for power and irrigation.

The temperature climbed all day, as we descended in elevation toward Phoenix, and the Tonto National Forest gave way to the rugged Superstition Mountains, folds of igneous rock lightly flecked in cactus desert. The blue expanse of the reservoir, Theodore Roosevelt Lake, looked cool and inviting. The bridge over it—apparently the longest

two-lane, single-span, steel-arch bridge in North America—echoed the attractive arc of the world's largest masonry dam (originally made of bricks, then later expanded with concrete).

Taking in all of that world-class "largestness," we rode on, passing a sign informing us that the next twenty-eight miles of the Apache Trail were unpaved. The narrow gravel road twisted along the canyon of the winding Salt River, past cactus and desert shrubs clinging to the carved banks of rock, shimmering in the heat.

Michael, Greg, and I had some thrills scrambling in the dirt, then the pavement began for another twenty miles, still with very few other vehicles, and still winding as it led downriver to Apache Junction. The pavement was nicely banked, the tight curves taken in second gear and sometimes first, and altogether it was about my favorite kind of riding, technical, engaging, and exciting, at a slow enough speed that I dared to lean *way* over, and use all of those tires. The Apache Trail definitely ranks in my handful of favorite roads so far this tour.

(Among the other candidates would be a couple of nameless tracks in West Virginia; Highway 129 in North Carolina, on the way to Deals Gap; a series of Washington state back roads from the Columbia River Valley to the Cascades; and the Sherman Pass in California, crossing the Sierras on the way to one of my favorite overnights, at Mono Lake.)

After the Phoenix show, Greg rode with us on the bus to a truck stop in Kingman, and next morning we set out for the MGM Grand in

Vegas (where it was fiercely hot, 107°F, but still nothing like as uncomfortable as that South Texas swelter). Once again, I had planned an adventurous detour, on a dirt road ending at a remote shore of Lake Mead.

Brian Catterson, editor-in-chief of *Motorcyclist* magazine, accompanied me across "Cop-orado." After the Salt Lake City show, we slept on the bus at a rest stop in Wyoming, then rode down the east side of Flaming Gorge. I had ridden the west side a couple of times, but Brian's brother Paul had recommended this route, and it proved to be a terrific series of linked, high-speed sweepers among majestic scenery.

Later that day, in the rangeland of western Colorado, Brian and I were caught in a violent thunderstorm. Lightning slashed down ahead to our right and left, and heavy rain was driven by crosswinds that swept spray across the road like . . . spindrift. Marble-sized hail began pelting us, painful even through our armored suits, and about then I considered it the worst storm I had ever ridden through. But in that remote, treeless area, there was nowhere to take shelter, and nowhere to go back to. I was leading at the time, and felt responsible for us both, but I could think of nothing better to do than slow down and keep moving. Like the Winston Churchill quote, "When you're going through hell, keep going."

I was relieved to learn later that Brian had the same instinct, under the circumstances. Slow down, keep riding, and hope our "angels" were on duty. Still, we both knew that lightning had the lethal potential to "charge" a heavy toll to a motorcyclist. Later we talked about the rider who had been killed by lightning on a *Cycle World* tour while Brian worked there, and I was pleased to hear what Brian told me the guy's widow had said, "If he was struck by lightning when he was riding his motorcycle, it was his *time*."

That's easier to take than the cliché, "Well, at least he died doing what he loved." Think about it: that's the *last* time anyone wants to die—when they're doing something they love!

After an overnight in the ski-boom town of Steamboat Springs (construction everywhere, but great restaurants), Brian and I joined the incredibly scenic (but painfully slow) parade through Rocky Mountain National Park. (This tour I have been pleased to add two new national park passport stamps to my collection, that one and Great Basin National Park in Nevada—hard to get to, but well worth a longer visit sometime.) Then we headed south on gently winding mountain roads that would have been posted at fifty-five mph in other states, but were "mysteriously" pegged at forty around there. Perhaps it had nothing to do with entrapment or revenue generating, but I also couldn't help noticing that my radar detector was blipping in my ear every few minutes, as patrol cars rode the range or hid in the trees.

Brian and I made it to Red Rocks unmolested by predatory patrol cars, but by the time Michael met us on his bike at the gate and led us into that fabulous venue, my nerves were even more on edge. Michael had traveled to Denver early to arrange for extra security for me there, because a schizophrenic "fan" was making insane accusations and threatening me with violent consequences.

Just another day at the office . . .

This issue's "Sports" report would also have to include deer hunting. Not intentional, alas, but an unfortunate encounter on a Texas road ended badly for a deer—and could so easily have ended badly for me. After sleeping on the bus in a truck stop in Junction, Texas, Michael and I set out early one Sunday morning through an area of the southern Hill Country I'd never explored. It began wonderfully, on a narrow, curving roller coaster of a road walled by low, thick forests of Texas live-oak trees and high limestone banks. In their shade, while the sun was still low, the hazy morning felt relatively cool (though it was indeed relative—the temperatures were already climbing from the upper 80s toward the 100s. But it was shady, and that is rare enough in the Desert Southwest).

Apparently the Hill Country has the highest concentration of whitetail deer in the United States, and they were certainly plentiful that morning, grazing among the dense trees, bounding across the road, or just standing in the middle of it. So we kept our speed down. Only last year, motorcycle journalist Lawrence Grodsky, who wrote a column for *Rider* magazine called "Stayin' Safe," from which I learned a lot in my early years of riding, was killed by hitting a deer just west of where we were, near Fort Stockton.

Grodsky's girlfriend was quoted in an obituary in his hometown newspaper, the Pittsburgh *Post-Gazette*:

"Larry was the most talented, experienced and competent motorcyclist in the country, but this is the one thing he knew he couldn't do anything about," said his girlfriend, Maryann Puglisi, with whom he lived in Squirrel Hill and Washington, D.C., and who helped run his business. "Just a few weeks ago he said to me, 'That's how I'm going to go, it's going to be a deer.' He could deal with all the idiot drivers, but at night when a deer jumps in your path, that's it and he knew that."

So that was in my mind, too, and thankfully I was only going about 40 mph when a blur of brown dashed right in front of me, so sudden that my first sight of the deer was when my front wheel hit it squarely. The handlebar wobbled between my hands and the adrenaline began to surge, as time seemed to hang suspended. The small deer was shunted aside, and I rode on for a few seconds, still taking in what had just happened—and already marveling that I was still upright.

I looked in my mirrors and saw Michael turn around. Riding behind me, he had seen me hit the deer, felt the start of fear you always get for your riding partner, then saw that I was still riding. He passed the deer where it lay twisted on the road, flailing its legs, its back obviously broken. He knew what he had to do.

I pulled up behind where he'd parked his bike, right on the road (we hadn't seen a car for many miles). I'll never forget the sight of Michael standing in the middle of the road in his riding suit, helmet flipped up, taking out his .40-caliber Glock 23, holding it in both hands and taking careful aim. I heard the sharp report even through my earplugs and saw the poor mangled deer give one final jerk. Michael took hold of its legs and dragged it into the bushes beside the road.

Everything was quiet for an awful moment. Michael walked back to his bike and said, "That's what I was always taught to do—stop its suffering." I nodded agreement.

Then Michael said, "I was looking for some confirmation that I did the right thing."

"No question," I nodded, "you did the right thing."

But it was still bad. I had the raw, dreadful sensation of having maimed a pretty little creature, caused it to suffer, and the sharp, equally dreadful awareness of having narrowly escaped death myself. Michael had the weight of having taken a life, however compassionately.

As the day went on, carrying us into the hot, flat rangeland of South Texas, we found ways to talk about it, at roadside breaks and over our evening whiskies. But like typical humans (or *my* kind of typical humans), we defused those heavy feelings with humor—humor so black and horrible we had to laugh. Because that's what you have to do.

Standing at the roadside, where we had taken refuge in the shade of a tall cottonwood outside a rancher's gate, Michael made a big-eyed, pouty face, spread his hands above his helmet for antlers, and squeaked, "Why? *Why* did you have to kill me?"

I feigned outrage, "Hey man—*you're* the one who killed Bambi, with your big gay gun. I'm pretty sure that deer was going to be all right." I brought my palms together, "I was *praying* for it."

"Look!" he squeaked, in his falsetto Bambi voice, spreading his arms wide, "Look around me. Here are the ghosts of *all* the little baby deer I was going to have—before you *killed* me."

It had been a young doe, all right, but certainly not pregnant in that season.

I gave my helmet a dramatic toss, "You *monster*! You horrible monster Bambi killer! I shall never speak to you again!"

But Michael got in the kicker the next day, on our way from an overnight at the Padre Island Holiday Inn to the show in Houston. We stopped at a shady roadside junction for a Red Apple break. (A *Roadshow* reader in our audience recently gave Michael an official Red Apple cigarette case, which must have been a promo item from a Quentin Tarantino film—he was thrilled.) When we were done smoking and had broken off the filters and put them in our pockets ("Don't Mess With Texas" is the Lone Star State's anti-littering slogan, but we don't leave our "scooter trash" anywhere), we got ready to ride on, sorting out earplugs, helmets, and gloves.

From my tankbag I pulled out a Ziploc bag containing the "bug rag," a damp washcloth for cleaning the helmet face shields. (Brutus invented that idea, and soon learned that you have to wash and dry that cloth at the end of every day—I take it in the shower with me—or it gets all stinky.) I wiped the insect splatter off my face shield and dried it with the yellow microfiber cloth. (I used to have a purple bandana for that, but it blew out of an open tankbag somewhere in Florida.) I passed them over to Michael, and he cleaned off his own shield, then as he went to pass back the cloths, he dropped the microfiber one on the dusty ground.

"*D'oh!*" he said, Homer Simpson style.

Then, a beat later, he added, "I bet that's what *you* said when you hit that deer! *Doe!*"

I don't mind confessing that by the time I got that *awful* pun, we were miles down the road, riding in fast formation toward the next little town, where we hoped to find a diner for breakfast. I would have to smack him for it then.

Deerslayer.

SHUNPIKIN' IT OLD SKOOL

SEPTEMBER 2007

That phrase appears on the back of a T-shirt Michael and I are designing for our two-man "biker gang," the West Side Beemer Boyz, to share among our coworkers on the *Snakes and Arrows* tour. I had run across the term "shunpiking" in car and motorcycle magazines a few times and thought it was fairly well known, but apparently many people are unfamiliar with the concept.

It goes back about 500 years, to a time when British roads were lawless, especially at night, prowled by highwaymen and footpads. Villages blockaded their entry roads with a long pole—a pike—stretched across them. Around the same time, toll roads were invented, and a similar pike blocked the way until travelers paid their fee, when the pike would be turned—hence "turnpike."

In those days, travelers who deliberately avoided toll roads called themselves "shunpikers." Lately, the term has been adopted by drivers and riders who deliberately avoid *all* major roads. On the *Snakes and Arrows* tour, as Michael and I have commuted to forty-nine shows and covered just under 20,000 motorcycle miles around the U.S. and Canada, we have become *major* shunpikers.

One night on the bus after a show, while Dave drove us to yet another truck-stop dropoff point, Michael and I were talking about our recent travels. We agreed that less than ten percent of those 20,000 miles had been traveled on interstates and freeways—or divided four-lanes or major secondaries, for that matter. (I dislike those the most; they are slow, congested, and unpretty.) Nearly all of those miles had been traveled on the smallest roads, through the smallest settlements.

Because we ride BMW GS bikes, the so-called adventure touring model, we feel obliged to ride some unpaved roads pretty much every day, just on principle. Given the present sophistication and adaptability of our GPS systems on the bikes, and our growing skill in using them, I have been tracing out routes over the very thinnest lines on the Rand McNally maps. In the afternoon before soundcheck, I spread the next day's state, or states, across the floor of the bus's front lounge and highlight a route.

In between Michael's errands on his security duties, and getting the bikes loaded and tied down in the trailer, he sits on the floor in front of his computer and traces my zigzags onto the software maps, then downloads the route to our bike-mounted units, Doofus II and Dingus II (who, as previously noted, are much smarter than their predecessors, but still occasionally earn their nicknames).

Like here. It looks like the Amazon rainforest, but it was a "road" in West Virginia—a road, it must be noted, that was indicated on the Rand McNally map, and on the GPS software.

We were somewhere near a dot on the map with the unlikely name of Volcano, West Virginia. After several miles of graded gravel through deep woods and occasional subsistence farms, the road had narrowed to a pair of gravel tracks with grass between them, then deteriorated to this abandoned old logging road. It might have been untended for fifty or a hundred years, and was apparently only used by hunters in deer season. Their high-clearance 4x4s had dredged deep ruts through mud, rocks, and roots, and we made at least twenty water crossings, the muddy surface a hazard impossible to guess until we plunged through it in a fountain of brown spray.

Michael later described the experience of trying to navigate our heavy, bucking motorcycles over that territory as "riding the bull," and that's as good a metaphor as any. When I took this photo of Michael standing astride his bike in a knee-deep rut, I had just called a halt and stopped behind him. I said I would walk up the hill ahead of us, to see if it got any worse.

I reported that it still looked bad, but perhaps not any worse. For myself, I was not keen to try to turn our bikes around in that spot, nor was I eager to ride back down over the same torturous way we had come. I hoped that going forward would bring us out . . . somewhere.

Michael agreed, and we carried on riding the bull for another mile or so, until we emerged from the woods at what looked like Jed Clampett's farm, and breathed easier to find ourselves back on "solid gravel" again.

Wanting to reach Gallipolis, Ohio, that night (because I had stayed there back in '96 one time, with Brutus, and always liked the name—though it took me ages to learn to pronounce it correctly, like "gallipo*lice*"—and because Michael hoped to meet his old friends Lance and Angie there), we set Doofus and Dingus for "Quickest Way." Even then, we had to ride at least another ten miles of gravel roads to get out of that shunpiker's maze.

Now might be a good time to explain why my website's book review department, Bubba's Book Club, has been growing cobwebs over there. Lately my life has allowed little time for reading, immersed as I have been in a world centered on my motorcycle and my drums. The brief snatches of reading time before sleep on the bus or in some backwater motel are of little substance outside my own current preoccupation—it's *Motorcyclist*, *Cycle World*, *Cycle Canada*, *Rider*, *BMW Owners News*, and like that on the nightstand. When you spend most of your daytime hours in the saddle of a motorcycle, no subject is of more urgent interest than motorcycling adventures, roadcraft and safety advice, equipment, and accessories. Fine to read about, but not so much to write about.

With two exceptions. Early in the tour, a fan in Florida sent me a hardcover edition of Ernest Hemingway's stories he had purchased at the Hemingway museum in Key West, including a nice laminated bookmark. (The giver signed his note, with reference to my comments about Florida in *Roadshow*, "from one of the 'friendly' Floridians.") Late at night while the bus roared down the interstate, or finally came to rest in a truck stop (I love that moment when the main engine dies into the hum of the generator, and I know my bed is not going to *move* anymore), I started to read a few of those wonderful stories, fresh again after so many readings. With writing of such depth and craft, it is true that you can never read the same book twice.

And as so often happens, by accident or design, art and life intersected. After a show in Indianapolis, with a day off before Detroit, Dave parked us in northern Indiana. In the morning Michael and I unloaded the bikes and headed as far north into Michigan as we could get (on the very smallest roads, of course, shunpikin' it old skool).

I had always presumed such Hemingway stories as "Up in Michigan," "Three-Day Blow," and "Big Two-Hearted River" were set in the Upper Peninsula of Michigan. Because I didn't recognize the towns he named from my travels in that area, I thought they were fictionalized. But when Michael and I got to the northern tip of Lake Michigan, up near Mackinaw City, I recognized signs for Hortons Bay, Boyne City, and Charlevoix (where Michael and I spent the night; they pronounce it "sharlevoy," not "sharlevwah," like we Canadians would)—and realized that this was Hemingway's Michigan.

The other two books I read this tour were both by Wallace Stegner, bought at the national park visitor center (always great book shopping) at Great Basin National Park, in Nevada near the Utah border. One was *The Gathering of Zion*, which relates the Mormon trek from Illinois to the Great Salt Lake (about which more later), and the other was *Marking the Sparrow's Fall: The Making of the American West*.

Again, art and life synchronized. I was reading that book at the same time Michael and I were riding the rural routes of the heartland, the corn and soybean country of Missouri, Illinois, Indiana, and Ohio. (After a few thousand miles of that, I said to Michael one day, "Corn and soybean fields are pretty and everything, but I really don't mind if I never see another one.") Apparently all of those crops are destined for animal feed, which would tend to support a theory I heard recently that the greatest cause of global warming is actually the meat industry. (As a wise journalist wrote a long time ago, "I only report this, I do not comment.")

A quote from Stegner's book nicely describes the small towns Michael and I passed through day after day in that part of the Midwest. (My routes also avoided any significantly populated areas, aiming to pass through crossroads settlements with no more than three stoplights, preferably *one*—or just a stop sign.) In a larger sense, Stegner's affectionate description illustrates the atmosphere of shunpiking:

> Whether they are winter wheat towns on the subhumid edge, whose elevators and bulbous silver water towers announce them miles away, or county towns in ranch country, or intensely green towns in irrigated desert valleys, they have a sort of forlorn, proud rightness. They look at once lost and self-sufficient, scruffy and indispensable. A road leads in out of wide emptiness, threads a fringe of service stations, taverns, and a motel or two, widens to a couple of blocks of commercial buildings, some still false-fronted, with glimpses of side streets and green lawns, narrows to another strip of automotive roadside, and disappears into more wide emptiness.

Wallace Stegner wrote that fifty years ago, and the description perfectly expresses the timeless feel of such places today. (Though "service stations" is an anachronism from my own childhood—replaced today by a Quik-Pay Self-Serve outside a C-store.)

Another of my favorite aspects of shunpiking is taking small ferries whenever possible. By nature, a ferry has endured into the modern era of freeways, bridges, and tunnels because its location is not "im-

portant" enough to require a bridge—and that is a good indicator to a shunpiker. (A title occurs to me, "Between the Bridges." Probably some musical metaphor there, too—I'll think about it sometime when my mindset isn't limited to rambling around on two wheels and hitting things with sticks.)

This third run of the *Snakes and Arrows* tour mainly covered the Midwest, Ontario, and Quebec, and as I scrutinized the relevant maps each day, I looked closely at where we had to cross a major river, seeking a ferry between the bridges. Michael and I ferried across the Wabash River from Illinois to Kentucky; across the Ohio from Kentucky to Indiana, and from Ohio to West Virginia; out in Lake Erie to Put-in-Bay on the Bass Islands; across the Ottawa River from Ontario to Quebec, then back again a week later; and two separate ferries across the St. Lawrence River from New York State, through Wolfe Island, to Ontario.

The back roads of America are also full of history—I'll never forget a bronze plaque I saw on a brick wall in a small Ohio town: "AT THIS SPOT, ON APRIL 14, 1864, DURING THE CIVIL WAR, ABSOLUTELY NOTHING HAPPENED."

Art and life were brought together once again when I was reading Stegner's *The Gathering of Zion* and planning our route between Columbus and Chicago. I sent us all the way across Illinois, to a tiny dot on the map hard by the Mississippi called Nauvoo.

The community was established in the mid-nineteenth century by Joseph Smith's followers, who eventually became known as the Church of Jesus Christ of Latter-Day Saints—the Mormons. Smith told his followers that Nauvoo meant "beautiful place" in Hebrew, and, as Stegner wryly notes, "without pausing to consult their Hebrew dictionaries," they set to work, with the cooperative qualities that would characterize their Utah home as "the Beehive State," building a thriving community there in just five years.

For complicated reasons, the Saints always seemed to alienate and infuriate their non-Mormon neighbors wherever they settled, and the "Gentiles" around Nauvoo were determined to drive them out. A mob attacked and murdered Joseph Smith and his brother Hyrum in the jail at the county seat of Carthage, Illinois, and soon the remaining Saints started west on the great trek of 1847, led by Brigham Young, that would carry them to the New Jerusalem, the Great Salt Lake.

That story is too vast even to summarize here, but I was sufficiently intrigued to lead Michael through several hundred miles of cornfields and soybeans to Carthage, where the Saints have rebuilt the courthouse where the murders took place, and to Nauvoo, where the church has created a massive shrine to Mormon history, centered on a reconstruction of the original temple from 1846, which had been destroyed by vandals, fire, and tornados—acts of man and God. (Nothing so fires religious fervor as a little resistance, from man or God, as proof of the "testing" of their faith.)

When we played Salt Lake City this tour, I noticed a cheer from the audience when Geddy sang the line from "Digital Man," "He'd like to spend the night in Zion." The Mormons in the audience might have taken it as a reference to their promised land, or to the magnificent national park in southern Utah I wrote about in *Ghost Rider*, but I had actually drawn the reference from the Rastafarian theology. Bob Marley also associated Zion with good, and Babylon with evil—as in his live recording, *Babylon by Bus*.

Note our motorcycles looking dwarfed in the left corner, and the water tower in the background—a study in contrasts. Here is a town of barely a thousand people that few "Gentiles" have even heard of, yet it attracts 300,000 visitors every year—chiefly Mormons, of course.

And shunpikers like us. We pulled up on our motorcycles and parked in front of the temple, and Michael said that while I was off taking pictures, the well-dressed people coming out of the temple were unusually smiling and friendly—no doubt figuring we must be Mormons, or why would we be there?

Well, because that's what we do—we explore strange new worlds and alien civilizations. (Michael actually made that comparison later that same day, at our motel in Burlington, Iowa, thinking back over some of the pockets of eccentric Americana we had been traveling through. He thought I would be Captain Kirk and he would be Spock, but I'm not sure about that.)

We do meet a lot of friendly people on those country roads, from the sheriff in North Carolina leaning back in a chair outside his office and waving as we passed, to the kids waving from the backs of school buses or Amish carriages, to the white-haired lady putting gas in her Buick at a crossroads gas station in central Illinois who called over to Michael and me, "I'll pay for yours if you'll pay for mine!"

That was a twist on our manager's old line about how my approach to touring was "a long motorcycle trip where you can earn a little gas money along the way." As our traveling circus of band and crew has continued to mount and perform our roadshow almost fifty times now, earning that gas money has continued to be a difficult, physically demanding job. As always seems to happen in the middle of every tour, when the routine grinds on into the third and fourth months, the mood at work among band and crew can sometimes sink to a tense, dark state of mind that combines homesickness, fatigue, edginess, frustration, friction, physical pain, and a feeling that threatens to approach "fed up."

Still, most of us "keep the shiny side up." Daily smiles and nightly jokes leaven the potential for tedium, and—most important—the band has continued to play to a high standard, supported by a first-rate and highly entertaining crew. (We entertain the crowd; they entertain us.) The audiences have been fantastic everywhere, and the shows have been going well, but—like the gas that goes into our motorcycles—it just keeps costing more.

And as for buying gas, sometimes just *finding* it could be a challenge for us shunpikers—one day in Missouri we had to ride ten miles off our route just to find a gas station. Restaurants, too, could be scarce. In the dog days of August, we would often set off early in the cooler hours, planning to stop for breakfast later, only to ride for hours before we encountered a suitable "family restaurant."

But that was another admirable facet of shunpiking: the adventure of searching out restaurants and places to stay overnight. (Late one afternoon as Michael and I cruised the motel offerings of Newberry, Michigan, in the middle of a thousand-mile ride from St. Paul, Minnesota, to London, Ontario, Michael pointed out that while I was judging motels by their charm, he was judging them by whether they

accepted American Express—for practical reasons, to keep his receipts in order.)

As a general thing, in the one-stoplight towns you won't find first-class luxury, but chances are you will find a clean room or cabin in a quiet, slowed-down world that offers open friendliness, a bag of ice for your end-of-day beverage, a plain and hearty meal, and maybe a little peace.

A moment's peace is a necessary way-point on our days off be-tween shows, because while it's nice that I can commute to work by shunpiking from job to job on my motorcycle, it should be remembered that when I wake up on the bus and wheel that motorcycle out of the trailer, there's only one destination I really want to set my GPS for:

Home.

Quickest Way.

4

Above Lake Windermere, England

HASTE YE BACK

NOVEMBER 2007

Late at night on the first of October, the bus pulled up to our hotel on the coast of southern Scotland. I stood in the dark forecourt, smelling the chilly sea-tang of the night air and feeling a little, oh, "psychedelic"—after an all-day bus ride, an eleven-hour flight, a nine-hour time difference, and all that disturbance in my circadian rhythms.

Brutus and I unloaded the bikes from the trailer, with help from Mark, our European driver. Once we had our bags and riding gear off the bus, Mark drove on to Glasgow with Michael, who had flown in from California with me. (In silent protest at not being my riding partner for this leg, he pretended to sleep through that whole operation. So passive-aggressive.)

The next day would be a setup and sound check day at the Scottish Exhibition Centre in Glasgow, followed by the first show (of fifteen) on this European run of the *Snakes and Arrows* tour. I had wanted to arrive a day early to start getting over that psychedelic state of mind.

While Brutus checked us in, I looked over the bikes, seeing how they'd weathered their overseas flight with the rest of the band's gear.

I turned on my GPS unit, Dingus II, which hadn't been activated since the last show, in Toronto. At first the screen showed its usual "Searching for Satellites" function, and worked away for a few minutes, searching its little heart out. Then suddenly the screen went blank.

A message box, small (as if tentative, or ashamed), lit up, and I could hardly believe my eyes.

It read, "ARE YOU CURRENTLY IN KANSAS?"

Um, no, Dingus, we're not in Kansas.

It seemed I wasn't the only one having a psychedelic experience.

Fortunately, we had two computer experts on hand, Michael and his associate, Kevin, who was helping with security in Europe. Over the next two days, the two of them spent *hours* downloading European maps and trying to get the software and the units to work together. Eventually, Dingus II and Brutus's new unit, Dork Deux, found their way out of Kansas and were ready for Europe.

The first couple of days helped to prepare Brutus and me, too. I defined the "Three Rs" of motorcycling in Britain as "Rain, Roundabouts, and the Wrong Side." We got used to all that surprisingly quickly, first with a fair-weather excursion to the Isle of Bute and the majestic country west of Loch Lomond, but especially after our ride on the show day in Glasgow. We caught a morning ferry to the Isle of Arran, and rode all the way around it in teeming rain. The narrow lane threading along the rugged coast reminded me of the Pacific Coast Highway up around Big Sur, only at about one-tenth scale. Carefully, even nervously, we picked our way around dozens of tight, steep turns, on a surface awash with rain, fallen leaves, mud, and sheep droppings, for sixty tortuous miles.

Such conditions demanded highly *technical* riding, as we needed to steer, shift, and brake with as much smoothness as possible. In subsequent days, I found the lessons and exercises I practiced so intensively on those sixty miles around the Isle of Arran had stayed with me. Somehow my riding was elevated to a previously unattained seamlessness of upshifts and downshifts, and after something like 200,000 miles of motorcycling, that was a revelation. Apotheosis, even.

Like country roads and drivers most everywhere, our travels and encounters on the Scottish lanes were pleasant, and sometimes charming. After one stretch of roadworks and detours, a sign politely apologized, "Sorry For Any Delay," and somehow it seemed sincere, like the sign outside the little villages in Ayrshire (Robbie Burns country) that read, "HASTE YE BACK." You had to smile at that, and hope that you might indeed haste back there one day.

Between the shows in Britain, from Glasgow to Newcastle and down through Sheffield, London, Birmingham, and Manchester, Brutus and I had some simply wonderful rides, with incredible scenery and radiant weather—at least most of the time. Unforgettable days carried us through the Lake District, the Yorkshire Dales, the postcard villages of thatched cottages in Devon and Somerset, and this day in the wilds of Wales, on the way to Aberystwyth for a night off between Birmingham and Manchester (passing signs for places named Abercegir, Bont Dolgadfan, Melinbyrhedyn, and—get this—Llanfihangel-yng-ngwynfa).

Overall, impressions remain of narrow lanes between weathered stone walls or tall green hedges, through farmlands, moors, dales, fells, tiny stone-walled villages, ancient oaks, autumn woodlands, and pastures dotted with sheep—so many sheep. I am pleased, and a little surprised, to report that sheep are actually smarter than deer (see "Every Road Has Its Toll"). Sometimes we crossed areas of "free range" grazing, and on one remote moorland road on our way to Newcastle we had to open and close five separate gates keeping sheep in or out; but although dozens of woolly balls clustered along the open road-sides, they had the basic good sense to stay off the road, and to get out of the way when we approached. We didn't have to kill *one*!

Puttering slowly along those tiny lanes (as I remarked earlier about similar American roads, they were the kind no one would travel unless they lived on them), we also startled many pheasants, red grouse, magpies (who fly off in a whirr of black and white wings like those little garden pinwheels), and a pretty hawk they call a common buzzard. (It deserves a nicer name.)

There were, however, less "picturesque" moments. Referring to the ups and downs of anyone's life, I always liked the title of Mel Tormé's autobiography, which played on a famous description of his voice as "The Velvet Fog." Mel called his life story *It Wasn't All Velvet*.

Early one morning as Brutus and I lingered over breakfast in our country hotel, before suiting up to ride to the next show, we were looking through the English papers. Brutus was paging through the *Times*, and said, "Hey, look at this." Even upside down, I recognized a live shot of us, and a headline that was snotty and dismissive. It was a review of our London shows, and obviously not a good one. I said to Brutus, "Never mind that," and he said, "Yeah," and turned the page.

Later that day, at the venue, I was checking my emails and saw a story on AOL titled "Worst Rock Lyricists." Curious, I opened it and read that some "hip" magazine had declared Sting the all-time worst rock lyricist, which seemed kind of dumb. Then, in second place, I was startled to see—gulp—*my name*. Ouch!

I felt my face burning with shame and anger, to be so publicly declared "the second worst rock lyricist of all time," and to read my work described in words like "an awful mix of science and fantasy." Though obviously written about songs from thirty years ago, and by someone whose choice for "great" lyricists would probably be, oh, Joey Ramone or Morrissey, it still stung.

After the show, as Mark, our European bus driver (who was incredibly helpful this tour, so attentive to the needs of us and the bikes—which are, of course, of equal importance), drove us to our overnight stop, we were followed by two cars, and Mark couldn't shake them. Now, imagine yourself sitting at home one night in your pajamas and making this statement, "I was followed home from work by two carloads of strangers, and they won't leave."

I couldn't confront these invaders without making matters worse, so poor Brutus had to go out and lay down the law—or at least threaten to summon them. For the second time on that British run I had to overhear the complaint that makes my skin crawl, "But we made them what they are." (As Katharine Hepburn once said, in a similar situation, "The hell you did!")

In a somewhat lighter vein, here's a bit of advice that Alex, Geddy, and I were joking about during an intermission one night, and agreed ought to be passed along: Guys, if your girlfriend *hates* Rush, don't bring her to the show. And if you absolutely have to bring her, buy her *earplugs*. At two of those British venues we looked out all night at a scowling female, front-row center, each with her fingers in her ears for the whole show. Hardly inspiring, for them or us!

But as the English like to say, after a good bout of complaining, "Still . . . mustn't grumble."

After the final British show, on October 14 in Manchester (which I felt was particularly good, especially the lively and responsive audience), we had a day off before a pair of shows at the Ahoy arena in Rotterdam, in the Netherlands. Those performances would be filmed and recorded for an upcoming concert DVD, and having seventeen cameras and a recording truck present is always a little unsettling. You just never know if the added pressure is going to be inspiring, or nerve-racking. On that occasion, Alex and Geddy and I were fairly ecstatic to feel that we played really well on those two nights. All things considered, they may have represented the true climax of the tour. Sure, there were many satisfying shows among those sixty-four performances, I am glad to report, but those two are *permanent*.

On the day off before, Brutus and I had slept through the ferry crossing from Dover to Calais. Waking at a bizarre roadside parking area in northern France, we unloaded the bikes once more and spent the day riding around that area and neighboring Belgium. We had decided to visit some of the World War I battlefields we had read about so often—from the poem we learned as schoolchildren, "In Flanders fields the poppies blow/ Between the crosses row on row," to novels depicting the horrors of trench warfare at places like Vimy Ridge, Passchendaele, Ypres, the Somme, and so many other bloody pieces of ground where Canadian boys had been sent to be slaughtered.

This memorial at Vimy Ridge commemorates the 66,000 Canadian soldiers who were killed in that "war to end all wars." Of awesome scale and presence, the monument is set amid grassy fields that remain humped and cratered from that long-ago artillery, and threaded with preserved trenches and tunnels. In that one battle at Vimy, in April 1917, 3,598 Canadian boys were killed and 7,000 wounded. In tribute to them, the land was given by France to Canada in 1922, and it became, uniquely, a Canadian national park on foreign soil. The magnificent memorial was finished in 1936, then restored earlier this decade, and rededicated by Queen Elizabeth II and representatives from the French and Canadian governments in April 2007.

That area of northern France and neighboring Belgium is thick with World War I battlefields and, inevitably, cemeteries, filled with foreign soldiers from Canada, Britain, Australia, New Zealand, and even Morocco—colonial outposts of the allies, Britain and France. Brutus and I stopped at several of those sites, and I couldn't help thinking, in my usual reductive manner, that it had all been so *stupid*—such a waste.

By the time we pulled up at a Canadian memorial in Belgium that commemorated a battle for an objective with no more significance than its name, Hill 62, and where another 8,540 Canadian boys had died so horribly, I said to Brutus, "This is starting to get to me."

He nodded, "Me too—let's head for the hotel."

So we rode on to the pretty city of Bruges, in Belgium, where we stayed for the two Rotterdam shows—only ninety miles away, and offering the novelty of a night ride back after the first one, on largely empty motorways and tunnels. I've written before that I seldom ride at night, for reasons of safety and lack of scenery, but once in a while it's kind of thrilling.

Other days were more uplifting than all those cemeteries, like a ride along the foothills of the Bavarian Alps in Germany, then north through the Black Forest, with the trees, grass, and rooftops frosted by an early snowfall.

At that time of the year (mid-October), the roads were not yet frozen, and thus were no more slippery than in the rain, but the whiteness around us made everything bright and somehow enchanted. I had visited Mad King Ludwig's castle, Neuschwanstein (the model for the Disney version),

several times, by bicycle, car, and motorcycle, but in that white-frosted setting, it seemed even more of a fairy-tale vision.

And such a story attaches to that castle, and to the poor bedeviled king, who, if not actually mad, was declared insane by his own ministers to stop him bankrupting the kingdom with his endless castle-building. He died under mysterious circumstances in a lake near one of his other fantasy castles, aged only forty, feeling sad and abandoned by his people.

Brutus and I did have one truly warm day, and it was perhaps my favorite of the European rides. Mark drove us from the show in Mannheim, Germany, to the next venue in Milan. After sleeping on the bus, as we always did on show nights, Brutus and I rode out on a day off, working our way from Milan to Monte Carlo over the French Alps.

With some difficulty, we discovered an ancient pass, the Col de Tende, which had been bypassed in the late nineteenth century by a tunnel. A single lane, mostly unpaved but for the hairpins, it twisted in dozens of tight switchbacks up the steep mountainside.

Brutus appears here, far below among the tight loops, with an abandoned stone building behind him. At the bottom is the main road, emerging from the tunnel.

At the top, high above us, we could see a massive-looking structure—the abandoned ruin of Fort Central, on the French-Italian border—but I realized it was going to take at least another hour to get up there, and another back. With serious regret, I decided we'd have to save it for another trip, and head for Monte Carlo.

I had long wanted to visit that fabled capital of the tiny principality of Monaco, whose fame far outscales its square kilometer, plus—rare delight!—my wife, Carrie, was going to be there, accompanied by Michael and his girlfriend, Danielle, driving in from Milan for the evening. Any other day, I'd have been up that pass no matter what, but my feelings that day were the opposite of the Scottish sign—Haste ye onward!

It is a pleasure to report that I found Monte Carlo to be . . . everything it ought to have been. After we negotiated the crowded, winding streets, our luxurious hotel had an incredible view over the yacht-studded Mediterranean, and we all shared a memorable meal and a visit to the famous Casino. (With Brutus as coach, Michael and Carrie both won a few euros at roulette, then were smart enough to stop.)

A few days later, as the tour, and Brutus and I, worked our way north to Scandinavia, things got *really* frosty. One morning in Norway, on our way from the ferry terminal of Kristiansand to Oslo, my motorcycle's thermometer showed –4°C (25°F). The landscape, so much like Ontario's or Quebec's, with glaciated rocks and lakes surrounded by second-growth boreal forest, was coated in translucent white frost. Signs pointed us toward names like Mjåvatn, Øynaheia, Åmli, and Vegusdal. The temperature barely rose above freezing all that day, and when Brutus and I made it to the arena in Oslo, I walked into the dressing room and said to the guys at work, dramatically throwing out my arms, *"I'll never be warm again!"*

Still, mustn't grumble—Brutus and I were relieved and pleased enough that we were even *able* to ride in Norway, Sweden, and Finland. Given the time of year, we hadn't taken that for granted. The ferry rides were enjoyable, too, especially the overnight sailing from Stockholm to Helsinki, with our large cabins looking forward, over the ship's bow.

But I was awfully tired by then, and so were Alex and Geddy. As we approached the end of the tour, it occurred to me that each of the three of us, in our own way, was quietly going insane.

Apparently, so were some of the crew members.

Everybody and everything had simply become beat up and worn down. Gump's careful maintenance was keeping the drums looking and sounding good, but little things still tended to wear out and break (and Gump himself was feeling pretty road-weary, like all of us). The bikes were scratched and dented (mostly from trailer mishaps, when rough roads caused the tiedowns to snap, and one of the bikes would break loose and fall into the other); our tires were worn, and a list of service and parts needs was growing at the back of my journal.

Day and night, my body was sore all over, "weary from my nose to my toes." In the bus lounge at night after a show, Brutus laughed when I struggled up from my seat with each motion accompanied by Germanic groans, "*Ach, der oofen-aufen, einbahnstrasse, gemütlich, schaden-freude.*" (Somehow German best expresses an aching body.)

But the general, all-over pain is only the natural result of exertion (and advancing years), and can be endured, and eased with a couple of Bufferins. It's the more specific pains that are worrisome.

For a few nights my left index finger had an agonizing bone bruise, which caused me to turn my grip on the stick a little so it wouldn't hurt so much. However, that tiny adjustment affected my shoulder, making it ache all the time, so I worried about the rotator cuff problems that have plagued other drummers I know. That means surgery, and a long recovery.

Later on, my right index finger developed a split callus between the first and second knuckles, a deep fissure into the tender flesh below. It throbbed all the time, especially when I was playing, from the impact of each stroke, plus the sweat getting into it. I couldn't even bandage it, because I needed the sensitivity of feeling the stick in that "cradle" of my fingers.

My right big toe also ached from a bone bruise for a few shows, and throughout this entire tour I had an ear infection that never had a chance to clear up, what with wearing earplugs on the bike all day, and the in-ear monitors onstage.

Right at the start of the European run, a crown came loose on one of my front teeth. I couldn't get it fixed properly until I got home, so I had to bite and chew around it. My socks had holes in them, my shaving kit was falling apart, and the bus's hot water heater packed up for the last few days, so I couldn't have a shower after a cold ride or a sweaty show.

Apart from the general fatigue, I also noticed some psychological signs of the "on the road too long" syndrome. During the previous break at home, one morning I took a shower and got dressed, then went to put my laminated "Tour Staff" pass around my neck—laughing grimly to think that I felt naked without it, even in my own house.

One night in a European hotel, I woke up in the dark and looked at the bedside clock. The red LEDs said 4:55, and I frowned in my dozy stupor, "Damn—only five minutes till soundcheck." It was, of course, 4:55 a.m.

Brutus in the Black Forest

Altogether, Brutus and I rode 4,543 miles in Europe, while Alex, Geddy, and I played fifteen shows. That brings me to a total of 24,412 miles of motorcycling on the *Snakes and Arrows* tour, on my way to sixty-four shows with the guys at work.

In summing up all of those travels, and all of those performances, I now realize that I learned a few new things on the motorcycle, and on the drums. As I mentioned in a *Modern Drummer* story written before the tour, I remain ambivalent about touring personally, but I have to admit it's good for my drumming. Night after night, in my pre-show warm-ups on the little drumset in the Bubba Gump room, new rhythmic ideas and figures were worked out and introduced into my solo, sometimes that very night. Such immediacy is possible because I have continued to improvise the first half of that performance each time, and find a way to open the solo with a different figure every night (though I did use "Wipeout" twice—on my birthday, to commemorate the first song I ever played on drums, and on the last night, in Helsinki, for the same reason).

I also find my playing and—especially—my *listening* are continuing to develop in a way I wrote about in an earlier story ("That's the Way We Roll"). I can still feel myself growing into an ever-greater understanding and control of *time*. Similar to discovering a new level of motorcycling technique after 200,000 miles, it may seem strange to find new musical attainments after playing for forty-two years, but . . . I guess that's how long it took me. (I never have been a fast learner—just stubborn.)

Another analogy between motorcycling and drumming is that many of the more subtle techniques can be *learned*, but not taught. In each pursuit, one level of understanding and accomplishment leads to another, and there are no shortcuts. That's certainly how it is with this idea of time sense—though one example I might offer is that I have begun to check my tempos in each song against Geddy's vocal phrasing. As I try to nail the "perfect" tempo, I listen to the way his singing falls against the time, especially at the beginning of the song. That can be a perfect indication of whether the tempo is too fast or slow.

When I told my friend Matt Scannell about that insight, he said (speaking for all singers, I'm sure), "I wish you'd tell *all* drummers about that." So I am. Spread the word.

One more comparison with these rarefied techniques on drums or motorcycle is that they remain elusive sometimes. One day you've got it, the next day it's gone. After that apotheosis on the Isle of Arran, I found that some days I simply could not attain that seamless shifting on the bike again, no matter how hard I tried.

Likewise with some of the new drum ideas I was coming up with on the practice kit—one day I'd nail it; the next day I couldn't. All you can do is keep trying—be stubborn.

And thinking of the "on the road too long" syndrome, it should be remembered that our families are subject to that, too. Big time.

The last ride, to the last show, in Finland

I am reminded of a print that hung on my grandmother's wall when I was a boy. Dating from World War II, it was a Norman Rockwell–style painting of a young girl, a mother, and a grandmother standing in profile, as if staring out to sea in a blue twilight. The caption was a quote from John Milton, "They Also Serve Who Only Stand and Wait."

As much as my life on tour can be exhausting and tedious, it is never boring. (Though to be honest, I don't think I've ever been bored for a single minute in my life.)

For our loved ones, left alone at home, the long months of a tour can be even harder to endure. It is well to remember that, and for others to realize it.

For those of us off on foreign campaigns, in Florida or Finland, we need the faith that our loved ones at home are feeling the way we do, like the signs in Ayrshire, "Haste ye back."

THE HOUR OF ARRIVING

5

DECEMBER 2007

This lighthouse was the centerpiece of the view from the balcony of my room at the Hotel Bayerischer Hof (Bavarian Court) in the island-city of Lindau, Germany. On a large lake called the Bodensee, or Lake Constance, near the present-day borders of Germany, Austria, and Switzerland, Lindau's history dates to Roman times, growing from a monastery to a fortified city-state almost a thousand years ago. A fair-sized island (about 170 acres), today Lindau is connected to the mainland by a causeway, and the city retains a picturesque, medieval atmosphere.

The clock on the lighthouse shows that it was 5:00—cocktail time—and that's what Brutus and I were celebrating. After a show the previous night in Oberhausen, we had slept on the bus in Mannheim, then unloaded the motorcycles and ridden 323 miles through cold, snowy weather along the Bavarian Alps. Now we were settled into our spacious and comfortable rooms, with a magnificent view over the lake and across to the Austrian and Swiss Alps. At the western end of the lake, where the Rhine flowed out, the sun was still bright. We clinked our glasses and stood on the balcony taking it all in.

Perhaps my favorite part of a long day on the motorcycle is that first hour of arriving and settling into a hotel, whether humble or luxurious. It feels so good to pull up in front of the hotel, kick down the sidestand, and lift a weary leg over the saddle, still keyed up from the day's adventures, yet gradually easing into a more relaxed state of mind. I peel off my gloves, lift off the helmet, pull out the earplugs, and slowly stretch my back into an upright posture again. Brutus goes inside to see about our rooms, while I lazily open the aluminum luggage cases and unload my soft bags, unhook the duffle from my saddle, and unzip the tankbag, piling them at the curb. At a hotel sufficiently luxurious as to provide a bellman, such as the Bayerischer Hof, I'll load up the luggage cart (at our hotel in Scotland, the doorman looked at me blankly when I requested a cart—they call it a trolley). Piling on my gear, hanging my helmet from the crossbar, I'll start adding Brutus's luggage, too.

Once the bikes are parked, we find our way to our rooms and start the usual sequence of rituals. First unpack the dress-up-for-dinner clothes (suit and tie in Europe, black cotton shirt and pants in North America) and hang them in the bathroom, to let the shower steam out the wrinkles. Clean the helmet's face shield with the "bug rag" I carry in my tankbag, and hang the grubby white cloth by the shower to be washed later, then draped over a chair to dry overnight (in plain sight, so you don't leave it behind—it's the kind of thing you miss when a bug splatters itself across the plastic in front of your eyes). Finally, spread the luggage bags across the bed and dig out the plastic flask of The Macallan.

Brutus will come by my room with a bucket of ice, and I'll pour us each a glass, sometimes omitting the ice on a cold day. (Once you've been chilled to the bone by riding in freezing weather all day, it takes a long time, and a hot shower, to finally feel warm again.) After toasting each other with a nod and a smile—a silent, shared tribute to the day, and to our continued existence—we admire the view, have a smoke, watch the tour boat come into the harbor, talk about some of

the day's adventures and encounters, and look through the photographs we've taken. We settle on a time to meet for dinner, and go off to take care of our own chores.

Dinner is always a big event at the end of a long ride. (Like that line from Byron, "Much depends upon dinner.") Brutus and I usually skip lunch, preferring to spend that time riding, and so arrive at our destination earlier. By late afternoon, we will be ravenous, but the wait is especially well rewarded in Europe, where great restaurants are so much more common.

Even on our first night off in Europe, a week or so before visiting Lindau, we had ended our day at a fantastic place—the Yorke Arms, in northern England. The small hotel described itself as "A Restaurant With Rooms," and boasted a Michelin star, so even more than usual, its dining room was an important part of the destination for Brutus and me.

In my years of traveling to places both exotic and ordinary, I have had many bad journeys to great destinations, and plenty of great journeys to bad destinations. The latter occurs more often in North America, which is far too large and scattered to have the concentration of sophisticated accommodations that Europe can offer. But of course the journeys can be monumentally grand, especially in the West.

At the end of the North American part of the tour, my American riding partner Michael and I had a T-shirt printed up that listed ten American motels we had stayed at for less than $100 (some of them *much* less, but still nice enough, and I do love being able to park right in front of my room). The column of motels, towns, and prices appeared above the slogan "THAT'S THE WAY WE ROLL." While Brutus and I swanned around between luxurious hotels in Europe, we joked about making a T-shirt with a list of all the fantastic—and fantastically expensive—places we stayed there, followed by the slogan "THAT'S THE WAY WE ROLL."

Our ride to the Yorke Arms in North Yorkshire had been a long day, but it was one of those journeys where the miles didn't begin to tell the story. Anyone who has traveled much in Britain would agree that 221 miles is a substantial day's journey under any circumstances, but for Brutus and me most of those miles were on tiny roads, often only one narrow lane, further crowded by stone walls, hedges, and woodlands in crooked lines, with endless blind corners. Pheasants and grouse started up in front of us from the roadside cover, sometimes causing us to duck reflexively, and sheep were a constant menace. Plus there was the occasional Land Rover or farm tractor appearing from nowhere and occupying most of the road.

We had started that morning near Jedburgh, in Scotland, waking on the bus in a quiet lay-by. Our driver, Mark, cut the oranges in half while I squeezed the juice (into glasses we kept overnight in the freezer—a recent innovation of mine), the coffee fragrant as it poured from the excellent little machine that ground the beans for each cup. While I ate my cereal and bananas, Mark and Brutus unloaded the bikes, then we got dressed to ride and gathered our luggage.

That day we rambled down through the Lake District (pictured in the previous story's opening photo, "Above Lake Windermere") and along some curvy little roads across wide-open moorland, grassy and treeless, in the Yorkshire Dales. On a bright sunny day, the stone-built villages and walls, the winding lanes through spacious countryside, and the variety of scenery from woodlands to open moors had made for an exciting and enjoyable ride. To arrive at a luxurious country hotel, the Yorke Arms, in the hamlet of Ramsgill-in-Nidderdale (a church, the hotel, and a few cottages, all in stone) nestled in a lush valley, with a Michelin-starred restaurant, was the proverbial icing.

Brutus and I have a particular appreciation for good food, perhaps because both of us do a lot of cooking at home (though I admit with all humility that Brutus is the more intuitive and sophisticated chef—

I'm just a recipe-follower). Apart from our Alex, Brutus is the only man I know who will spend hours preparing a meal for friends and loved ones—and it was from the two of them that I learned *why*: Cooking is an expression of love. When Brutus visits me at my house on the lake in Quebec, if the weather is bad we might spend hours in the kitchen making ourselves an amazing meal.

For myself, it's only in the past ten years that I have taken any interest in cooking; before that I couldn't do much more than boil an egg. That process of learning and refining techniques in the kitchen parallels my comments about motorcycling and drumming in a previous story—many things can be learned that cannot be taught. (My friend Mike Heppner, a novelist and writing teacher, points out that writing is the same way.)

By gradually learning to prepare dishes that I liked to eat (and that pleased my wife), from fish, vegetables, and rice to key lime pie and chocolate cake, beginning to shop wisely and often (every day or two, in the European fashion), and moderate heat and time precisely (a recipe for good drumming, too: heat + time), I have built up a fair repertoire of simple meals.

That minor accomplishment not only impresses women no end, it has changed the way I look at a restaurant menu. Now I automatically dismiss anything I could make myself, and choose dishes that are difficult or especially time-consuming to make. The Yorke Arms menu offered a perfect example of this policy, as I ordered a scallop soufflé, roast grouse, and a chocolate soufflé (soufflés are famously one of the hardest dishes to produce successfully, and grouse is—well, not generally available in my neighborhood grocery store). The meal was absolutely superb, and a bottle of great burgundy, Echézeaux, was an ideal complement, finished perfectly by black coffee and a snifter of Hennessy XO.

The Yorke Arms experience was already a dramatic contrast to some of the utilitarian motels and humble meals Michael and I had resorted to in North America. Though at the time we had certainly appreciated those "hours of arriving," too, our destinations were more-or-less accidental, chosen because they were on our route, and it was time to stop. In Europe, Brutus was able to choose a great destination, then design a fantastic route to get there. It is hard to imagine how an establishment as sophisticated as the Yorke Arms manages to exist in the wilds of North Yorkshire, but Brutus and I were glad it does.

The next day off, between shows in London and Birmingham, carried us to another fantastic destination. After a long day's ride through the West Country, Devon and Somerset—part of Thomas Hardy's "Wessex"—along many more winding little lanes, we rode into the curving gravel drive of the Buckland Manor in the Cotswolds.

The evening light was golden on the gardens and the manor house (my room on the front right, top floor) and neighboring chapel. Built from the famously buttery local stone, parts of the building dated back more than a thousand years. At a place like that, we would carry

our drinks with us and go for a walk, take some photographs, and feel good about life.

Another unforgettable overnight stop was the Bühlerhöhe Schlosshotel (described glowingly in *Roadshow*) in Germany's Black Forest. During that same magic hour after arriving, I made a journal note expressing my awareness of these contrasts in my life.

> Sometimes I can only laugh.
> After today, last night, the last two days–*almost* too much.
> But really just enough.

With that note I was trying to reconcile playing two hard shows in Rotterdam, filming for a concert DVD with the attendant pressure to play well, feeling good about having captured two decent perform-ances on those nights (a little extra sore, too), then sleeping on the bus and waking up to ride all day on the challenging roads of southern Germany and the Black Forest, and finally arriving at a truly magnif-icent hotel—where I had been given the ridiculously large, ornately

decorated Presidential Suite. Brutus and I guessed that upgrade was due to our stay at that same hotel last tour, when we had complained (okay, I had complained) about not being able to get a reservation in the main restaurant. Perhaps they'd made a note that they "owed us one." In any case, after those action-packed days and nights, to stand in that palatial suite and look out at the breathtaking view was indeed "*almost* too much. But really just enough."

Clearly, this was not a scene to be taken for granted, and in the same way the view from my balcony in Lindau had fascinated me, I kept watching as the sky changed. Again and again I picked up my

camera and tried to capture the ultimate sunset over the Black Forest, the Rhine Valley, and, in the far distance, the low Vosges Mountains of French Alsace.

That evening, I contemplated a title for a story about such experiences, "Europe Is Different." With the intended irony of understatement, that title seemed to hint at a whole host of differences between traveling in North America and Europe. Under the title, I added a wry parenthesis, "(plenty of eggs go in that basket)," and I was certainly thinking of *good* eggs. As I wrote in *Roadshow*, referring to Brutus's and my European travels on the R30 tour in 2004, "Europe has . . . seduced me."

On a show day, the hour of arriving is completely different. It is not the end of the day's labors, but merely the beginning. Not least, there's still a three-hour *show* to perform. Soundcheck at 5:00 is the first "scheduled activity," but there is always plenty to do before that. We like to arrive between two and three, after pausing just before we pull up at the venue to call Michael (who handled security in Europe) and let him know our ETA. Michael will advise us on the easiest way into the building or parking area, and he or his associate Kevin (former Canadian soldier, now firefighter and computer forensics expert in Calgary, Alberta, moonlighting as Michael's fellow Praetorian for the European tour) will meet us out front to wave us in.

The amphitheaters in North America are the nicest to arrive at, because they are usually in rural areas, so we don't have to fight through city traffic, and because they have a private, enclosed area for the buses and trucks, so I am able to walk freely from bike to bus to backstage anytime I want. The arenas in North America and Europe are usually in the middle of a busy city, and the buses and trucks are often parked on the street or in a public area. There is no privacy for me outdoors, so if I want to, say, change the oil in my bike, it takes some . . . logistical strategy—like at the Ahoy in Rotterdam.

Before Brutus and I arrived, Michael had Mark park the bus close along a wall near the backstage entrance, then arranged to have some free-standing curtains from the building placed at each end of the bus, between it and the wall. When we rolled up, Kevin pointed me behind the bus and trailer, and pulled back the curtain at one end for me to ride through. Thus I had a private area to work on the bike, hidden from gawkers, rockers, talkers, and stalkers. (An audience is very good to have when you're performing, but not so much when you're lying on the ground changing your oil.)

In its way, that first hour at work is almost as special as it is on a day off. It is not so pleasurable, of course—it's work, and there is more urgency to get things done, take care of business—but there is time for all the chores, and that is satisfying in a "practical" sort of way. Carry the luggage onto the bus, unpack the dress-up clothes and hang them in the locker, clean off the face shield and hang the rag to dry— beside the salt-stained stage clothes from the previous show, dry now and ready to give to Donovan for cleaning, so they are shoved into the "gig bag" with my used towels from that show, and my drumming shoes. (Actually dancing shoes, inspired by my teacher, Freddie Gruber. When I first studied with him, back in 1995, he shook his finger at me and said, "Don't play drums in sneakers!" Freddie's method was centered on teaching me to *dance* on the drums, so I tried some soft-shoe dancing shoes, and now I can't play properly without them.)

I leave that bag by the bus's door, ready to go inside later, then gather the tools, oil, filter, and rags to do the oil change. Twenty minutes later, with Brutus now working on the other bike, I have the pleasure of washing my dirty hands and noting the mileage in my journal (especially satisfied when the interval is close to my target of 3,000 kilometers between changes).

Then on to check phone messages, skim through accumulated emails, maybe have a shower and a nap, and before I know it, it's soundcheck time. Then dinner with the guys at work, a bit of quiet time to phone Carrie, read, even close my eyes for a few minutes, then fifteen or twenty minutes on the little warm-up drumset, change into stage clothes, and on to another show . . .

When the show is over, there is another kind of hour of arriving. As the bus drives away from the venue, and I change out of my sweaty clothes and into pajama bottoms and a T-shirt, then sit in the front lounge to enjoy what I called in *Roadshow*, "my humble workman's re-wards: a glass of booze and a smoke," there's a similar feeling of keyed-up peace that only lasts a little while, but feels pretty good.

The nature of the reward at each of those hours is the feeling that you have traveled a long way to get somewhere, and now you're there. Such a feeling is necessarily transitory, because all too soon you're on your way to somewhere else—another ride, another hotel room, another show. But when that destination is *home*, and you've got more than a few days to spend there, that hour of arriving can open into a delightful passage of unfenced time.

As if a long-held breath has been released at last, tension eases, fatigue slowly melts away—one muscle group at a time, it often seems. After about two weeks of rest, I notice that one shoulder will ache for a day, then the other one, then a daily succession of forearms, biceps, quads, calves, and elbows. Likewise, the split calluses on my fingers start to itch a little as they heal over, and my hands don't look and feel so inflamed and swollen all the time.

After the past two years of more-or-less steady work, recording and touring, there are practical matters to attend to as well—like visits to the dentist, which may not be *delightful* as such, but need to be addressed. Along with getting cars serviced and mail sorted, I am able to provision my long-neglected kitchen with all the fresh and varied ingredients I might need to "feed inspiration"—onion, garlic, dill, tomatoes, multicolored peppers, lemons, that sort of thing. Just to have them on hand, so that while I'm cooking, if I think, "Hmm, some fried onions would be good with this," I can do it.

There is time for *indulgences*, too, like writing these stories. (I have decided to define them as a combination open letter and meditation.)

I'm not sure what they're "for," or where they're leading me, but I enjoy the process, and *I can do it*.

Likewise, I have ordered 100 postcards, with a picture of me and my drums on the front, intending to write and mail one as a thank-you note to each of the people who sent me gifts on this tour. (Inevitably, as I traveled around and collected so many cards and letters in the dressing room case, on the bus, and in my luggage, some of them went astray—like the card from the "friendly Floridian," for example—so I apologize to anyone I missed, and thank them now.)

Back in April of this year, just before the *Snakes and Arrows* tour, I did a

TV interview for the Canadian music channel, MuchMusic. The cameraman placed the interviewer and me in the rehearsal hall, in front of my drums, where I had been laboring for several weeks by then. Some of the interviewer's questions seemed to angle toward a certain starry-eyed view of my work, especially the touring side of it, and I tried to explain to him that I didn't consider touring, or even drumming, to be my *life*.

He seemed perplexed, and to appraise me as clearly jaded and cynical, because his next question was "When did you start to feel that way?"

I paused to think for a couple of seconds, then was glad to feel the mental light bulb illuminate a true and clear answer. I was able to answer honestly, "About a month into the first tour, in 1974." That really was when I started to feel that touring was "not enough," and turned to reading books as a way to make more use of the days and nights.

Partly out of sheer contrariness, but partly out of a desire for *context*, I often refer to playing the drums, with deliberate disrespect, as "the job"—hitting things with sticks. Obviously it means much more to me than that and has been a central focus in my life. But still, it seems rather sad to hear anyone say that their work is their life.

Not family and friends? Not reading and writing? Not hiking or cross-country skiing or birdwatching or motorcycle riding or swimming?

Just work?

I don't think so.

Earlier in the tour, when we played in Portland, Oregon, someone in the audience had apparently seen that interview, and ventured to disagree publicly with my opinion on the subject of my life. Far back on the stage-left side of the house I saw a large sign, with big block letters reading, "NP—THIS IS YOUR LIFE."

Well, thanks, but no thanks.

Of course it's just my opinion, but to me, my life is not dedicated to the *place*, but to the journey, and to the hour of arriving.

All the while knowing that, all too soon, there will come the hour of departing.

6

THE BEST FEBRUARY EVER

MARCH 2008

That's a bold claim to lay before a reader, I know, but as baseball great Dizzy Dean put it, "It ain't braggin' if you can back it up."

Start with the weather. The words "February in Quebec" sum it up pretty well, though there are people for whom those words might evoke something more like . . . fear and loathing. For me, other seasons in other places have their charms, and the world offers plenty of great scenery and weather, but way down in my Canadian soul, I am profoundly stirred by that cold heart of winter—the short, bright days, the flying snow, and the deep blue freeze of winter nights. As French-Canadian songwriter Gilles Vigneault sang, "*Mon pays ce n'est pas un pays, c'est l'hiver*"—My country is not a country, it is winter.

And the *air*—so fresh and crisp and bracing, so delicious to breathe, even as it pinches your nostrils shut. It would be hard to prove, but I swear there is such a thing as the smell of snow. One time I was trying to name my favorite drink, and thought of the morning ritual of fresh orange juice with half a blood orange squeezed in (for sweetness and color), the full glass placed in the freezer for a few minutes to get that Popsicle zest, or perhaps the end-of-day Macallan on ice, with its fiery amber glow. But eventually I decided my favorite drink is February in Quebec.

Whenever I'm not off plying my trade in other parts of the world, I am mainly based in Southern California these days, but I always try to arrange my life and work to spend a few weeks in Quebec around February. Perhaps my affection for that time of year in the Laurentian Mountains comes from my love of cross-country skiing and snowshoeing, but even beyond that—even just looking out the window—it is soul-stirring. Snowscapes, woodsmoke, and a frostbitten, dripping nose have been part of my reality since childhood, and that season, in that part of the world, must be my favorite combination of time and place.

Considered in those terms, February 2008 in Quebec was just about *perfect*. The storms of December and January had piled the snow waist-deep, and white billows and pillows rounded the trees and rooftops. The daily temperatures were generally in my ideal cross-country ski range, five or ten degrees below freezing, and the skies were either crystal blue or dashed with flying snow. One morning at first light I woke up and looked through the window above my head to see a million snowflakes dancing in the air, swirling in patterns like a ballet of white atoms, a life-size snowglobe, and I found myself saying, automatically, "Hello, beautiful!"

Words like that came into my mind on many days, and many nights, too, like looking up through that same window at the piercing stars and latticed treetops. But the beauty was most keenly felt when I was out *in* it, wandering the woods on cross-country skis or snowshoes. Nearly every day I dressed in my multi-layered winter wardrobe and headed for the trails, and this year it happens that such an aerobic, full-body workout was a perfect fitness program for pre-tour conditioning. In just a few weeks I will have to put on my drummer

hat instead of my black balaclava and "Be Yourself" wool cap (bought at a London performance of the excellent musical *Billy Elliot*, which I attended with Carrie while we were there on tour last October). Early in March I will have to start preparing for another series of concerts, a "continuation" of the *Snakes and Arrows* tour. (The *Snakes and Arrows* "surge," I call it.)

We had planned to end the tour in Europe last fall, but apparently more people want to see us, or see us again, so we were asked to do more shows. Some of them will be in places we haven't got to for a while, like New Orleans, Oklahoma City, and Winnipeg, and that is nice, plus we plan to make a few changes to the setlist and presentation to freshen it up a little. Although the world knows by now that I'm not crazy about touring, I sure don't discount the good fortune that we can still *do* it, personally and professionally—that we can play better than ever, and that people will come and see us. That's not something I have ever taken for granted. As I have said to friends who might be having their own work difficulties, "At least if I have to work, I'm glad I *can*." And not just any old job, of course—pretty much the best job there is—but none-the-less a hard one.

Another semi-professional (literally) activity this season has been getting back to playing the marimba. My old beginner's instrument had been disassembled and stored for a few years, but I was moved to set it up again in my front hallway, which is like a small chapel (a chapel to *nature*, with big windows open to the view of white forest and lake). The marimba had a warm resonance in that setting, as I riffed on my older exercises, "Pieces of Eight" and "Momo's Dance Party," and improvised more-or-less aimlessly on some new ideas. Just for fun.

During those few precious weeks when I remained free and unfettered by schedules or itineraries, out wandering on the snow-covered trails, I tried to take at least one photograph every day. A little over a year ago I started experimenting with the use of photos in these stories, and found the combination of words and images inspiring, so from then on, and for that purpose, I made the effort to take more motorcycling photos on tour. Similarly, this winter I wanted to try to fully capture this very different experience and setting.

Carrying my camera every day in my backpack, and looking around me at all the fetching combinations of landscape and snowscape, I experimented with different ways of framing the scenery. One innovation I came up with was the "Ski-Cam™," where I would bend down to shoot a scene across the tips of my skis, to give it more perspective.

Here is an example, where I was about to enter an avenue between groves of silver birches.

While I skied through the woods on all those glorious winter days, kicking and gliding along the flats of the old railroad tracks, as pictured here, or flying downhill between the leafless trees and snow-dappled evergreens with mingled fear and excitement, or laboring uphill with my skis splayed out herringbone style, I tried to find the words to express what it was about cross-country skiing that I love so much.

For one thing, I believe that no sport is more beautiful in its setting than cross-country skiing. The only possible comparison might be wilderness hiking. Long-distance cycling and running, for example, must usually be done in less picturesque surroundings—public roads in most cases—and endurance swimming is too often confined to counting laps in an indoor pool. But the snowy woods, and the trails through them, are *always* pretty. And unlike roads, urban paths, or swimming lanes, there is no traffic.

On weekdays, I could ski for two or three hours and in that whole time maybe encounter one or two other skiers, and often no one. On weekends, when more people were on the ski trails, I could snowshoe into the neighboring woods on remote paths and see nothing but animal tracks.

But cross-country skiing is my favorite, for its rhythmic swing, and the special state of mind it engenders. The southern Laurentians have a world-class network of cross-country trails, and by the time I get on them, in early afternoon, any fresh snow on the trails is already broken, either by other skiers or the local association's snowmobile trail-groomer. Many times I have noticed that as soon as I plant my skis in those parallel tracks in the snow and push off, it seems as though my mind is suddenly *transported*. It's almost like a kind of trance, especially on one of my favorite trails, a ten-mile, multi-textured loop that I can only compare to the rhythm of a good flow yoga practice.

The opening meditation is a mile or so of that old railroad track, pictured above, where I just groove along with a steady, fairly effortless pace. Then the Sun Salutations, as I turn uphill for a long ascent through varying degrees of gentle climb and laborious herringbone. The summit leads to several miles of alternating ups and downs, the *chaturangas* and standing poses, working different parts of the body as well as the core, so that despite the cold, my inner clothes are soaked with sweat. And all the while, the winter woods flow by, the fractaled deciduous trees and the piebald evergreens, snow beneath, sky above, the delicious air drawn in with relaxed *ujjayi* breaths.

Choosing a sheltered grove or open overlook, depending on the wind, I might pause to snack on a raspberry yogurt granola bar and apple juice (this winter's favorite combo—last year it was peanut butter cups and cranapple). Then on again, up and down, until a couple of hours later I close the loop, and glide down the long slope to the same stretch of meditative flats I started with. My mind is at rest, knowing the hard climbs and perilous descents are behind me, and that final, easy cruise feels like the equivalent of *shavasana*, the traditional closing to a yoga practice. That's when all you have to do is *lie there*, which is no big deal in itself, but it feels so blissful after the arduous workout that led up to it. As I have written before about such spiritual states of mingled satisfaction and relief, like after a hard show or a long motorcycle journey, you can't just wake up and feel that good about lying down—it's a *reward* that only has value according to how much you have paid for it.

While I'm skiing along, my arms and legs are working away like a locomotive, but require little thought to guide them, especially after all these years. (I first learned to cross-country ski while working at

nearby Le Studio, in the early '80s.) Above it all, as it were, my mind is spinning like a generator, taking that energy and converting it into a train of thought that can go anywhere. And does.

Tangents both shallow and deep, from cars to literary analysis, problem-solving to wool-gathering, pondering how to answer a strange email from a friend, or a decision on this or that question, re-solving to write soon to another neglected friend (I have so many neglected friends), searching for words to capture the world around and within at that moment, and often, an old song plays in the back-ground of all those thoughts.

Yet the cross-country skiing state of mind has a wonderful sense of *composure*. That word seems absent from running, in my experience, with the jarring impacts and heavy breathing, and is even rare in cy-cling, unless you're spinning along a flat, empty road. On the ski trails, while I'm kicking and gliding through the snowy landscape, thoughts parade through my mind in a somehow *stately* fashion, without ur-gency. Even issues that, at home or in the car, were stressful can be considered calmly, one at a time. Or not at all, as I choose.

However, I did have other, more serious matters to think about, for this was a *working* vacation. (That might be a recipe for an ideal life: a working vacation that never ends.) Apart from preparing for the up-coming shows physically, there was a lot of "executive" work to take care of, and I could only try to deal with all that in the mornings, leav-ing the afternoons free for snow sports. With Hugh Syme doing the real work, I still had to supervise the cover for a CD of our shows from Rotterdam last October, plus a revised edition of the tour book to in-clude photos from earlier this tour, review the live mixes, and field countless questions from bandmates, crew members, and the office, about arrangements, schedules, and decisions. And I did feel I ought to contribute something new to Bubba's Book Club, after a long hiatus because of last year's busy touring schedule, so I spent a few mornings working on that. But at least those jobs could all be handled by the relatively unobtrusive email. All I care is that my phone doesn't ring, and that every day I can get out in the woods.

And thus the high-tech world definitely has its place in my winter wonderland. Why, this year I even made the leap to modern fiberglass skis, instead of the antiquated wooden ones I had been clinging to for many years. The new ones steer better, are much lighter, and I learned to choose a wax a few degrees "warmer," and apply it more frequently, to get the same versatility as the wooden ones.

Same with snowshoes. I had always stayed with my quaint varnished-wood-and-sinew racquets, but this year I finally surrendered to the undeniable advantages of man-made materials. Perhaps they are not quite so elegant, but—as I feel about vintage drums, motorcycles, and cars, for example—some things were always nice, but new ones are better.

Home from the snowy trail, showered and changed, "it's good to rest my bones beside the fire," as Roger Waters put it in that great old Floyd song. As the light fades, I build up the fire, savor a Macallan on ice, and look out at another winter sunset. The last spark of orange filters through the snow-covered hemlocks and firs to the southwest, and the snow is gilded with soft light. Twilight is a magical time here, as the snow gradually fades and glows through an unbelievable range of tints and shadows. Carrying my glass, I move from one window to another to watch the show.

I am also glad that February in Quebec is a gift that can be *shared*, and after a couple of weeks on my own, it was great to have Carrie join me for ten days of the finest winter she has experienced (being a native-born Californian facing her husband's native land in its harshest season). As she stepped out in her own new snowshoes, and joined me on the cross-country trails, I christened her *Notre Dame de la Neige*—Our Lady of the Snow.

And here's a telling moment—a few years ago, after twenty-five years of having a place in Quebec, I was thinking about moving away from certain disturbing memories, and building a new place on a piece of land I'd bought in Ontario. That summer Carrie was with me in Quebec, reveling in the area's excellent grocery stores and restaurants, and the lovely scenery and serenity, and one day she said to me, "Are you sure you want to leave this area?"

Well, no, I wasn't sure, and before long I decided to stay. As I explained it in *Traveling Music*, this is my soulscape. I went ahead and sold the old place, and built a new one across the lake—a place to collect *new* memories. This February was my first stay there, other than a few days in December to organize the place, so that was another reason why it was the Best February Ever.

One first-time visitor to the area was my friend Matt Scannell, who arrived for a weekend visit soon after Carrie's departure. Matt lives in Los Angeles now, but grew up in Massachusetts, so he is no stranger to winter. He took to snowshoeing right away, and as we tramped around the nearby woods or across the blinding white, wind-blown Sahara of the lake, he and I dreamed up a spectacular new stage production, on a scale with Riverdance, Cirque du Soleil, and Ice Capades, that we are going to call "SNOWDANCE: Lord of the Snows."

As we traded ideas, the vision grew into a concept for a massive, over-the-top production, on a vast stage of artificial snow, with dramatic lighting effects, soaring synthesizer music with dynamic percussion, lasers and pyro, dry ice, and a huge cast of performers, all on snowshoes. Just imagine the choreography . . .

Uniquely among my friends, Matt and I have developed a certain "arch" tone of conversation, so that sometimes we discuss absurdities as if we were serious. As the subject matter veers into deliberate sur-reality, we go on talking with complete sincerity, a kind of *faux* earnestness built on conscious irony. In that spirit, we envisioned a logo consisting of a sparkly snowflake beside the word SNOWDANCE, spelled out in big silver glitter letters against, say, powder blue. I figured that every woman of a certain age would want a sweatshirt like that. Matt thought probably everyone in the *world* would want a sweatshirt like that.

I spread my arms, all innocent frankness, and said to Matt, "I know it might seem shallow to jump straight to thinking of ideas for the *merch*, when here we are conceiving such a vast enterprise of artistic genius, but hey—I can't help but see the entire creative rainbow that lays before us." I shook my head with amazement, "You know, when you and I are together, all I can say is, 'Magic happens.'"

From then on that was the theme for our weekend together in the north: "Magic happens."

Here is Matt, making some magic happen on the 'shoes—"Bustin' a move, kickin' it old school, all right, bring on the noise, bring on the funk." This is just a hint of what will be brought to the stage in "SNOWDANCE: Lord of the Snows." Watch for it.

After Matt's visit, I had a little more time to myself, then a brief appearance by Brutus, who also did some impressive snowdancing on the snowshoes—though unintended, in his case. He just fell.

I also shared my February with the woodland animals, whose tracks I tried to decipher in the snowy woods, identifying deer, fox, squirrel, and snowshoe hare. My man Keith, who looks after the property while I'm off, you know, *paying* for it, and his helper, Pierre, installed the new location of my multi-leveled bird feeder, Bubba's Birdbrain Café. The black-capped chickadees discovered it on the first morning, and I was happy to see them flitting in and out in their cheery, gregarious mobs. The chickadees were soon joined by a calmer, but no less sociable group, the common redpolls, with their delicate russet plumage and bright vermilion caps. Mrs. Hairy Woodpecker dropped by to sample the suet, and a solitary red-breasted nuthatch was an occasional diner, seeing off the chickadees if they crowded him too much. I recognized the spirit of a fellow cranky hermit.

In any account of this Best February Ever, I would have to include the lunar eclipse. Around 10:00 on the night of the seventeenth, Carrie and I watched Earth's shadow start to slip across the bright moon, framed among the bare, black trees. Like the Christmas song, "Brightly shone the moon that night, though the frost was cruel"—it was minus twenty outside, so we watched from *indoors*, with all the lights off but the fireplace. "A world lit only by fire," as an eloquent historian described the not-too-distant past.

Across the radiant, silver-blue snow, the trees stretched dark, sharp-etched shadows, silhouettes that gradually faded as the darkness crossed the moon. Finally the sphere turned a dull orange, and the stars shone brighter in the eerie dimness. Long minutes later, a spark of silver fire returned to the opposite edge of the moon, and crept across its mournful face. The light radiated down across our snowbound world, and the forest began to glow again. Magic happens.

Back in the early twentieth century, before color photography was widely seen, Canadian landscape painters exhibiting their work in Britain were derided by British art critics for portraying such obvious absurdities as pink and purple snow. Any resident of a Nordic country knows the palette of winter colors ranges from delicate pinks to sparkling silver to deep soulful blue to a brilliant, blinding Arctic white with prismatic, diamond-like sparks. When I look at paintings of winter landscapes by artists from other northern countries, in Scandinavia or Russia, I see the same qualities of light and color.

And they make me smile. Because magic happens.

SOUTH BY SOUTHWEST

MAY 2008

From San Juan, Puerto Rico, to Los Angeles, California, April and early May carried me through seventeen shows and more than 7,000 miles of motorcycling. That journey quite literally stretched from the far-thest southeast to the farthest southwest of the United States, and the scenery varied from tropical rainforest and Caribbean beaches to the Everglades, remote bayous, the Deep South's lofty trees bearded with Spanish moss, the sage and mesquite rangeland of West Texas, the massive, eroded towers of Monument Valley, the cactus desert of southern Arizona, and the wide-open, creosote-dotted expanse of the high Mojave Desert, with its Joshua trees and the distant snowpeaks of the Sierra Nevada.

These images are part of my latest series of experiments in travel photography, a collection titled "Action Self-Portraits with Scenery." While I ride along (on a straight and empty road, of course), I hold my camera out to the side, or over my head, and snap away. The technique yields many failures, and ongoing lessons in "remote framing," but oc-casionally it captures the desired effect—the perspective of a helmeted rider passing through a backdrop of natural beauty.

The idea evolved when my usual riding partner, Michael, was called away on other duties, and I rode alone for a few days. Without a model, or designated photographer, I was trying to figure out how to continue my attempt to document the combination of motorcycles and landscapes. Scenery doesn't seem nearly as interesting without a kinetic, human element, I don't think, and parking an empty bike in front of a landscape isn't very satisfying. Not wanting to fiddle with any kind of on-bike camera mount (especially after watching Brutus struggle to get one to work for the whole European run last October), I had to come up with something comparable to the "Ski-Cam™" I introduced for my cross-country skiing photos. Or like the method I made into a theme on my *Ghost Rider* travels—parking my old 1100GS in the middle of the road on its centerstand, with scenery all around, and the road ahead diminishing to its vanishing point.

In that spirit, when I made the long solo ride to Monument Valley during a two-day break between shows in Oklahoma City and Albuquerque (eventually riding 1,000 miles in two and a half days), I was determined to recreate the cover shot from *Ghost Rider*. On the same stretch of road where that photo had been taken ten years ago (ten years ago? Ten *lifetimes*), I posed my current 1200GS.

It was a stirring moment for me, haunting, resonant, and almost surreal. In those two simple images of stationary motorcycles in a stark, dramatic landscape, I connect all the journeys of the past ten years, throughout the world and throughout myself.

(Fun Fact: *Ghost Rider* still outsells my other books by more than double, despite its dark mood. As they used to say, go figure.)

Before the first show in San Juan, the band had already rehearsed for several weeks in March and early April, getting back into performance shape after a few months away. As usual, I began with two weeks on my own, this time at home in California, commuting to Drum Channel's new multimedia facility just up the Pacific Coast Highway. Terry Bozzio, the ingeniously innovative percussion virtuoso ("drummer" doesn't seem sufficient), is more-or-less the artist-in-residence at DC these days, and it was inspiring to share our lunch breaks with owner Don Lombardi, watching films of masters like Buddy Rich— even slowing down Buddy's snare break in "Love for Sale" and trying to figure out, "How is he doing that?"

(Fun Fact: Buddy had a technique of turning his left wrist over, reversing the "cradle" of the stick so it approached the drumhead sideways; thus he could strike it in both directions, like a guitarist's style of alternate-picking. That's just *sick*.)

On my final day in that intense drum-immersion course (including playing along with our CDs and rehearsing my solo for hours every day), I took part in an impromptu percussion trio with Terry and another of my favorite drummers, Joey Heredia. That experience was both inspiring and humbling (a healthy combination).

After ten days in Toronto rehearsing with "the guys at work," we spent almost a week in San Juan for full production rehearsals.

When our manager, Ray, suggested that idea back in Scandinavia last October, when Brutus and I had been freezing on the bikes every day, the notion of starting a tour in the tropics sounded pretty sweet. And it was—more than I could have imagined.

My only experience of Puerto Rico had been changing planes in San Juan many times on my way to the British Virgin Islands years ago, so my impressions were hardly ideal. With a few free days between rehearsals, or earlier on the work days, Michael and I were able to get out on our motorcycles and explore pretty widely around what proved to be a fascinating and richly scenic island. Carrie joined me for a few days, and we spent an enjoyable day poking around the ancient fort, narrow streets, and European ambience of Old San Juan. Altogether, Puerto Rico proved to be a delightful combination of influences, mingling elements of West Indian, Spanish, African, American, and Mexican culture and atmosphere.

(Fun Fact: Rum was introduced to Puerto Rico in the early 1500s by Spanish governor Ponce de Léon—who, incidentally, never once mentioned a "fountain of youth" in his writings. However, a few centuries later the piña colada was invented in Puerto Rico, and it has probably helped to rejuvenate full many an aging Yankee libido with tropical languor.)

When Carrie had flown home, Michael and I had a free day before the show in San Juan, so we set out across the island's spine on a series of little roads called the Ruta Panorámica. We had made a symbolic visit to the lighthouse on the northeastern point of the island, el Faro de las Cabezas, and now headed for the lighthouse on the far southwestern point, el Faro de Cabo Rojo. In the valleys and up the mountainsides, we rode through deep rainforest, with hanging vines and an incredible tapestry of different greens.

Most of my tropical sojourns in recent years have been to the Hawaiian Islands, whose remote location in the middle of the Pacific Ocean naturally limited the diversity of its flora and fauna (though not its lushness and beauty). Riding through the dense greenery in El Yunque National Forest, on our first ride in Puerto Rico, I was struck by the seemingly numberless variety of plants and trees, from ferns and cycads (the oldest plant form on earth—dinosaur food) to banana

palms and bamboo, delicate little blossoms at the roadside, velvety mosses, and a mosaic of interlocking leaves overhead.

It might almost be said that Hawaii's relatively limited palette of greenery suggests a creationist simplicity, a pristine Eden, while Puerto Rico, collecting from North America, South America, and even the ancient supercontinent of Pangea, overflows with a complex hurly-burly of evolutionary struggle and burgeoning life. Even the smell of the Puerto Rican forest was richer, darker, and more pungent. It reminded me of another Caribbean island, Montserrat, where we recorded at Air Studios back in the '80s, and the primeval smells of the night forest as we drove back to the guest house at night after work.

(Fun Fact: Puerto Rico is classified as a United States Territory, acquired from Spain in 1898. In 1950, there were outbreaks of violent liberationism, including the attempted assassination of President Truman and a volley of shots in the House of Representatives that wounded five Congressmen. More recently, the people have held several indecisive referendums on whether to become a republic, a state, or retain their present status.)

The tiny, winding roads led us up across high ridges with majestic views, the rich green valleys sloping down to the glittering turquoise and blue water—the Atlantic Ocean to the north, the Caribbean Sea to the south. The riding was challenging, over crumbling pavement in tightly wound, narrow switchbacks, and I was reminded of certain roads in Mexico—especially el Espinazo de Diablo, "the spine of the devil," in the Sierra Madre. Other similarities to Mexican roads were the hazards of chickens, dogs, iguanas, cows, horses, ancient smoking cars and pickups, erratic driving, non-functioning brake lights and turn signals—not only unused, in the fashion of thoughtless drivers everywhere, but actually not working, their bulbs seemingly shaken to bits on the local roads. Potholes and broken shoulders were sometimes repaired with a patchwork of lumpy asphalt, and if a section of road had washed away down a cliff, they simply moved the guardrail in, greeting the oncoming rider with a sudden stretch of one-lane road. And perhaps an oncoming truck or school bus.

For all of those reasons, most of our cross-island ride was taken in first gear, creeping around blind hairpins with the ever-present possibility of . . . anything. In steeper country, where the road was carved into loops down a mountainside, the houses were perched at the pavement's edge. With no flat ground for a driveway, say, if a guy needed to work on his car, he simply parked it on the road and jacked it up— offering yet another surprise as we rounded a blind corner.

Michael prepares to descend the steepest road I have ever ridden. Narrow, too.

With all that, it took Michael and me seven and a half hours to cover only 150 miles, but after such a long, hard day, we parked at the Parador Guánica 1929, a charmingly restored old hotel on the mangrove-fringed bay of Guánica.

(Fun Fact: There is a bay in Newfoundland humorously called Useless Bay, and as I looked around the inlet surrounding our hotel, a monotonous circle of mangroves broken only by an abandoned, rusting sugar mill, and signs warning against swimming—"It is prohibit"— I decided this must be Puerto Rico's version of Useless Bay.)

The next day continued with more of those sinuous mountain roads, heading north through the rugged interior, with lush vegetation, some picturesque villages, and occasional vistas of distant valleys. (To adventurous motorcyclists—Puerto Rico is *definitely* a recommended destination, especially if there is a motorcycle rental company there. If there isn't—start one.)

Passing the famous observatory at Arecibo, we reached the northern coast, then detoured onto a small road that followed the shore for a few miles of undeveloped beach (increasingly rare on any tropical island). After that we surrendered to the busy multi-lane toll road, and made our way to the conurbation of San Juan, and the arena. The idyllic moment pictured here is thus not representative of our "riding dynamic" that day, nor of the hellish traffic in which we were about to be embroiled getting into San Juan, nor does it suggest the oppressive heat and humidity. But it is a pretty picture.

For once I'll offer up the fantasy . . .

For many years I have looked longingly at a little road on the Florida map that runs all the way south through Everglades National Park, ending at a dot called Flamingo, right at the southernmost tip of Florida's cape. Once before I described the road atlas of the United States as "the Book of Dreams," and this is a fine example of the kind of elusive, remote little road that tantalizes my imagination.

That particular road, though, had always been just too far from any show for me to get there and back, even with a day off. This time I made it happen—though I paid a heavy price: a long slog north on the so-called Florida's Turnpike, which might be my version of hell on earth, to the next show in Orlando.

The Everglades, the "River of Grass," like many of America's landscapes, can only be appreciated by traveling through it, and getting some sense of its sheer scale. Riding through the heart of the Everglades, I noticed that the roadside vegetation had the same quality as the Western deserts—the added precipitation from the pavement's runoff resulted in a greater variety, and especially size, in the plant life at the road's margins, like a naturally unnatural hedgerow. Beyond that narrow line, to every horizon stretched a vast savannah of brownish-green grass, broken only by occasional groves of tall, spindly pines.

The Everglades birdlife is famously spectacular, white egrets, herons, storks, cormorants, anhingas, and other water birds plainly visible from the road. During my travels right across the South, in that season of spring migrations, I saw a great variety of birds, mostly on the fly (them and me!). Ducks, geese, hawks, falcons, grackles, doves, crows, jays, vultures, and the characteristic birds of the West, yellow-headed blackbirds, magpies, and horned larks.

(Fun Fact: You never actually *see* horned larks—you just know it's them by the sudden flurry as they rise in front of you from a Western road, missing you by seeming inches as they disappear in a blur.)

And speaking of national parks (as I was just before the birds distracted me), I was able to add a few more of them to my collection—and their passport stamps to the front of my journal. With a rare two-day break between shows in New Orleans and Austin, Dave drove us through the night back to Texas. Almost as soon as he had parked the bus at a truck stop in New Braunfels, I dragged Michael out of his bunk and all the way west to Big Bend National Park, which I hadn't visited since the journey recounted in *Traveling Music*, back in 2003.

The first 400-mile day brought us to Marathon, Texas, and a delightful old hotel called the Gage, which seemed to be popular with traveling motorcyclists. About twenty bikes were lined up in front of it, on the Route 66–style main street of Marathon—nearly every business huddled along a two-lane highway. At night it was a brief oasis of neon over a ribbon of pavement that flowed in and out through a wide desert of darkness.

The next morning we headed south and through the park, reveling in the

mostly straight, empty roads framed in majestic scenery and a sense of limitless space. As I have noted before, referring to the Grand Canyon, it seems impossible to hold a landscape of such grandeur in memory. Every time I see Grand Canyon, or the Big Bend country, I am freshly amazed.

Riding north and east, putting in another 400-mile day (in 106° heat), we worked our way back toward the next show in Austin, stopping for the night in San Angelo. For the first time ever, in any of my day-off rambles, we had trouble getting rooms there. Most of the motels were filled with investigators, victims, and counselors dealing with that fundamentalist, polygamist Mormon sect in nearby El Dorado.

(Fun Fact: "Reformed" Mormons might not like it, but it could be said that those people, however benighted, and unquestionably victims and perpetrators of what right-thinking people would call abuse, were *true* Latter-Day Saints. They remained faithful to the divine revelations preached, and practiced, by Joseph Smith and Brigham Young—that God *commanded* the men to have multiple, ever-younger wives. In order to achieve statehood, back in 1896, the "reformed" church put those inconvenient truths aside. Sometimes even divine revelations have to bow to good business.)

When Michael and I visited Nauvoo, Illinois, last summer, we genuinely admired the life-size equestrian statue depicting Joseph Smith and his brother Hyrum riding to the courthouse in Carthage, knowing they rode to their deaths. (They could as easily have escaped West, and abandoned their people to an increasingly violent struggle with the neighboring "Gentiles," but as Wallace Stegner pointed out about Joseph Smith, "whatever he was, he was not a scoundrel or a coward.")

Somehow Michael got it into his twisted mind that he and I were reincarnations of Joseph and Hyrum (never mind—I didn't even ask), and here is what might be our equestrian portrait. It is the alternate variation of the "Action Self-Portrait with Scenery," holding the camera above my head and shooting backwards.

Collecting that Big Bend National Park passport stamp on April 22, a few days later I was on my way back from Monument Valley (not a national park, but a *tribal* park, being part of the vast Navajo reservation), riding solo, and decided I had time to make a brief stop at Mesa Verde National Park. (Note to riders: worth it just for the fifteen-mile ride up to the Visitors Center.)

Two days after that, I began my day at Petrified Forest National Park. Usually I wake up and look out the bus window at a line of tractor-trailers in a truck stop, but that morning I was delighted to open my blinds and see the familiar arrowhead logo of the National Park Service.

That was a fine sight to contemplate from my bed, and the beginning of perhaps my favorite day of solo riding. Through the Petrified Forest National Park, where many of the fossilized logs lay right at the roadside, broken into sections like shattered columns, I rode south into the colored strata of the badlands in the Painted Desert, then down to a simply wonderful piece of road: Highway 191 in eastern Arizona. Empty, endlessly winding in well-engineered curves of varying radius and banking, ascending through fragrant pine forests to spectacular vistas, patches of snow remaining at the roadside, though it was almost May (and in *Arizona*), then snaking and looping down again, the two-lane roller coaster offered a technically engaging and deeply satisfying thrill for almost a hundred miles.

I had been a little spooked about riding that highway, though, remembering that the only time I had ever been stranded by a motorcycle was on that road. As recounted in *Ghost Rider*, some warranty work on the 1100GS had been improperly reassembled, and the clutch shaft failed—in about as "middle of nowhere" a place as I could possibly be. Back in that fall of 1999, I sat at the roadside, reading, writing, and sipping Macallan, for about four hours before the truck and trailer arrived from the Tucson BMW dealer.

(Speaking of helpful BMW dealers, my thanks go to the service departments in North Dallas, Austin, Oklahoma City, and Reno, for some quick, friendly, and skillful work on the bikes during those 7,000 miles.)

Even nine years later, I recognized that spot at the roadside very well as I zoomed past it, and continued south (with a little superstitious relief) into the mesquite grasslands around Chiricahua National Monument. Late in the afternoon, I arrived at the Copper Queen Hotel in the old mining town of Bisbee, Arizona (another revisit from my *Ghost Rider* travels).

Dave met me at the Copper Queen, riding my back-up bike, an older 1200GS. As he had done from Taos to Albuquerque, Dave was going to ride into Phoenix with me on the show day. (Though I don't mind riding solo, it seems irresponsible not to have a "wing man" on a show day. One bad puncture or mechanical mishap could not only leave me stranded—on the farthest reaches of a lonely road like Highway 191, say—but my failure to show up at work could disappoint an awful lot of people.)

Dave has a great affection for the Old West, and thus appreciated the preserved and restored century-old town of Bisbee, the Copper Queen Hotel, and especially, our brief pause the next morning in Tombstone.

Farther west, I was joined by Greg Russell, fellow drummer and self-described "Master of All Things Creative" (including designing my website, and creating the film behind my drum solo, and "Red Barchetta," this tour).

(Fun Fact: Greg shot that footage with three cameras mounted in the back of his pickup, then reversed the motion.)

Greg and I rode from a truck stop in Kingman, Arizona, up through the wilds of western Nevada on a nice stretch of remote gravel road. In this Action Self-Portrait, you can also see how *windy* it was, by the dust-trails swept away beside us (nicer for the following rider!).

We crossed into California through the Silver Peak Range, over the fantastic Westgard Pass. I had taken that road a few times before, first led that way by Brutus on the *Test for Echo* tour in 1996. Narrow—sometimes one lane—and little used except by the odd RV or rancher's pickup, the Westgard Pass is a symphony in three movements, three separate stages to the crossing, with plateaus between, and each twisty section presenting different dynamics and topography.

Riding down the final stretch to the Owens Valley, we were facing those snow-streaked Sierras (as shown in the second photograph, way back at the beginning of what has become a colossal epic). The next photograph, taken by the Master of All Things Creative, captured something rarely pictured in, say, motorcycle magazines. The vastness of the landscape, the flow of its contours laid bare by a low, intricate pattern of vegetation, and a banking motorcycle arcing through the distant center. I call it art.

And speaking of art, particularly "performance art," let us recall that all of this motorcycling was part of a *concert* tour, after all. Between the days off in Monument Valley or Mono Lake, I had to show up at arenas and amphitheaters and "earn my gas money."

(Fun Fact: The fuel bill for our tour buses alone these days is a whopping $6,500 *per week*.)

But the shows have been going very well, too. It may be my imagination, but it seemed to me that the audiences in places we hadn't played in many years, like New Orleans, Austin, and Oklahoma City, were especially appreciative, and excited that we were simply *there*.

(As I stood beside a bayou in Louisiana, this alligator slowly surfaced in front of me. It seemed excited that I was simply there, too. I soon wasn't.)

At the very end of the show in Dallas, when I stood up to bow and wave and the lights were bright on the audience, I saw a sign way back on the stage-left side: "LET NEIL SING." I laughed out loud at that. As the old saying goes, "Be careful what you wish for."

Hoping not to appear immodest (to quote Dizzy Dean again, "It ain't braggin' if you can back it up"), I have to say that I think the band is playing at its absolute peak. (And I guess that's not bragging—I'm only talking about *our* peak, not anybody else's!)

But each show takes so much out of us that we live in a world of hurt, especially toward the end of a long run like this one. But—it's a good hurt. It is well earned, and well rewarded. (Some of the pain comes from those 7,000 miles in the saddle, too.)

There is a saying in French: "*Ça vaut la peine*"—it is worth the grief or pain. That's how I feel about those journeys, and what it takes to deliver the kind of performances we've been giving lately.

(Fun Fact: The drumming-induced calluses on my fingers sometimes split open, which lets the sweat into the tender flesh beneath. As described in "Haste Ye Back," it causes a kind of nerves-on-edge torture, and finally, in desperation, I tried filling the split with a drop of Krazy Glue. It really works!)

After the show, tired and sore and sitting back on the bus, I struggle to my feet to refresh my glass of Macallan with a litany of German imprecations: "*Einbahnstrasse, gemütlichkeit, hauptbahnhof, ausfahrt, schadenfreude.*"

Which is to say, "one-way street, friendliness, train station, exit, and taking pleasure in the pain of others."

That last would describe Michael, who laughs at my pain.

(Fun Fact: Michael is an evil and unfeeling monster. I don't know how I've put up with him for three tours and 75,000 miles. Maybe it's because I enjoy insulting him so much.)

Often enough, though, my world of pain is balanced by moments of pleasure. In *Roadshow* I wrote about one of my favorite roads, California's Highway 33 up above Ojai, and about one of my favorite flowers—Spanish broom, which explodes in clusters of yellow blossoms in early summer along the highway edges of the West. Apart from brightening a somewhat stark palette of arid, rocky landscape, scrubby chaparral, and dark green California live-oaks, during their short blooming season, those yellow flowers fill the air with an intoxicating fragrance that compares to only two other floral perfumes: lilac and jasmine.

Exemplifying the favorite road and favorite flower theme, here is one of my favorite of the Action Self-Portrait with Scenery series—riding down that glorious Highway 33 toward home, swooping through the bends with my helmet filled with Spanish broom, after a show up in Concord, California, and after sleeping on the bus in a truck stop at the junction of Interstate 5 and State Highway 99.

A final quote (which is often attributed to Mark Twain, but was actually written by the French scientist and philosopher Blaise Pascal): "I am sorry this letter is so long, but I did not have time to make it shorter."

(Fun Fact: The theological default called Pascal's Wager is a pusillanimous theorem stating that it's "safer" to believe in God than not, because you have nothing to lose if you're right, and everything to lose if you're wrong. All I can say to that is "Man up, Pascal!")

A final Action Self-Portrait with Scenery, this one of a very happy rider, motoring along the Pacific Coast Highway near Malibu, bound for home.

WHEN THE ROAD ENDS

JUNE 2008

Witness my dismay at finding the road ahead—the road to *work*—buried in several feet of snow, on the first of June. You can see it was a paved road, with painted lines, proper signage, and the tracks of a four-wheeler whose journey had also ended there. Ahead you see my beloved "winding road" sign (one of our "snakes and arrows" logos, the one that marks the door of my warm-up room, otherwise known as Bubba Gump, backstage at shows). Clearly, on that day, the speed limit behind the winding road sign would only apply to snowmobiles.

(Metaphor alert: This photo, the "winding road" sign, and the story's title all contain potentially meaningful quantities of metaphorical resonance. I.e., I'll be jamming on those riffs.)

That rudely interrupted road was near Mount St. Helens, not far from a jobsite near Portland that Michael and I were on our way to, after sleeping on the bus up near the Tri-Cities, at the confluence of the Snake and Columbia. It was obvious we would have to turn back and find another way to work, but it was also strange for us to remember, facing that impassable wall of snow, that back in 2004, on the R30 tour, Michael, Dave, and I had ridden that same road together. However, that had been in July, when all that snow would finally have melted. Not in June, apparently.

In the mountains of the West, like the Rockies, the Cascades, and the Sierra Nevada, many high-elevation roads are simply closed in winter, because they are impossible to keep clear—some of those areas might be buried in up to *forty feet* of snow. This tour, in May and June, Michael and I seemed to arrive too early for quite a few of those roads. We were turned back by snow in the Sangre de Cristo ("Blood of Christ") Mountains in New Mexico, in the Cascades in Washington State, depicted above, and in the Blue Mountains of eastern Oregon—on the very next day.

After sleeping on the bus near Pendleton, Oregon, I had planned an adventurous day off, a 400-mile ramble from eastern Oregon into Idaho on tiny back roads. By early morning, Michael and I were already *way* out there, on a remote U.S. Forest Service road. The moderately rough and twisty gravel track followed a boisterous river, swollen with snowmelt (a clue, perhaps?), as we climbed ever upward, pounding and sliding along between leafy hardwoods and pines. After an hour or so, we met an unexpected sight: a sudden swath of sophisticated pavement in both directions, all "official" looking, with painted lines, metal signs, and everything.

Trouble was, it was another "Closed in Winter" road, and as we followed its high, winding curves, things began to look bad.

A few miles on, bad turned to worse, and once again we halted at deep banks of snow that completely covered the road. We tiptoed over the first patch, pushing my bike through, then Michael following in my wheel-ruts, but all too soon the road disappeared again, this time under a massive snowfield. Even after a reconnaissance on foot, it went on as far as I could see, broken only by the tracks of an elk. Once again we had to face the grim reality—this road had ended.

Unless a particular road ends at the ocean, say, or at a high-mountain retreat, it is an uncomfortable feeling to have your way suddenly blocked. I don't know about other travelers, but my whole being recoils at the thought of going back the way I have come, and I'll do anything I can to avoid it. (Another road metaphor, of course.)

With the help of our (usually) trusty GPS units, Doofus and Dingus,

and the paper map, we navigated our way out of that mess, but had lost so much time that we had to resort to the interstate (though not a bad one: I-84 across open stretches of eastern Oregon and into Idaho) for 300 miles.

Usually, wherever we happen to find ourselves in late afternoon—whenever I'm ready for our road to end—I start looking for somewhere to stop for the night, watching for billboards or pausing to peruse the list of accommodations programmed into Doofus and Dingus (incomplete, rapidly out of date, and sometimes incredibly *wrong*, but occasionally helpful). That day, however, I had a particular destination in mind: the Sun Valley Lodge, near Ketchum, Idaho. I had stayed there with Brutus on the *Test for Echo* tour, in early 1997, and again during my *Ghost Rider* travels, and I knew it would be the rare combination of a fantastic journey and a great destination.

Opened in 1936 with a fanfare of visiting movie stars like Errol Flynn, Clark Gable, Gary Cooper, and Ingrid Bergman, the Sun Valley

The snowy heights in the background are exactly where we were when that road ended

Lodge remains a luxurious hotel in a winter playground. These days it fills the rest of the year with conventions, judging by my out-of-season visits.

Ernest Hemingway spent his last years in Ketchum, where he is buried—under a plain flat stone next to a matching one for his fourth wife, Mary. Near the Sun Valley Lodge there's an artful memorial, set among the trees along a stream.

The inscription reads, "Best of all he loved the fall, the leaves yellow on the cottonwoods, leaves floating on the trout streams, and above the hills the high blue windless skies. Now he will be a part of them forever. Ernest Hemingway, Idaho, 1939." The words had been written for a friend's eulogy, but resonate well for the writer, too.

During dinner at the Lodge that night, Michael and I had a table overlooking the outdoor skating rink. We looked at each other and nodded, "We *have* to do it." After dinner we rented some skates and made like Brian Boitano and Elvis Stojko for a while. (To the tune of the song from the *South Park* movie, "What Would Brian Boitano Do?")

In further "sports" news, that day and the next we enjoyed some spectacular rides in Idaho. I have described the state before as seeming under-rated for its roads, scenery, and lack of much other traffic. We took a roundabout route (naturally) into Boise, north through Salmon and west along the Payette River. Some grayish snow banks remained at the roadsides, among the characteristic crisscross rail fences and coniferous forest, and (quoth the anchorman, "now here's Bubba with the weather report") the gray sky gave way to rain showers, sometimes light, sometimes heavy.

Riding in the rain does not appeal to every rider, but I don't mind it. (In any case, there's nothing I can do about it, so might as well enjoy it. My chosen motto this year has been, "What cannot be altered, must be endured"—about which more later.) Faced with wet roads and diminished visibility, I can adapt to the slower, gentler pace, and the somber, pensive mood. (Another metaphorical bit of roadcraft: "There is no such thing as bad weather, only the wrong clothes." Or the wrong attitude.)

Plus, I *had* been wanting to capture an Action Self-Portrait of riding in the rain. You can see from the rider's intent expression behind that rain-dappled face shield that it is a serious business.

Speaking of faces telling stories, I spent one day off *not* riding, as I tend to do once every month of the tour, and was able to view something like that in myself. A luxurious hotel in Chicago made a nice change from our usual cheap motels (however "atmospheric"), and I was satisfied not to see anyone all day but the room service waiter. (Even not visiting *one* gas station was a symbolic treat.)

During that day I watched the finished edit for our live DVD from last October in Rotterdam. It looked really good, and we had played well, so it was enjoyable to view, but I could not get over how *composed* I looked. Such a contrast to how it feels, mentally and physically— brain frantically trying to keep everything "under control," and body pounding away at full strength all the time. It doesn't seem fair that it should look so easy. But as I learned a long time ago, "Ain't no why, ain't no fair."

My friend Jamie Borden, a drummer in a Vegas band called Phoenix, wrote me that a friend of his who might be described as "an old Vegas hand" told him after seeing our show, "Neil is up there just whaling away and never makes an expression that fits how much energy and concentration it must take to do what he does. He has the best poker face I have ever seen."

A kind of high praise, I suppose—and perhaps an idea for a future vocation. When the road ends.

Meanwhile, back in Boise . . . I was joined by Brian Catterson, Editor in Chief of *Motorcyclist* magazine, for his fourth annual appearance as guest rider—and his fourth annual good fortune to ride with me in rainy weather. Michael flew to Denver to take care of some unpleasant business involving a menacing psycho, while Brian and I made our way down from a truck stop in Wyoming (spotting a golden eagle on the road, a rare thrill) into Colorado, and into plenty of rain. Cold, too.

We stopped for the night in the pleasant town of Gunnison, and I said to Brian at dinner, "Nothing is better for your riding technique than twisty roads in the rain."

He nodded, still shivering.

The next day we faced more rain, and an impromptu side trip to a nearby national park, Black Canyon of the Gunnison, for a passport stamp. I told Brian it was "about forty miles," but it was more like sixty, and I'm pretty sure he appreciated an extra 120 miles of riding in the rain. And worse was yet to come, for when we climbed the 11,312-foot Monarch Pass, we found ourselves riding through a full-blown *blizzard*. An early title for this story was "Snow in June," given all the previous encounters with the frozen elements, but this was the capper. Near the summit of that pass, the pavement was clear, if shiny wet, but the roadsides were solid white, and the air was filled with flying snow, covering our windscreens and face shields. The temperature hovered at exactly the freezing point. (I nervously kept an eye on the thermometer on my bike's instrument panel, while wiping snow off my face shield with my left glove—which has a pad on the back of the index finger just for that purpose. Clever.)

That time we made it through, but unfortunately the show we were on our way to—Red Rocks, near Denver—had been canceled due to impending bad weather. The same front that delivered us a blizzard brought thunderstorms to Denver, and tornadoes to Kansas. Our equipment trucks and crew buses had already been on-site at Red Rocks that morning when the decision was made to cancel, but we'll be making it up at the beginning of the next run.

Knowing the weather was threatening that show, I checked my cell phone at the park and saw I had a message, but there was no cell service until an hour later, back in Gunnison. I led Brian into a roadside spray-wash (a rare and valuable shelter for a motorcyclist on a rainy day—more roadcraft), and called tour manager Liam to discuss alternatives for the make-up date, and bus driver Dave to plan our logistics. I arranged to meet Dave and Michael in the parking lot of an arena in downtown Denver, where I did a quick oil change, then we loaded the bikes in the trailer and climbed on the bus. Dropping Brian at his hotel, Dave drove Michael and me to a truck stop in western Kansas. The following day we would enjoy a pleasant ride on the back roads of the Great Plains, without snow, rain, cold, police, or traffic.

Some travelers are unimpressed by flat country, but on the back roads I find there is a certain *calmness*, a feeling of space to let your mind relax. There's little to fear, and plenty to look at: the farmhouses scattered among the open fields, occasional crossroads towns. (One, Hoxie, Kansas, has the motto on its sign: "Good Crops, Great People"; another in Saskatchewan has the alarming sign, "Tisdale, the Land of Rape and Honey." Of course they meant what Encarta defines as "an annual plant of the cabbage family that has bright yellow flowers and is grown commercially for its oil-bearing seeds and as a fodder crop," but . . . don't they know?) In early summer, the fields of Kansas were low and green, plush and velvety, stretching to the horizon. Hawks perched on fence posts, lines of cottonwoods traced the banks of slow, muddy rivers, red-winged blackbirds and goldfinches flitted across the road, and often we passed those Aermotor wind pumps, solitary and iconic. I studied different ones for many miles across the West and the Great Plains, to find just the right one, at the right distance from the road, with the light on the right side, and all that "artsy" stuff.

On the back of my bike is a one-gallon gas can, which I always carry west of the Mississippi and east of the Coastal Ranges—in the Great Plains and the Great Basin, where gas stations can be a long way apart. Once again, I never had to use it, but I felt so reassured just knowing it was there. (Metaphor alert.)

And now that my story's meanderings have followed the tour's itinerary back eastward, I would point out that in the middle of the country, our road ended a few times just because of *water*. Last summer I wrote about my traveling mode of "shunpiking," choosing the least-traveled roads, and seeking out ferries across rivers and lakes when I could find them. This year I was determined to ferry across the Mississippi, the Father of Waters, and first tried one at St. Francisville, Louisiana, between shows in Jacksonville and Houston. After a long ride, Michael and I learned the ferry was not running, because of what the sign announced as "High Water." We could see that for ourselves—the road to the dock was underwater—and we had to scramble down to the interstate and ride for Houston that way.

That was very early in the season, and in the tour—April 20—but a month later, May 21, I tried to take another ferry higher up the Mississippi, from Cassville, Wisconsin, over to Iowa, but it was also closed due to high water (at least I knew by then to check in advance—always learning). That rising water in the Mississippi headwaters was soon to wreak devastation in the area, as the huge, sluggish volume backed up into the other slow-moving rivers of the plains.

(My friend Chris Stankee has posted a story, "The Accidental Drum Tech," on the Sabian website, and it recounts some of the other dramas from the first few days of this run.)

The state monuments of North Dakota seem to be abandoned farmhouses, which are common along the country roadsides, and a little sad to contemplate. The combination of the state's depopulation, and the amalgamation of marginal family farms into agri-corporations, leaves behind these desolate memorials. Places where people have

North Dakota wetland, with
bird in flight (rider, too)

lived and loved, grown up and grown old, now moldering in the harsh
prairie weather.

However, the *national* monument of North Dakota, and neighboring Manitoba and Saskatchewan, ought to be the prairie wetlands.
Environmental slogans like "Save the Wetlands" can sound a little
dull, but start to seem *vitally* important when you see the constellation of ponds, sloughs, and small lakes surrounded by reeds, and
the millions of migrating birds that use them as stopovers and feeding stations.

Meanwhile, on our own spiraling migrations through the states
and provinces on this second summer of the *Snakes and Arrows* tour,
we were continuing eastward by mid-June. One morning, in the woods
of Pennsylvania, bright with flowering dogwoods, it looked like another road was about to end. A sign at the beginning of the road,
running through a state park, had read, "Drivable Trail, Open for use
by Licensed Motor Vehicles, No regular maintenance, 4-wheel drive
recommended."

And at first it wasn't too bad. Here I look back to make sure Michael is still with me.

But the track soon got much worse. A high-clearance, specialized off-road truck might have got through there, but no ordinary four-wheeler or "Licensed Motor Vehicle." We only just made it through some of the roughest sections (but again—go forward, or go back!), bounding over deep ruts, through wide, brown puddles, over mossy rocks, and into slippery mud. Here Michael negotiates a particularly dodgy stretch of the "Drivable Trail."

That too was a show day, on our way to Philadelphia, and once again we made it out to a real road, and got to work in plenty of time. Pennsylvania has been my "discovery" this tour (though when I said that to Geddy at dinner in the dressing room one night, he said, "I'm pretty sure it's been discovered already—they have people living there and everything"). The back roads of north-central Pennsylvania are as good as any in the East, for their curves, scenery, and relative empti-ness, and it is also one of the few Eastern areas where you might ride twenty miles without having to stop—along with parts of Virginia and West Virginia, maybe, and always the Adirondacks. (I saw a bumper sticker on a battered pickup there: "It ain't a damn park. It's the Adirondacks. It's where we live, and where we work." Some local conflicts between the natives and park authorities, I guess.)

Just one more show remained, in Boston, and by then we had made it to thirty-two, and brought our motorcycling total to almost 14,000 miles this summer.

During those miles, I have had plenty of time to think. In the middle of a grueling tour, I mostly just live from day to day, not counting how many more days until I get home, or how many until it is over (psychological roadcraft, like immediately changing your watch to a new time zone, and not thinking in terms of the previous one anymore). But from time to time I do allow myself to think about "when the road ends."

People often ask, "What's next for the band?", but we learned long ago that when you're in the middle of a big job, you don't need to talk about another one. So, in the middle of a tour, we never talk about making another album, and in the middle of recording, we never talk about another tour. One job at a time, even in your own head, is easier to deal with—you don't need another burden if you can keep it "in storage" for a while.

For fifteen years people have been saying to me, "I hear this is your last tour" (I've been saying it myself since 1989), but subjects like that don't even get raised among the three of us. Certainly after the last two summers of heavy touring, which will eventually add up to well over a hundred shows, there will be no more of that for a while.

(I adopted my current motto, "What cannot be altered, must be endured," around New Year's, and actually found it useful in such occasions as, say, flight delays. Only much later did I realize that the reverse was equally true, in a less passive way: "What cannot be endured, must be altered.")

Some fresh challenges await me, no doubt. Later this year, I have agreed to take part in another big-band project, a Buddy Rich tribute concert in October, and that will be a huge occasion to try to rise to. I'm thinking a lot about that these days.

While I ride the open roads, from time to time I have given a little thought to trying to write another book. It seems to me that the stories I've been writing for this website are laying a good foundation for another challenge I might like to undertake: a book called Roadcraft: How to Work the World. If I could draw together all I've learned about traveling, in the literal sense and in a larger, metaphorical way, it might be worthwhile. It wouldn't be just for motorcyclists, of course, or even just for travelers—but I would love to make the particular elements of roadcraft apply to the larger journey: life.

The gas can, the oil changes, the rain gear, the maps and signs.

How to make the most of the road you're on; what to do when the road gets tough; what to do when the road ends.

That would be a tale worth telling.

(Hint: In reference to the question, "What to do when the road ends," the correct response is not, "Pout.")

INDEPENDENCE DAY

JULY 2008

It was Friday, the Fourth of July, Independence Day, and Michael and I were riding to a show in the eastern United States. I can safely wager that few readers would identify the state pictured (no cheating and looking at the band's itinerary). In *Roadshow*, I ventured that every state had interesting roads, you just had to look for them, and a prime example I cited was the Garden State—New Jersey.

This dirt and gravel track (sometimes sandy, too—a particular hazard to us on our heavy bikes) framed in pinewoods ran through the Wharton State Forest in the southern part of the state. The area, known as the Pine Barrens, is officially designated the Pinelands National Reserve, a million acres of pitch pines and other vegetation adapted to the sandy, acidic soil and frequent fires. It is one of New

Jersey's more attractive areas, and Michael and I also traveled many pretty little roads in western Jersey, passing verdant farms, luxurious rural homes, and lush woodlands.

Independence Day was not a holiday for me, but I did exercise a measure of independence in how I got to work—traveling by motorcycle, and seeking out the roads less traveled: shunpiking. Even on a busy holiday weekend, when I design our route to follow roads no one drives unless they live on them, or dirt roads few travel anyway, I can navigate fairly enjoyably through even the most populous states. On this Fourth of July, we were on our way to Atlantic City, yet our road was a million acres away from cities, suburbs, and casinos.

The arena in Atlantic City was inside a garish casino, where the management held back (denied us and our fans) the front section of seats. Those were "comped" to the "high rollers" (by definition, big losers), and thus we looked out from the stage at the first few rows (the ones we could *see* most) filled with people who had no idea why they were there except that it was free.

In contrast to our real fans farther back, who would mortgage their *Hemispheres* picture discs, and perhaps internal organs, to get closer to the stage, we were confronted by mild curiosity at best, and at worst, rude indifference. As the show went on, we started to see empty seats where bored big losers had slipped away, a woman looking down and *texting* through whole songs, and a pair of slack-jawed, sulking teens (the Beavis and Butthead of the *Guitar Hero* generation—as Cartman from *South Park* says in the hilarious sample that Geddy uses in "The Trees," "Real guitars are for *old* people") actually *yawning*. Anyone would agree that yawning is not appropriate behavior at a rock concert. (Vomiting, yes, but not yawning.)

These casino specimens are only noteworthy because they represent such an utter contrast to the audience around them, and to the front rows every other night—smiling, singing, dancing, and cheering people pressed along the barricade and stretching to the far distance. Several nights this summer, during the opening song, "Limelight" ("*Living on a lighted stage, approaches the unreal*"—still so true!), especially when we were playing outdoors and I could see everybody, I couldn't help shaking my head in disbelief at the sheer *number* of people out there. "Unbelievable," I thought, "all of those people spent their money and their time, on this night in this place, to come and see *us*."

That realization is somehow humbling—you feel you have to try to *earn* support like that, because it's obvious that those people deserve the best you can give them.

Another unstereotypical New Jersey scene–a hayfield and maple tree among horse farms and tree-shaded mansions

A couple of years ago my father sent me an anecdote about baseball great Joe DiMaggio, telling how a journalist asked the Yankee Clipper why he went out and played so hard every day. Joltin' Joe replied, "There is always some kid who may be seeing me for the first or last time—I owe him my best." Dad added that this attitude reminded him of someone else he knew, which made me feel good.

All through that Independence Day weekend, Michael and I were motorcycling to shows in the Northeast. I was looking over the maps each day with a combination of apprehension and claustrophobia. Yes, there are good roads to be found everywhere, but the heavily populated East is a challenge. Like lyric writing, designing an enjoyable route is a kind of puzzle—sitting on the floor of the bus's front lounge in the afternoon before soundcheck with maps strewn about, tracing my orange highlighter along the gray lines, trying to avoid major roads, larger towns, and suburban sprawl. Then Michael takes on the puzzle of transferring that zigzag scribble to the computer mapping software, "Mother," and "the boys," our GPS units, Doofus and Dingus. (I've noticed that both Michael and I talk to ourselves while we're mapping.) In the East, so many lines that look like rural roads on the map (that lying map!) turn out to run through strip malls and subdivisions. In addition, I have ridden nearly all of the "interesting" roads in that area before, plus it was a holiday weekend—no road is fun when it's jammed with traffic.

So, my glance wandered over the map to the only open area, the blue part, and I had a flash of inspiration: "*Go to sea, Billy!*" On the morning of July fifth, Michael and I rode down through the pretty, but busy, back roads of Connecticut and onto a ferry from Point Judith, Rhode Island, to Block Island, thirteen miles off the coast, in Long Island Sound. (I had long understood that Rhode Island's name came from a metaphor for an "island of tolerance," but it actually derives from a mix-up between Block Island, first called Rhode Island after its resemblance to the Greek island Rhodes, and the mainland. Block Island was renamed by a Dutch explorer, coincidentally named Block, while Newport's island was changed from Aquidneck to Rhode Island, which later became the name of the state, one of the Original Thirteen.) The only town on Block Island, New Shoreham, with an off-season population of barely 1,000 souls, calls itself "the smallest town in the smallest state."

Block Island felt like a smaller version of other New England islands, like Nantucket or Martha's Vineyard, with large old white-painted, shuttered hotels in the Colonial style beside seafood

The Great Salt Pond on Block Island with Canada geese just drifting and reflecting (like the Canadian rider)

restaurants and souvenir shops along the waterfront, gray-sided salt-box houses tucked among the dunes and salt-resistant foliage, a pair of historic lighthouses, and a few tiny roads through a tumbled green landscape that was fragrant with sea air and flowers.

Here Michael and I have reached the end of the road again (continuing a theme from my previous story, "When the Road Ends," we were turned back a couple of times this run, in Kentucky and Ohio—once because, as a local advised us, "a crick runs through that road"). We were at the island's northern tip, with the North Point Lighthouse in the distance. I was pretty sure we could make it all the way across that rocky beach to the lighthouse, but Michael always discourages me from trying stunts like that. Not that Michael is above breaking the law—why, I've seen him exceed the posted speed limit, oh, every day—but, given his credentials as a private investigator, and contract work with federal law enforcement agencies, he draws the line at breaking *federal* laws. Like the time in Puerto Rico when he didn't want to follow me into a national forest road just because there was a government sign prohibiting anyone but "authorized personnel" beyond that point.

"Well," I said, "*I'm* authorized—by me! Let's go!"

Michael said he considered my argument specious, and my behavior unconscionable. (What he actually said was less articulate, and less quotable.) I said, "Hmpf," tossed my helmet, and turned around.

Block Island proved to be a restful getaway, even just for one night, and after a decent dinner and some spectacular "Fifth of July" fireworks, I opened my hotel room window to the sea air, and had a deeply refreshing and much needed sleep. (A few days later I smiled at a sign along the New York shore of Lake Ontario for a place called "Point Salubrious," a Latin name meaning "beneficial to health.")

In the morning, while Michael and I waited for the ferry back to the mainland, and to a show in Connecticut, we decided to ride a short loop around the southern part of the island. Because it was hot and muggy, and island traffic was light and slow-paced, I followed Michael's bad example and rode without helmet and jacket—just to see what it was like, really. "Going commando," we called it.

Michael goes commando on Block Island

In a couple hundred thousand miles of motorcycling in the past fourteen years, only twice have I tried riding helmetless—one time around an open stretch of hardpacked sand in the Sahara, for a mile or so, and that morning on Block Island. It was the kind of place where residents and visitors typically rode around on bicycles and scooters, though I read in the local paper that thirty percent of the island's emergency medical calls were for bicycle and scooter accidents.

As we rode along the island's narrow lanes at 20 or 30 mph that morning, I was surprised to find I actually didn't *like* the feeling at all. Even at such a slow speed, the wind was loud, and buffeted my face and head, so I found the experience of being bare-headed uncomfortable and distracting. I can only imagine what that would feel like on a 400-mile day, or a 1,000-mile day, compared to wearing a full-face helmet. With my own head encased in that light, airy, transparent cocoon, I still feel plenty exposed to the elements—every degree of cold or heat; every waft of fragrance in the air, from blooming flowers to burning brake pads—yet I feel more focused on the road, able to observe, plan, and handle the motorcycle with a sense of *composure*. (Interesting that I've now applied that word as a desirable component of cross-country skiing, drumming, and motorcycling.) On the bike, that calm, yet sharply aware feeling is especially apparent when wearing earplugs, which attenuate the wind noise while still letting in "necessary" sounds—horns, sirens, and shouted conversations with your riding partner at gas pumps (Michael and I notice people staring at us sometimes). In my clear-lensed bubble, I eliminate the sensory overload and ride with a sense of peace.

That experience of riding "naked," as it were, and a couple of other coincidental experiences around that time that will soon be told, had me thinking about the helmet question. Perhaps surprisingly to non-riders, helmets are a *huge* issue in motorcycling politics, with many American states having passed helmet laws, then repealed them in deference to "individual rights" lobbyists. It occurs to me that the combination of principles—freedom of choice, personal responsibility, and social responsibility (taking care of those who don't take care of themselves, which often results in a severe dichotomy of compassion and tyranny), and, yes, a question of simple *independence*—has resonance to other issues in modern life.

I have no wish to deliver a sermon, but would offer these thoughts as more like . . . a *meditation*. Something I've been thinking about for many miles.

So, meditating as a quasi-libertarian (left-wing conservative, right-wing liberal, what have you), helmet laws are not an issue at all to me, on motorcycles or bicycles; I just wear one. Questions of "individual choice" in your wardrobe do not apply if you are, say, a race-car driver, a jet-fighter pilot, a skydiver, a firefighter, or a fragile human being perched on an unstable two-wheeler in a demolition derby. Such activities are just too hostile to be casual about. When you place yourself in harm's way, you might as well protect yourself as best you can.

About motorcycling, it has been said that there are two kinds of riders: those who have fallen down, and those who are going to fall down. I mostly know the first kind, for no one can ride many thousands of miles without some kind of mishap. And it has to be remembered that, as I read once, "a motorcycle is so

"Hope for the best, and dress for the worst." Off-pavement in the Adirondacks.

stupid it can't even stand up by itself." I've seen several of my riding partners go sliding down the road, then get up and walk away (how-ever gingerly) because they were properly dressed. Most of my own tumbles have been when the bike wasn't moving—turning around on a gravel road, say, and losing my footing. I've fallen a number of times while riding slowly in mud or sand, and had one fairly serious "get-off" in Belize, recounted in *Ghost Rider*. On a rain-soaked and oily wooden bridge, my tires slipped out from under me and before I knew it the bike was down and it and I were sliding helplessly along the planks, my arm banging into a guardrail. Those few seconds would have been *extremely* painful for a long time after without an armored leather suit, boots, and helmet—though the tropical heat represented exactly the conditions some riders complain are "too hot" for protec-tive clothing, and when helmets are "uncomfortable."

Well . . . it's not hard to conjure images of other conditions in which an unprotected rider might feel hot or uncomfortable. A full-body cast, say.

One Saturday morning in late June, Michael and I were riding a back road through southern Indiana toward Kentucky, and we saw flashing lights ahead of us. Two police cars and an ambulance framed a big chrome-laden motorcycle in the middle of the road, and a rotund deputy raised his hand to stop us. The cruiser-style bike was scratched and dented, and must have been picked up after a fall, while the rider was being attended to on a nearby lawn. We killed our engines and stood astride our bikes, feeling a little dread that we were witnessing a tragedy (a statistic, too, alas). I noticed a long gouge in the asphalt where the bike must have scraped along the road on its side. My best guess was that a car had pulled out of a driveway in front of the rider, he'd grabbed the brakes and locked the wheels, and gone down.

A friend of the victim drove up and rode the scarred cruiser off the road, and we watched the gurney being wheeled to the ambulance. The victim's legs and feet were bare where his jeans and shoes had been cut away, and his head was swathed in white bandages. His friend said he was going to be all right, but, "His face is smashed up pretty good."

When the ambulance had driven away, the deputy waved us on, and Michael and I started our engines, lowered our face shields, and rode east toward Kentucky. Witnessing that crash scene would not be a "sobering" experience, a cautionary tale that would urge us to take it easy that day (or any other), because—in a deep distinction—we were not doing what that guy was doing. Anyone can be undone by an unavoidable accident, and suffering is *always* evil, but how awful to know your fate was the result of a series of thoughtless mistakes.

(Another of my riding mantras, which guides so many of my choices and actions on the motorcycle—my roadcraft: "It mustn't be my *fault*.")

Later that same day, near Lexington, Kentucky

Like many motorcyclists, I resent non-riders harping about the danger, even folly, of motorcycles (or, ha ha, "murder-cycles"), and the jokes about doctors calling motorcyclists "organ donors." However, to my shock and horror, that last part is no joke.

Recently I happened to see a story in the *New York Times* (July 13, 2008) titled "The Pros of Motorcycle Helmets," in which reporter Jerry Garrett wrote that victims of motorcycle crashes were indeed favored by the medical community as organ donors. He recounted how a motorcyclists' rights organization had contacted a hospital to enlist their support for a "freedom of choice" coalition—specifically, to support the right of motorcyclists not to wear helmets. The hospital directors were concerned about the ethics (or at least, ramifications) of such an endorsement because, as one doctor stated, "Motorcycle fatalities are not only our number one source of organs, they are the highest quality source of organs, because donors are usually young, healthy people with no other traumatic injuries to the body, except to the head." The hospital's "ethical" issue was actually about (surprise) *money*—the loss of income the hospital would suffer as a result of a reduction in available organs for transplants if motorcyclists wore helmets. They decided to stay out of it.

Granted, the figures on motorcycle fatalities, especially from head injuries, are alarming, but a look at the details shows that those tragedies are so often *unnecessary*. The majority of such incidents share common causes: the victims were young, inexperienced, drunk, and bare-headed.

One hot Sunday in July, Michael and I were riding to work in a state with no helmet laws, and many other motorcycles were on the road, some with wives, girlfriends, or children as passengers. Michael, being more easy-going about such matters, remarked that he really could understand guys not wanting to wear protective clothing, but—he shook his head—"How could you put your *loved one* on the back like that?" It's one thing to risk your own skin, if you think the odds are in your favor, but how would you feel if something happened to your passenger?

But a sermon won't change anyone's mind; you can only "preach by example." I always wear a full-face helmet and an armored suit (I follow the example preached by motorcycle racers, who wear leather, because nothing saves a fallen rider's skin like the skin of a cow). Years ago Brutus and I were fueling our bikes in sweltering Lake Havasu City, Arizona, and a woman said to Brutus, "Aren't you *hot* wearing all that?" Without missing a beat, Brutus shot back, "Yeah, but I've grown attached to my *skin*."

Happy, happy helmet-head, crossing the Ohio River, barge-tug in background, the road ahead reflected in my face shield

If others feel invulnerable, confident in their own skill and concentration, and that of others on the roads around them, then "go with God." (Or Darwin.) It just makes me wince to see them—if they can't imagine what might happen, I can. I have said before that such behavior seems like a failure of *imagination*, and in trying to safeguard my own place on the road, I'm always picturing some terrible thing that could occur, and guarding against it. (I call it the "what if?" game— what if around this curve there's a tractor or patch of gravel, or what if that car turns left in front of me?)

Early experience was instructive for me—even on a bicycle. I first started carrying a bicycle on our tour bus in the early '80s, getting it out to ride around on days off and the afternoons of show days. On about the third day of that experiment, I was pedaling through Portland, Oregon, among a crowded afternoon throng of pedestrians and cars. Suddenly, amid all that, I had an epiphany—I was *invisible*. "These people don't even see me!" Observing more experienced cyclists around me, I decided that putting a bright white "brain bucket" on top of my head would help, and stopped at a bicycle shop that day to buy one.

That first impulse to put something on my head was about visibility—conspicuity—but further bicycling experience opened my eyes to the protection factor. On one of my first bicycle tours, in the mid-'80s, I was laboring up the Rogers Pass in the Rocky Mountains of British Columbia in pouring rain, and was struck on the head by a fist-

sized rock falling from the mountainside above. Without my dorky white helmet, that *really* would have done damage. Another time, in Greece, a woman in a group I was cycling with hit a bad pothole and went over the bars of her bike (I heard the crash behind me, sounding like a shopping cart being dumped on its side). She landed sprawled on the road, with a badly gashed chin, cuts around her eyes from her glasses, and a deep gouge in her helmet that would have been . . . something much worse. Experiences like that are "exemplary," to say the least.

On a motorcycle, after so many years and miles on every kind of road from Alaska to Tunisia, my helmet has been struck numberless times, by insects large and small, stones and gravel, snow, sleet, hail, and rain, tree branches, debris thrown up by other vehicles, an outbreak of big June bugs in Georgia—they hurt even through a leather suit—and a good-sized bird just the other day, bouncing off my helmet. Striking a bare head, any of those flying objects would have been uncomfortable, painful, and potentially worse. Consider the impact of a bird hitting your face at highway speed.

So yes, I understand the fine point that helmet-wearing might be a matter of "individual choice." What I'll never understand is why it's a "matter" at all.

But, as our gay friends say, "That's a whole other *Oprah*."

Changing channels, this Action Self-Portrait shows me passing a farm in Vermont and thinking, "I'd like to stop right now, buy that farm, and live there." I must admit I often entertain such fantasies (and entertain my wife with them—hearing my rhapsodies on the phone about some new part of the country I've explored, Carrie will sardonically reply, "Where are we moving to *now?*"). Thinking back, I remember having similar flights of fancy in the '80s, on my bicycle, when I'd be riding in the country on a day off, and stop under a tree for a rest and look at a cozy-looking farm for sale. I would think, "I could buy that farm and hide out there—just park my bike in that barn. They'd never find me . . ."

Or even in my earliest days of touring, in the '70s, I would get fed up with too much "carney life" (like the *Gummi Bears* theme song, "Bouncing here and there and everywhere"—and never mind how I know that), and would fantasize about running away to the airport, and just going home.

Those were fantasies of *independence*, of course—in reality, I had a place to go, and a job to do, and I would go there and do it as well as I could, like Joe DiMaggio. Still, I suppose it's harmless to pretend that someday I might *not* have a place to go and a job to do.

Speaking of country roadsides, in front of a farm in Southern Ohio I saw a homemade sign posted: "I Do Not Recommend G & R Plumbing." That seemed to be a polite, and probably fairly effective, form of consumer protest.

And, most important, it was an *independent* protest. (No lawyers.)

Earlier this summer, in the West and Midwest, when Michael and I rolled into a town at the end of a long day on the road, I had been finding it increasingly difficult to search out motels and restaurants that weren't part of some grimly identical chain—another question of independence: where have all the independent businesses gone?

Well, the answer is obvious—*vox populi*, the people have spoken—and they speak loudest with their patronage. (Hello, Walmart; Goodbye, Mom and Pop.) I try to choose towns for our day-off destinations that are small enough to be enjoyable to get to, but big enough to have a few amenities—Hutchison, Kansas; Summersville, West Virginia; Spirit Lake, Iowa; Williamsport, Pennsylvania; and like that. However, in such places it seemed that more and more I had to settle for the *blandest* of ticky-tacky McMotel chains, those aiming for that ol' lowest common denominator. Cheap, and worth it. The people have spoken.

(A Broadway musical version of my quest for character over conformity, as expressed in themes of independent motels and restaurants versus chains, might be called "Unchained Melody." All-singing, all-dancing visits to American towns—oh yes! *Our Town* meets *Oklahoma!* meets *In the Heights*. I'll get together with my usual collaborator on such fancies, Matt Scannell.)

Late one afternoon in Austin, Minnesota, I diligently searched the town, and my GPS's database, for any independent lodgings, yet ended up at the ultimate archetypical national chain—Holiday Inn. That night I made note of some thoughts on the matter: "I am not the first

A study in motel signs in North Battleford, Saskatchewan—no prizes for guessing which one I chose

to bemoan the vanishing of individuality in American towns, but I may be among the last. Folks, it's all but gone."

In the Northeast, where more people mean more customers mean more variety of businesses, my quest was more often rewarded, and hope revived. I found many independent establishments still surviving, if not thriving, and it seems that in more seasonable areas, like seacoasts, ski towns, and northern holiday destinations, there are more independents—perhaps because the abbreviated business year scares off the chains.

One such town that absolutely charmed me was Littleton, New Hampshire, even from the road into it, overlooking thick summer foliage with church spires and the town hall's tower poking up through the trees. Michael and I stayed at a quaint little family motel, "The oldest motel in New Hampshire, 1948"), a short walk from downtown. We dined at a truly fine restaurant, Bailiwick's, and strolled back to the motel on a classic summer evening. (Later, on the phone, Carrie had another opportunity to say, "We're moving *where?*")

The next morning, I let Michael sleep (his usual breakfast is a Red Bull and a Red Apple [a fictional brand name for cigarettes]) and walked along Main Street, past prosperous-looking stores, to a perfect little diner, delightfully named Topic of the Town. A spare, white-haired lady brought me a menu, then the orange juice and black coffee I requested. While I waited for the morning special, two pancakes and two eggs ($4.99), I set down my book (*A Voyage Long and Strange*—excellent—you can find the review in Issue 10 of Bubba's Book Club) and decided to try to figure out how the self-timer on my camera worked. . . .

After that idyllic interlude of solitude, nourishment, and peace, I walked back to the motel and woke Michael, and we set out for the road up Mount Washington, the highest mountain in the East, at 6,288 feet. Years ago, in a book of weather trivia I was reading ("That is *not* pathetic, Michael!"), I learned that the highest winds ever recorded had been measured there—231 mph in 1934.

At the toll booth, we collected our tickets for the Mount Washington Auto Road (stickers reading, "This Bike Climbed Mt. Washington"), then headed up the narrow, winding, seven-and-a-half-mile road, nearly all of it paved. Above the treeline, the landscape took on the bare rock and sparse green austerity of the mountains in Wales. The summit wasn't too windy that day, but it was plenty cool, and the road up and down was certainly dramatic.

As we get toward the end of a tour, I find I feel a little nervous—

Independence half hour

not about the shows, but about the rides. "We've got this far okay—don't let anything happen now to spoil it."

Michael descending the Mount Washington Auto Road

And nothing did, really. In almost 20,000 miles on the bikes this summer, and 24,000 last year, I and my various riding partners had just enough misadventures to be able to say, "Adventures suck when you're having them," and to laugh about them later.

The forty-nine shows (added to the sixty-four last year) were exhausting all right (and some of the rides, too), but satisfying, on the whole. Alex and Geddy and I were talking before the Atlanta show, one of the final ones, and agreed that the overall quality of our performances this summer has been better than ever before—that's something to be able to share, after all these years. The audiences, as I wrote last summer, were "wonderfully large and unbelievably appreciative (adjectives interchangeable)," and—crucially—we remained mostly healthy. (Though we all had our sufferings, and toward the end, I lived in a world of hurt. My days began and ended with a couple of Bufferins, which almost rhymes with "sufferings.")

Michael's and my motorcycles were also kept healthy by a few more excellent BMW dealers around the U.S. and Canada: Gateway in St. Louis, Bloodworth in Nashville, Cross Country in New Jersey, and BMW of Toronto. Our thanks to them.

The proverbial silver lining,
Suches, Georgia

And now, as our traveling circus folds up its tents once again after a successful season, crew members, buses, and trucks go their separate ways, and the gear goes back into the warehouse, I still have many notes and Action Self-Portraits that haven't found their stories yet. But that's all right—as Ernest Hemingway once advised writers, "Always stop working when you know what's coming next."

For now, I look forward to a long, slow recovery, and to a whole series of Independence Days. They will be sweeter for being so hard-won.

10

THE DRUMS OF OCTOBER

NOVEMBER 2008

In my time, I have climbed some serious mountains, from hiking to the top of Mount Kilimanjaro and bicycling over the Simplon Pass in the Alps, to facing down the uphill battles that life throws up in all our paths. However, one of the hardest climbs I ever had to make was just four steps—up to the stage of the Hammerstein Ballroom in New York City, on the night of October 18, 2008.

Final rehearsal, Buddy Rich tribute concert, Oct. 17, '08. "Look, Ma—I'm smilin'!"

In forty-three years of playing drums, I have walked onto thousands of stages, of course, and I am *always* tense and anxious—tense with determination to play well, and anxious about not playing well. But this stage, this performance, was, as my teacher Freddie Gruber would say, "a whole other thing." Earlier that day, friends asked me how I was doing, and I shrugged and said, "Terrified!" They laughed, but that was a pretty accurate confession.

Final rehearsal

I felt I had a lot to live up to on that stage—the weight of *expectations*, my own and the audience's, and of course, the peerless drumming deity under whose name we were performing: Buddy Rich. I wanted to do my best—better than my best!—and I would only have one chance: right now. The house was full of great musicians, in the band and in the crowd, and, oh yes—the show was not only being recorded and filmed, it was streaming live on the Drum Channel website, all over the world. . . .

So as I stood at the bottom of those four little steps waiting for the stage manager's cue, my "fight or flight" instincts were powerfully active. I must admit the "flight" option had its appeal: "Just run away, out that door over there and onto 34th Street, and don't stop—they'll never catch you." But, with a supreme act of will, I decided to "fight"—go up there and . . . face the music. I could only hope all my preparation would carry me through.

The path that led me to those four little steps had been a long and tangled one, and like so many stories, it started when I was a child. The music my father played on his prized hi-fi was big-band records by Duke Ellington, Count Basie, Glenn Miller, Tommy Dorsey (I would have heard Buddy Rich with the Dorsey band, or Harry James, way back then, without knowing it), Nat King Cole, Frank Sinatra, and other greats of that era.

At the age of eleven or twelve, my first inspiration to play drums came from the movie *The Gene Krupa Story*, so big-band music was deeply engrained in my memories, but, strangely, never in my drumming. In my teens I fell madly in love with rock music, and every day I practiced by playing along with the hits of the mid-'60s on the AM radio in my bedroom. When I started playing in local bands, together we discovered, and covered, the "underground" hits of the day: Jimi Hendrix, Cream, the Who, Moby Grape, King Crimson, Jethro Tull, Grateful Dead—all that adventurous, ambitious, and ardent rock music—and that became *my* music. That's what I listened to, and that's what I played, for the next—well, forty-three years and counting.

In 1992, I had my first opportunity to play with a big band, when Cathy Rich, Buddy's daughter, invited me to play at a Buddy Rich Memorial Scholarship Concert in New York City. Though powerfully intimidated by the challenge, and naturally inclined to avoid it, I forced myself to accept. The results were . . . let's say, "mixed." With too little time to actually rehearse with the band (a serious handicap!), it wasn't until we were onstage playing the first tune, "Mexicali Nose," that I discovered two things: I was too far away from the horns to hear them (as far as could be: they were upstage left; I was downstage right), and, second and far worse, the band was playing a different arrangement from the one I had learned!

That situation is usually the stuff of a performer's nightmares (musicians, stage actors, and professional athletes all seem to have them), but all of a sudden it was horribly real. Barely a minute into "Mexicali Nose," I went into what I knew as the first four-bar drum break, only to hear that the rest of the band—what I could hear of them—was still playing! Pushing away the panic, I just played steady time, holding it together while I strained to hear something in the arrangement that I recognized.

Though I survived that "train wreck," it's not the kind of psychic shock and trauma I am able to take lightly, or recover from easily. I played through the rest of the show, "Cotton Tail" and "One O'Clock Jump," and a drum solo, but I was shaken, and—it has to be admitted—wretched.

Later, I resolved that the only remedy for that bad feeling was to do it again, have another try, only this time under more *controlled* conditions: in the recording studio. In 1994, I produced and played on the *Burning for Buddy* tribute recordings, and that was a much more rewarding experience (as it remains—I still like listening to that music).

And yet . . . I still had a nagging feeling that when I played in that style, I was just *imitating* it, not really *feeling* it properly. As the old Duke Ellington standard goes, "It don't mean a thing, if it ain't got that swing," and I didn't think I did.

So, in early 2007, when Cathy Rich and I began discussing another Buddy tribute concert (agreeing, "It's time"), I started thinking about trying to upgrade my "swing skills." That notion was reinforced by my old friend Jeff Berlin, a virtuoso bass player (perhaps *the* virtuoso bass player), in the kind of brutally honest advice only a really good friend—a really *outspoken* good friend—would offer.

Jeff and me, final rehearsal

Jeff and I, and my bandmates, have been friends for nearly thirty years, going back to Jeff's days with Bill Bruford's band. Since that time, Jeff and I have stayed in touch, however sporadically, and earlier this year, when Rush played in Orlando, Florida, near Jeff's home, I arranged to get together with him in the afternoon. When I told him I was going to be playing at the Buddy Rich tribute in October, he immediately offered to be my bass player. (Maybe "demanded" is more accurate—Jeff's the kind of guy who combines apparently boundless self-confidence with deep-seated neuroses and insecurity. I know many people like that—I see one in the mirror every day!)

Later, as Jeff and I exchanged emails about schedules and material, he offered a suggestion. Though phrased in more diplomatic language, the essence of what he said was, "Whyn't ya get some lessons, kid?"

And I said, "Oh yeah?"

And he said, "Yeah!"

And I said, "Oh yeah?"

And he said, "Yeah!"

So—it was *on*.

But seriously, the only real question for me was *who*. Jeff mentioned a couple of drummers he had worked with who he thought would be suitable teachers for me in the particular discipline of swing drumming. I consulted with my longtime teacher, Freddie Gruber, now eighty-two years young, but pretty much retired from the "game," and another knowledgeable adviser, Don Lombardi, founder of Drum Workshop, and now spearheading an exciting online resource for drummers, Drum Channel (about which more later).

Now, here's a chain of happenstance that strains credibility. Back in the early '80s, I played on a couple of songs for a Jeff Berlin album, and in the Bay Area studio where we recorded, I met Steve Smith for the first time, as he was playing most of the other tracks on Jeff's album. A decade later, at that Buddy Rich tribute concert in '92, Steve also performed, and we met again for the *Burning for Buddy* sessions in '94.

That's when I met Steve's teacher, Freddie Gruber, who became a hugely important musical influence and friend to me, and introduced me to the products of Drum Workshop (showing up at my house with one of their bass-drum pedals, to replace the antediluvian device he had frowned at on my practice kit—Freddie had also taught Don Lombardi, and been involved in the early years of DW). Earlier this year, at Freddie's eighty-second birthday party in a nightclub in the Valley, where our friend Joey Heredia was playing, I met another former student of Freddie's, Peter Erskine. Peter had taught Steve Smith years ago, when they were both teenagers. What a web of connections.

Freddie and me watching Joey play

Peter began his drumming career with the Stan Kenton big band, then went on to cement his reputation with perhaps the preeminent jazz group of the '70s and '80s, Weather Report. All along, Peter remained a teacher—for more than thirty years now, and he is currently Professor of Drumset Studies at the University of Southern California—and has continued to record and perform with a wide variety of artists, including Steely Dan, Chick Corea, Joni Mitchell, Diana Krall, various classical ensembles, and do studio work ranging from big-band jazz to film scores.

All that—and the guy lived fifteen minutes from my house!

As the English would say, "S'obvious, innit?"

During a break in this summer's *Snakes and Arrows* tour, I scheduled a lesson with Peter. When I parked in front of his house in Santa Monica and walked up to the door, sticks in hand, I had to smile at myself. I was a thirteen-year-old beginner again, climbing the stairs to the Peninsula Conservatory of Music on St. Paul Street in St. Catharines, Ontario, for my Saturday morning lesson with my first teacher, Don George.

And of course, that's how I *had* to feel—there's no point in taking lessons if you're not going to surrender to the teacher. That's what I had done with Freddie back in '94—followed his guidance to the extent of changing just about *everything* I had done before, in thirty years of playing: the way I held the sticks, the way I moved my hands and feet, the way I set up my drums, the way I sat at them—everything.

When Peter welcomed me into his backyard teaching studio, he told me he had watched my *Anatomy of a Drum Solo* DVD, and had appreciated it.

I said, "Hey, as far as I'm concerned, I'm a butcher, and you're a surgeon."

Peter laughed and spread his hands dismissively, "You're not a *butcher*."

I raised a hand up high, palm out, and smiled, "Hey—I'm a *good* butcher; I'd just like to get a little more *surgery* into it!"

So we began. The object of this course of study was to make me a better big-band drummer, but that proved to be a complicated assignment, and it started with the most basic element. Peter asked me to play slow quarter notes on the ride cymbal, just "ding, ding, ding," and I did, with a kind of circular flick of the wrist between each beat. That was part of what I had learned with Freddie—to think about what happens *between* the beats, and make it part of the music, a kind of rotary motion that makes your playing a *dance*.

But Peter pointed at that little flick of the wrist, and said, "What's that?"

Well, Peter had studied with Freddie too, so he knew what I was doing, and I was puzzled. I looked at him and said, "Um—timekeeping?"

Peter shook his head and put his fist to his chest, "Timekeeping is *here*. It's internal, and doesn't come from waving your hands in the air!"

He paused and raised a magisterial finger, "*Own* the time!"

So we started with that, working on remaking my ride stroke—again, the most basic of drumming techniques—with Peter offering visual metaphors like, "Pretend you're scolding your dog," with his index finger extended. "Your stick tip is a *laser*," with his fingers indicating the range of motion it should have—a thumb and forefinger apart. As I tried to replicate his instructions, I would slip into old habits, and Peter raised his finger in the dog-scolding gesture, and scolded *me*: "Quit waving!"

I laughed and tried again.

Thinking about it later, I came to understand that Peter's method didn't actually contradict Freddie's at all—it was simply a "higher evolution." Perhaps now I was ready to take that understanding of "the dance" and *internalize* it—make it part of my thinking, part of my feeling, part of my time-sense, but not part of my actual *motion*.

After that first three-hour lesson, which seemed to fly by, Peter gave me a printed list of exercises to work on, and a CD of music to listen to and play along with—but, he stressed, on high-hat only.

I drove home that day feeling dazed by this flood of information, and a little unsure. Could I do this? Devote myself to months of daily practice? Would it do me any good?

But I resolved to try. Because that's what I do—I'm a heck of a "tryer." I had warned Peter right away, "I'm a slow learner—but I'm stubborn!"

During the final run of the *Snakes and Arrows* tour in July, I started working on Peter's exercises in my pre-show warm-up. When the tour was (finally!) over, I retreated to my Quebec house, where I set up a little practice corner in a spare room—just a throne, a high-hat, and a metronome (a lot more neighbor-friendly than a whole drumset, especially if you live on a lake in the woods). Every day I made time (in both senses) to keep working on Peter's economy-of-motion ride stroke, and exploring time and rhythm at different tempos. Then I would put on the headphones and tap along with one of Peter's "play-along" selections.

When I got back to California in early September, I scheduled another lesson with Peter, and the first thing he asked me to do was play a quarter-note ride on the high-hat. Peter watched me for a minute, then nodded and said, "Perfect." What a glow of satisfaction (and surprise!) I felt at that moment.

As an adolescent, when I worked Saturdays and holidays at my dad's farm equipment dealership, he would send me off to do something—polish a tractor, clean out parts bins—and when I finished, I would say, "Is that good enough?"

Without even looking at what I had done, Dad would say, "If it's perfect, it's good enough." So in my father's scale of values, my ride stroke was "good enough."

It's nice when hard work pays off.

Peter gave me some more exercises to work on, and I continued practicing every day. By then I had played nothing but high-hat for over two months (though I must say it never became tedious), and one day I sent Peter an email, titled "Epiphany."

Today, September 24, 2008, at precisely 4:32 p.m. Pacific Standard Time, for the first time in recorded history, I commenced to SWING!

It was as if I was looking down from a great height, for I watched my right hand ticking away on that high-hat, and it was OWNING THE TIME!

You know what I'm talkin' about!

Professor Erskine expounds for the cameras

At my next lesson, Peter said he wanted me to play along with "Love for Sale," one of the Buddy Rich arrangements I would be performing at the upcoming tribute concert, on his drums—right now. *¡Jesu Christo!* It would be the first time I had played an actual drumset in two months, and the first time I had *ever* played that song on a drumset. And not only was it in front of my master teacher, but he was going to record and film it ("for reference," he said).

I struggled through it as best I could (at least I knew the arrangement, if only on high-hat!), then had to stand aside and watch ruefully while Peter sat down and played it—properly. (I thought that was *really* unfair!) His playing was delicate, eloquent, and economical—a kind of artful, effortless surgery that expressed supreme musicality. I have written before that I believe the first deadly sin for humans might be *envy*, but right then it was hard not to feel a little of that poison.

But fortunately, Peter teaches drumming with the same attitude my editor, Paul McCarthy, brings to my prose—an attitude I have described as "critical enthusiasm." Rather than telling you what you're doing *wrong*, they tell you what you're doing *right*—then suggest how you might do it better. That works for me.

The lesson pictured here was conducted for the cameras of Drum Channel, in their state-of-the-art multimedia studio in Oxnard, California. For nearly two years now, Don Lombardi has been developing and nurturing his "baby," building a team to create an online resource for drummers with unlimited horizons—a teaching forum, an archive of drumming history, a faculty of instructors impossible to match in any other medium, and an online "community center" for all those who worship at the Altar of the Drum.

Earlier this year, while I was preparing for the summer 2008 part of the *Snakes and Arrows* tour, I rehearsed in Drum Channel's studio for a couple of weeks, and in return for that opportunity to do my preparation at home instead of in Toronto, I filmed some instructional material for Don.

Drum Channel is a separate enterprise from the Drum Workshop factory, but is adjacent to it, so the number of prominent drummers who come through there is staggering—and exciting. Just while I was working there in April, and again for ten days in October before the Buddy Rich show, I encountered such an inspiring variety of great drummers, from artist-in-residence Terry Bozzio to old friends and new who were also contributing material for the Drum Channel: Gregg Bissonette, Doane Perry, Joey Heredia, Chad Smith, Danny Seraphine, Alex Acuña (Peter's predecessor in Weather Report), Ralph Humphrey, and Steven Perkins. I saw bits of footage Don's team has shot of other drummers, and I can tell you, it's wonderful stuff—of the moment, and for the ages.

In early October, once again I traded some instructional filming for the use of Drum Channel's studio as a rehearsal space, the presence of my master drum tech, Lorne Wheaton, and the world's best commute—up the Pacific Coast Highway through Malibu to the farmlands of Ventura County, one day smelling of onions, another of cilantro.

Don and I thought it would be worthwhile to film a session of Peter teaching me—not only instructive in its substance, but also in its *spirit*, its message: after forty-three years of playing the drums, a guy like me could still try to learn something. (Jeff Berlin's advice to me applies to all musicians, really: "Whyn't ya get some *lessons*, kid?")

I also spent a day hanging and playing with my young friend Nick Rich, Buddy's grandson. I have known Nick since he was six, when we were both nervously awaiting the start of our first Buddy Rich

Memorial Scholarship concert (that year, Nick's contribution was break dancing to Michael Jackson!). We "bonded" then, and kept that bond as he was growing up. Twenty-four now, decorated with all kinds of skin ink, body ornaments, and striped hair (I call him *el Tejón*, "The Badger"—he calls me "Uncle Noyle," after my grandfather's nickname for me, or—ha ha—"Grandpa"), Nick has become a fine drummer. He studied with the great Dave Weckl (another student of Freddie's), and has integrated some of Dave's fluid, intricate funk style with his own natural exuberance.

Jamming with *"el Tejón"*

Nick and I played "drum duets" for a while, and it was great to discover that our drumming interlocked as tightly as our characters always have. (I love that crazy mixed-up kid.)

This time Nick would be playing drums at his grandfather's tribute, and it meant a lot to him (he was only two and a half when Buddy passed, in 1987). Nick was going to perform two of Buddy's more rock-oriented charts, "Beulah Witch" and "Mercy, Mercy, Mercy" (originally a pop song by the Buckinghams, written by Joe Zawinul, founder of Weather Report—Peter told me that when he joined Weather Report, Joe gave him some "homework": the works of Nietzsche). That weekend Nick and I had a chance to rehearse our material with a real, live band, along with the other West Coast drummers in the show, Terry Bozzio and Chad Smith.

Don had suggested bringing in some music students from the nearby California State University at Northridge, where our bandleader, Matt Harris (Buddy's last keyboard player), taught. Matt had also written some special arrangements for Terry and Chad, while I had commissioned a big-band treatment of Rush's "YYZ" from one of

Buddy's other longtime musicians and arrangers, John La Barbera. That arrangement had never been played before, so it would be a good opportunity to check it out, along with the chance to play through my other selections: Buddy's trademark arrangement of "Love for Sale" (a supreme challenge, but it was probably my favorite of all Buddy's vast repertoire, and I just *had* to try it—never mind that it had already been played so superbly not only by Buddy, but by Steve Gadd and Dave Weckl), "Time Will Tell," which had a good bass showcase for Jeff Berlin, and the traditional swing numbers, Duke Ellington's "Cotton Tail" and Count Basie's "One O'Clock Jump" (both of which had featured in my drum solos with Rush in past years).

For two days in mid-October, the Drum Channel studio was crammed with four drumsets and drummers, fifteen other musicians, an arsenal of video cameras, and a platoon of operators and engineers. It was a surreal scene, really, that perfectly exemplifies my title, "The Drums of October." Drums have never been a bigger part of my life than they were that month.

And the actual drums I played in October were pretty special, too. DW's restlessly innovative drum designer, John Good, imbued them with all his "Wood-Whisperer" magic, and they glittered in classic white marine pearl, like Buddy's, with gold-plated hardware for a little modern bling. My cymbal array was also completely redesigned for the performance—different ride, high-hats, and lighter Paragon crashes—with help from Chris Stankee in onsite testing, and, in the Sabian factory in New Brunswick, Mark Love, the cymbal alchemist ("literally," I told him, "turning base metals into gold").

Even the sticks I held in my trembling hands at the bottom of those four little steps were different. For this music, Peter had recommended something with a narrower shoulder and smaller bead than my usual "rock knockers," and out of a huge selection sent to me by Kevin Radomski at ProMark, I immediately gravitated to a pair of Joe Morello's signature models. They just felt "right" in my hands and when striking and rebounding off the high-hat. (Coincidentally, that very day, in the car, I had listened to Joe's lovely playing on "Drumorello," on the first *Burning for Buddy* volume—and it had been sitting beside Joe in the studio while we recorded that, hearing him make those DW drums *sing*, that inspired me to try out their drums myself.)

Now, back to those four fateful steps. Short version: I climbed them. As quite a few of us in the show seemed to agree later, "It could have been better; it could have been worse." That, of course, is because we all apply my father's values: "If it's perfect, it's good enough."

For myself, once I was on that stage and behind the drums, I felt like I was in a kind of kinetic trance, my mind spinning in frantic orbits. At one point I remember watching my hands and feet play a certain figure correctly—all by themselves! That was proof enough that the hours of rehearsal and preparation had paid off. Generally, I just tried to play it safe and straight, not taking too many chances, and in the end . . . it could have been worse.

Though I had watched all the rehearsals at Drum Channel and in New York, I didn't watch the actual show. I shut myself away in my dressing room and tried to escape the tension by reading a book. (I know, weird, but it works for me, and I had chosen a perfect book—*Case Histories*, a gripping mystery by Kate Atkinson, whose genre is referred to as "literary thriller," which apparently doesn't have to be an oxymoron.)

But my dressing room was right beside the stage, so of course I could hear every note of the show, and it clearly offered such a wonderful range of styles, in the drummers and the material—largely from Buddy's catalogue, plus some music specially commissioned for the event. As onstage host, it was Cathy's job to stitch the whole evening together (as she realized suddenly, with a little trepidation, just before the show), along with video clips of Buddy and us performers (as I stood twitching beside the stage while my long-winded video introduction played, I called over to the headsetted stage manager, Don Sidney, "Tell that guy to *shut up!*").

The audience was treated to a fantastic band, assembled by one of the featured drummers, Tommy Igoe (in a single word that I mean to convey much, Tommy's playing is "accomplished"), along with John Blackwell ("prodigious"—after watching John play at rehearsal, and talking with him a little about our lives, he told me *Ghost Rider* had helped him through a similar tragedy of his own, and the way he said it made my eyes prickle. I told him, describing his playing and his nature: "You're a *monster*—with a beautiful spirit," then added with a laugh, "and you can put that in your bio!"), Terry Bozzio ("inimitable"— the more time I spend in his company, the more I am inspired by his example of total creative dedication, and he was joined onstage by percussionist Efrain Toro, who can only be described as "delightful"— such a warm spirit in his playing and his demeanor), Chad Smith ("effervescent"), Nick (*el Tejón*) Rich ("formidable"), Donnie Marple ("promising"—the young winner of a drum solo contest), and a last-minute guest appearance by Peter Erskine ("masterly"). Peter happened to be in town recording, and when he told me he was going

to be at the Buddy show, I made a wide-eyed grimace and said, "It's a good thing I work well under pressure!"

But Peter was very kind, and sought me out after the show to offer some encouraging words. While watching Peter play at rehearsal the day before, I had turned to a friend and said proudly, "That's my teacher!" When I told Peter about that, he aimed a thumb at me and said, "That's my student!"

I gave him a big hug and said, "I'm not finished with you yet!" I already had the notion that I would want to continue studying with Peter, for I had learned one very big lesson: understanding more about jazz drumming is simply understanding more about *drumming*. That's got to be good—even in the "October" of my own years.

So, as Freddie would say at the end of telling a long story, "That's the way it went." I warned at the outset that this tale would be "long and tangled," but there was so much to tell. In such cases, I often think of the title of a novel by the Senegalese writer Mariama Bâ, *So Long a Letter*, because it carried the same meaning.

Sure, it might have been better if I had taken time to write some of this between my previous report in August and now, but . . . I was busy doing all that. It always seems that the more I have to write about, the less time I have to write it.

But I'm not complaining.

My life is not perfect, but it's good enough.

Facing the Music, onstage
October 18, 2008

11

DECEMBER IN DEATH VALLEY

DECEMBER 2008

In the dark early hours of December 4, 2008, I rode down the Pacific Coast Highway through a black void of ocean and sky. A few pairs of headlights glared toward me, and the Ferris wheel at Santa Monica Pier was outlined in shifting circles and lines of colored light. The air was chilly, but I was warmly dressed, and excited to be heading for the desert.

Riding east on I-10, keeping a semi-legal pace in the outside lane, I was hoping to slip through the entire width of Los Angeles before the morning gridlock. The sky began to brighten around the downtown towers, and lines of traffic were building to the east, but luck favored my journey. I kept moving steadily, out past San Bernardino and the San Gorgonio Pass to Palm Springs. Then at last I reached open highway, climbing the long grade up to Chiriaco Summit, and turning off into Joshua Tree National Park by about 8:00.

There the real journey began—the part that made that long freeway drone worthwhile. I stopped at the Cottonwood Spring ranger station and paid my fee (and collected the passport stamp in my journal), then cruised along the park's narrow, winding roads, with hardly any other vehicles. The sky was pale blue now, mottled with white, and the high desert air remained cool. I passed the tumbled formations of huge, rounded boulders spread among the midwinter desert vegetation in pale shades of brown, and the namesake Joshua trees. They grow only in certain areas of the Mojave Desert, north of I-10, where the elevation rises above 2,000 feet, and not at all in the lower Colorado Desert, south of I-10. Coincidentally, the freeway pretty much traces the border between the high and low desert. Some of the Joshua trees are thought to be more than a thousand years old, and a few groves reach into Arizona, Nevada, and Utah. (The Mormons named the trees, as I have noted before, after the biblical prophet raising his arms to beckon the Saints to the Promised Land. Wild.)

For forty miles I cruised through the rocks, Joshua trees, fuzzy cholla and prickly pear cactus, and tall, spindly ocotillo. Leaving the park at Twentynine Palms, I continued north on the road to the ghost town of Amboy, and Roy's Motel, which appeared in *Ghost Rider*. In fact, unknown to most people, Amboy also appears on the booklet cover of the *Snakes and Arrows* CD, and lately, on the new concert DVD, plus at the beginning of the "What's That Smell?" film that played before "Far Cry" during our concerts this past summer. I watched it every night from my "waiting chair" behind Geddy's ampline (er, rotisseries), before the second set, and it always gave me a smile.

Back in 2006, when Hugh Syme and I were trading ideas for that *Snakes and Arrows* cover, we discussed a surreal desert highway scene. As a reference, I sent him one of my Ghost Rider photographs, taken on a stretch of old Route 66, looking west toward the cluster of crumbling buildings at Amboy, with the unmistakable Amboy Crater in the distance. Hugh ended up "building" the scene on that original photo, which had been taken in 1998 (as a *slide*, in those days). Like the Monument Valley ten-years-apart photo that appeared in a story earlier this year, "South by Southwest," I decided to pause for a ten-year anniversary shot of Route 66 and Amboy.

The old *Ghost Rider* bike from the original photo, a 1996 R1100GS long retired after 100,000 miles of sterling service, is now in the Motorcycle Hall of Fame Museum near Columbus, along with my R30 drumset.

After a few miles of Route 66, I turned north on the Kelbaker Road (it took me years to figure out that the name is derived from the simple fact that the road runs through Kelso and Baker), between wide vistas of brown, wrinkled mountains and speckled vegetation of creosote and winter-brown grassy clumps. The Mojave Desert gives a peerless feeling of space, openness, emptiness, and peace. On roads like that, I ride along feeling no sense of urgency, danger, or stress. Just cruising and looking around. You know—happy.

In the tiny settlement of Shoshone, I stopped at the worthy Crowbar restaurant for lunch. (They serve soft drinks in Mason jars, which is quaint and original, and they fry up a fine burger.) There were only two other diners, a corpulent couple raving about their milkshakes. After lunch, I filled up with gas at the station across the way, then headed off on a road I'd never traveled. My favorite.

Looking over the map the previous day at home, planning my route to Death Valley, and browsing for anything new I might explore (always trying to find at least one new road), I noticed a dot just over the Nevada line called Devils Hole. (Note the lack of apostrophe—almost no official American place names have them, I've noticed, even if it's Browns Mill or Toms River. Apparently the Board on Geographic Names of the United States Government—yes, there is such a thing—*hates* apostrophes. According to Wikipedia, only five names of natural features in the U.S. are officially spelled with an apostrophe, one example being Martha's Vineyard.)

The site was labeled as part of Death Valley National Park, yet it seemed to be inside Ash Meadows Wildlife Preserve, which was about ten miles east of the park's borders. Curious. Best of all, a couple of high-desert roads I had never ridden would take me there, so I thought, "Yes—go to Devils Hole."

From Shoshone, I set off to the east, crossing into Nevada, then at Pahrump, I looped back to the west. The road to Devils Hole was indicated on the map by a dotted line, meaning unpaved, and I thought the turnoff would be marked by a sign, but it wasn't—in fact, the place was pretty well hidden. The state map brought me to the Ash Meadows Wildlife Refuge, then a handout at an information sign showed me the network of gravel roads leaving to Devils Hole. Still there were no signs on the unnamed tracks, so I tried the GPS. Under local "Points of Interest," it listed Death Valley National Monument, though it's been a national park since 1994. Sometimes the most modern information is the least up-to-date—but it helped.

Far from anywhere, in a particularly bleak region of gravelly desert, sparse brown vegetation, and barren rocks, I spotted a chain-link enclosure, and a small wooden sign reading "Devils Hole."

For scale, that's my shadow in the upper middle, standing on the observation platform, looking downward through the fence. That little patch of water at the bottom of the rocky gash is home to the Devils Hole pupfish—its only home in the world (hence the national park designation for this isolated spot, to protect it), though a few have now been transferred to other places for safety.

The waterhole is a remnant of the ancient lakes that once covered this region, the basin and range province—and like a desert island in reverse, Devils Hole is a spot of water surrounded by an extremely arid land. The pupfish, iridescent blue and less than an inch long, have been marooned there for something like 12,000 years, when the massive lakes that once flooded the Great Basin faded away. The few hundred remaining pupfish live as deep as eighty feet down, but feed and breed on one small, shallow patch of algae. Because of this, the water level is critical to their survival, and apart from the national park designation, a unique Supreme Court decision in 1976 protected the local water table from overpumping, to preserve the level at Devils Hole. (In the old days, it was called Miner's Bathtub, because the water is a steady 86°, and was easily reached before the chain-link fence was installed.)

Scuba divers have explored the cave to depths of 300 feet, and still didn't find the bottom (two divers were lost and never recovered). From the observation platform, I couldn't see the little pupsters, of course, but I was thinking about those unlikely survivors after my visit.

So often books and travels coincide for me in a remarkable serendipity, and around the time of this Death Valley getaway I happened to be reading *The Song of the Dodo* by David Quammen (sent to me as a gift during the tour—thank you, "Norde"). The theme of the book was the biogeography of islands, and the razor's edge balancing point of survival for every island species. By extension, the fragmentation of habitat in the modern world threatens the continued existence of uncountable species in a similar way: even if we save a bit of rainforest here, a piece of desert there, it's just a fragile island, and won't be enough. (Cheerful reading, no, but nonetheless fascinating to a nature lover. As I've noticed lately with a few good non-fiction books, the key is that the writer travels to—and takes the reader to— the places he's writing about.)

But in context of the pupfish, I was thinking that nature also changes in ways that can seem cruel and arbitrary, and leaves behind "islands" of species that may or not survive. Over millions of years, the great "extinction events" have killed off ninety-nine percent of species that ever lived, making the odds already long, as Stephen Jay Gould described in *Wonderful Life*. Even the most recent period of glaciation, ending around 12,000 years ago, left behind islands of life stranded in much-reduced environments, in higher, cooler elevations, say, or like the pupfish in their cave in the desert.

Here I will resort to the old bike-parked-in-front-of-landscape shot. Because what a bike—and what a landscape.

The motorcycle is a new BMW R1200GS, and this was our first adventure together. Strangely, BMW did not offer the bike in red this year (are they *insane?*), so I had to have it painted—because all my motorcycles have been red. I've never been comfortable driving a red car, you understand, but it just seems right for a motorcycle. And I didn't want to settle for a silver, blue, or (gasp!) yellowish-orange one. After having the paint done, and the accessories installed—Jesse luggage cases, Motolights on the front for extra conspicuity, GPS (Dingus III), power for the radar detector—I finally brought the new bike home in late November. I stood looking at it in my garage for a while, and wondered, "Where will we go together?"

My two previous 1200GSes had certainly carried me far. For the *Snakes and Arrows* tour in 2007 and 2008, my two "working bikes" had been a 2004 1200GS, with over 70,000 kilometers (42,000 miles), and a 2007 model, with over 60,000 kilometers (36,000 miles). Both bikes had been purchased in Canada, and although the '04 had later been registered in California, it would be difficult ever to sell or trade the bike there, given that state's strict regulations. During the tour, one of our crew members, Kevin, said he wanted to buy my older bike, and because he lived in Calgary, there was no problem with its Canadian origin. I agreed to sell the '04 to him, then planned to buy a new one in California, keep the '07 in Quebec, and everything would be kosher.

So that's the bike. As for the landscape, it is Death Valley, from Dante's View (no apostrophe on the park map—but this time I think it looks funny without it), at 5,746 feet, looking down to Badwater

Basin, at –282 feet. From Devils Hole I had continued west about thirty miles toward the main part of the national park, which surrounds the valley itself, and when I saw the sign for Dante's View, I immediately turned off on that isolated road to its high overlook. (Those two names are good examples of the dark humor that shades several of the place names in Death Valley, like the Funeral Mountains, Coffin Peak, Hells Gate, Devils Cornfield, and Devils Golf Course.) The road was a challenging combination of tight, technical curves on narrow pavement, and in early December, I had it to myself, as I did the cold viewpoint at the top.

The Dante's View road had been closed for some years, after a devastating flash flood in August 2004 that swept away several roads—not to mention cars and buildings—and I had been told it would likely never reopen. Away on tour that year, I hadn't been making any local road trips, but when I visited Death Valley the following spring, I saw photographs at the Furnace Creek General Store that showed the Inn completely enisled by a flow of water spilling out of the canyon behind it. That visit was in April 2005, and while I was there I hiked to the top of Wildrose Peak, at 9,046 feet. From the summit I looked down at the Furnace Creek Inn, pretty much at sea level, through my binoculars, and saw a brand new alluvial fan, or *bajada*—a sloping field of eroded debris, in this case washed down by the flood—spreading all around it and across the valley floor like a chocolate-brown apron. Geology in action.

Long shadow on the road from Dante's View

And biology, too—riding back that evening in April 2005, I noticed there were already tufts of vegetation in the tumbled debris, after only five months. Desert life is necessarily opportunistic and hardy, and some desert seeds are only germinated by the action of grinding stones in a flash flood. Thus they have a better chance of sprouting with the necessary moisture for survival.

This time, in December 2008, it was mid-afternoon when I came riding down from Dante's View, and I rode into the valley at Furnace Creek and stopped at the Visitor Center for a passport stamp and hiking information. Alas, it was a moment symptomatic of many bureaucratic evils in our times: I asked the lady in the ranger uniform about hiking advice, and she confessed she was "only a fee taker"— she didn't know anything about trail conditions, and there was no ranger on duty. That's just wrong. (Tax money is rarely better spent than on the national parks, but apparently not enough taxpayers, or their elected representatives, agree.)

As I rode across the valley floor around 4:00, ready to check in at the Furnace Creek Inn, the sun was already sinking behind the Panamint Range. A soft light lay across the alluvial fans, the even, gradual slopes at the base of the mountains, between flat ground and the folds of dark rock. In the glimmer along the peaks, I saw a dusting of white around the highest summit, Telescope Peak, where I hoped to hike the following day.

Telescope Peak was an important place in *Ghost Rider*—and in my life, really. In October 1999, when I had been rambling aimlessly around the West for the better part of a year, trying to find some way to face the world again, I hiked to that 11,049-foot summit. The next day, I rode on to Los Angeles, where I met Carrie, and my whole life changed completely (and needless to say, positively). An irresistible metaphor seemed to arise there—that I had climbed to the highest point in Death Valley from the lowest, then descended to travel onward and find Life again. In the book *Ghost Rider* I had used Telescope

Peak as an important symbol, and had written some lyrics called "Telescope Peak," too, around the refrain of "the last lonely day."

Those lyrics hadn't found a musical home with my collaborators, Alex and Geddy, during the songwriting sessions for our *Vapor Trails* album in 2001, but fair enough—those guys shared enough of my grief, in life and in art. In any case, the best lines from "Telescope Peak" were recycled into other songs, like "Ghost Rider" and "How It Is," so nothing was lost.

Listening to some of that music just before setting out on this journey, as the three of us reviewed a couple of remixes of songs from *Vapor Trails* for an upcoming anthology, I can still sense my emotional state then—an underlying mood of anger and confusion that comes through even in my drumming, never mind the lyrics.

I still have the anger, all right, but I think I've left the confusion behind.

There's my shadow riding alongside, caught in the low December sun as I rode through Death Valley. In the song "Ghost Rider," I described my feelings on those lonely, aimless travels: *"There's a shadow on the road behind/ There's a shadow on the road ahead."* Those shadows are still with me, alas, but at least these days I can say that they are mostly behind me, but will always remain beside me—inside me.

And, inevitably, ahead. (Taking the Tragic View.)

Early next morning I rode about sixty miles across the valley and up Emigrant Canyon Road, aiming for a hike in the Panamint Mountains. I was still thinking of going for the "big one," Telescope Peak, as I wanted to close that circle of more than nine years ago—revisit the place that had also inspired another line in "Telescope Peak" that ended up in "Ghost Rider": *"From the lowest low to the highest high."*

All things considered, though, I decided that would be foolhardy. It was a fourteen-mile round trip, the days were short, and there was that snow. If other hikers had packed it down, it would freeze again into solid ice, and on a steep trail, it would be extremely treacherous. With the temperature falling into the 30s, and lower at night, one slip, one injured ankle, knee, or hip, and I would be in big trouble.

Wildrose Peak trailhead: the charcoal kilns

My rule number one of roadcraft applies to hiking, too: If something happens to me, *it mustn't be my fault*.

By the time I got to Emigrant Canyon Road, I had convinced myself to go for the prudent option, Wildrose Peak. Its trailhead was on the way to the Telescope Peak trail—in fact, that mountain's snowy pyramid would dominate my view through most of the Wildrose climb—and it was still a serious hike, starting at 7,000 feet and climbing over four miles to its 9,046-foot summit.

About thirty miles up Emigrant Canyon, as I sped along the narrow, twisty, deserted road (yahoo!), it turned to gravel, and I slowed and adjusted to the loose surface (weight on the pegs, assertive hand with the throttle, light on the rear brake). I parked in the empty gravel lot in front of the charcoal kilns, where the trail began.

A sign explained the purpose of these beehive-shaped stone structures: They were giant ovens to render the local pinyon pine trees into charcoal for the smelters at mines in the desert below. Built in 1877, they were only used for one year before the mines were abandoned. The kilns were "designed by Swiss engineers and built by Chinese laborers," and that got me thinking about those Chinese laborers. What must their lives have been like? (Not fun.)

One fascinating aspect of the Death Valley area is the history. Part of that history is geological, from the huge Manly Lake that once filled the valley to the faulting and subsidence that have made it the hottest, driest, and lowest place in North America, but there is a surprising amount of human history, too. Because Death Valley is perhaps the most inhospitable region in North America, short of the Arctic, the stories are rich and endless. They begin with the Timbisha Shoshone, who still occupy a small reservation on the valley floor of perhaps a dozen families, then the wagon trains heading West and choosing an ill-advised shortcut, and the miners and prospectors living and working in what are now ghost towns: Skidoo, Rhyolite, Ballarat, Wildrose, the Eureka Mine.

I remember a TV show from my childhood called *Death Valley Days*, one of television's longest running series, from 1952 to 1975 (one host was Ronald Reagan, just before he entered politics). *Death Valley Days* began as a radio show, from 1930 to 1945, and was sponsored by the U.S. Borax Company. The company had been harvesting borax (used for detergents, plastics, and many other industrial purposes—including, Wikipedia says, "curing snake skins") in Death Valley, and as the borax played out, they were looking to publicize the region for tourism. I dimly recall the commercials for "20 Mule Team Borax," with a miniature mule team skittering comically around a kitchen floor—a pretty fancy effect for 1950s TV. The screenplays for all 558 episodes of the TV series were at least based on true events, so there were some stories in Death Valley, all right.

I changed out of my leathers and into khakis and hiking boots, then shrugged into my daypack (carrying tuna sandwiches, cheese, peanut butter cups, lemonade, two bottles of water, binoculars, a pair of light gloves, my motorcycle rain jacket as an extra barrier if it got too cold, my camera, and—of course—a Swiss army knife). I headed up through the pinyon pines and junipers, the air cool and fresh, but thin already above 7,000 feet. The trail was steep, and sometimes faint, winding among roots and small, loose rocks that demanded attention to where I planted my boots. I was soon sweating, and feeling the burn in my leg muscles.

Toward the top I encountered some snowy patches, the loose scree of the trail coated in hard bluish ice. Once again, the fear of falling

Wildrose Peak, 9,046 feet, December 5, 2008. Patch of snow above left boot, and distant Furnace Creek—and its alluvial fan—almost two miles down, above right boot.

and injuring myself was daunting, and I tried to be careful (it doesn't always come naturally). Sometimes I could step around the ice into the crusty snow, and kick my toes in to gain purchase and hoist myself uphill. A few times I had to grab onto a nearby bush for support, and once I smelled the most delicious perfume, piney but with a hint of vanilla and citrus (I sound like a "wine bore"). I discovered that the fragrance was coming from my hands, and looked back to see that it was a limber pine I had grabbed. I knew them as one of the characteristic high-elevation trees of the Western mountains, but I never knew they *smelled* so good. After that I occasionally crushed a few more branches in my hands on purpose, just to inhale that subtle perfume again.

On a climb like that, my mind is always working furiously. All the way up and all the way down I was having conversations with myself, and mentally "writing" things into sentences—descriptions, reflections, ideas. My friend Kevin Anderson hikes the mountains of Colorado and dictates his novels into a recorder while he walks. Obviously that needs a serious focus and discipline, to shape descriptions and dialogue into the story he's building. My thoughts are more random, and I simply *imagine* how I might put them into words. I often do that on the motorcycle, too, and I figure in that three-day journey I "wrote" about 10,000 words. Now I just have to work until I take away those quotation marks . . .

That day I was giving myself a "talking to" about something, and resolving to kick myself out of my usual shyness, my usual comfort zone. The previous night, as I walked from my room at the Furnace Creek Inn to the main building for dinner, I saw two BMW GSes like mine (one red) in the parking lot. They had Ontario plates, and I thought, "Hmm."

I walked into the lobby a few minutes before my 7:15 reservation, and had a look through the gift shop, and at some of the old photographs on the lobby wall. From the corner of my eye, I saw two guys hesitantly moving my way, and I thought, "Hmm."

One of them called out my name, and I gently corrected his mispronunciation, then nodded, "Yes," and offered a small (careful) smile. They were fortyish, I would say, quietly friendly and polite (Canadian, after all—we're famous for saying thank you to ATMs), and introduced themselves, shaking my hand. One of them said, "We've read your book!" and I guess he meant *Ghost Rider*, where I talked so much about Death Valley. Though embarrassed as always by attention from strangers, I have to admit I was secretly a little pleased by this fresh kind of fame—not about hitting things with sticks, or writing mildly cryptic lyrics that people interpreted their own way (for better or worse!), but as a traveler, a travel writer. That was nice. I was still embarrassed, but it was nice.

They went off to the dining room (unusually busy for the time of year, as a marathon was being held the following morning), and I saw them across the room as the host led me to my table. They left me alone to scribble in my journal, while I enjoyed a fine dinner of tortilla soup, lamb with couscous, ice cream with cherries, and pinot noir and coffee. On my way out I stopped by the two riders' table, smiled and said, "Have a good ride!" They returned the sentiment, and that was it.

But when I thought about it later, I wanted to know their story. For one thing, how did they get their bikes from frozen Ontario to Southern California in December, unless they had been traveling a while—like I had done in '98 and '99? ("The Wilderness Years" just occurred to me as a title for that time. I see it was the title of a movie about Winston Churchill.)

Where did they come from? What did they do for a living? What about their families?

So as I hiked up the steep trail, I decided I wanted to make myself

Death Valley sand dunes

do something *bold*. I promised myself that if those two guys were still at the Inn when I got back that afternoon, I would invite them to join me for dinner. That was about the most unlikely thing I—or anyone who knows me—could imagine me doing.

Hiking down to the trailhead, I felt weary but contented. Changing back into riding clothes, I lifted my right leg over the bike's high saddle and heard myself utter an involuntary "ow." But it was a "good hurt."

The bike's thermometer read 35°, which surprised me, as it didn't feel that chilly. ("It's a dry cold.") The air must have been even colder at the top, 2,000 feet higher, but I had been comfortable enough while eating my lunch and reclining on a pile of sharp stones—which also felt remarkably comfortable after the hard climb.

I rode back across the valley, admiring the graceful shadows on the dunes and the golden light on the furrowed brown mountains. As I gradually descended from 7,000 feet to sea level (and below), I watched—and felt—the temperature climb to 77°. Back at the Inn, I kept an eye out for those two bikes and their riders, but they were gone. I never got to put my bold resolution to the test.

But still, I wondered about those two Canadian motorcyclists on their adventure-touring bikes—wondering if it was their first visit to

Death Valley, and what they thought of it. After all, it wasn't the kind of place everybody would appreciate. (In a story for *Motorcyclist* magazine, I once wrote about a certain humble motel, and on a subsequent visit, the new owner told me people had been showing up to stay there because of me—even wanting the same cabins Michael and I had stayed in. Although the place was perfectly adequate, and even charming for me, I felt a little concerned that other people might find it less so—and blame me!)

I would certainly never forget my own first visit to Death Valley, in the fall of 1996. Brutus and I had spent the day rambling around big, empty Nevada, then crossed into California through the fantastic Westgard Pass. We had made a late start because of a snowstorm in Tahoe City, forcing us to wait until the snow softened up a little so we could "tiptoe" over the pass to Carson City. Thus by the time we reached Lone Pine, the turnoff for Death Valley, it was already getting dark. As we fueled up and headed east on winding Highway 190 into the jagged mountains, a full moon rose ahead, lighting the stage for one of the greatest rides of my life.

Brutus told me later he could see I was "getting into that groove," speeding ahead into the tight curves and pouring on the steam. Sometimes that happens to me late in a long day—I feel myself ease into that perfect *focus*, my whole being concentrated on reading the road ahead, and handling the motorcycle as smoothly, and rapidly, as possible (with some regard for *consequences*, of course). Brutus said he saw me start to pull away from him, and he just "let me go," shaking his head and riding his own pace.

When we emerged from the mountains, riding together in formation again, I was elevated by the adrenaline generated by that on-the-edge riding, and exalted by the radiant light of that full moon. It flooded Death Valley, shining silver off the mineral lakebeds, and shadowing the dunes and clumped vegetation of the Devils Cornfield. We followed our headlights south to Furnace Creek, glad to be there, and glad to be alive.

In the morning we got up before sunrise and rode to Dante's View, then sat on the hillside out of the chilly wind and watched the valley gradually bloom into light, like an old-time photograph developing in a chemical bath. Then back to the Inn for breakfast, and on to the next show.

That's how the first visit to Death Valley was for Brutus and me, and I hope it had some of that unforgettable magic for our two fellow Canadian explorers. While I was riding to the trailhead at Wildrose, I passed the turnoff for Scotty's Castle, and was reminded of the second time Brutus and I rode to Death Valley. We were on our way to start the second half of the *Test for Echo* tour in Southern California in early 1997, and we had allowed an extra day for the cross-country journey from Toronto, in case of trouble. When we didn't have any trouble, we spent that day in Death Valley. I started adding up how much Brutus and I had seen and done that day, and it didn't seem possible.

Traveling with Brutus was like that—I have described him before as "Mr. Carpe Diem," and he can pack more action into a day than anybody I know. We started painfully early (of course) and rode sixty miles up to Scotty's Castle (itself another fabulous story, perhaps for another time) and took the tour. Then we stopped to look at Ubehebe Crater and followed a long unpaved road to a place called The Racetrack (a dry lakebed where good-sized stones actually "sail" after a rain, driven across the slick surface by the wind, and leaving eerie trails in the thin layer of mud).

We backtracked a few miles to Teakettle Junction (with its solitary tree hung with a multitude of teakettles), and south on a *very* rough Hunter Mountain Road. That was a challenging thirty or forty miles of slippery dirt edging along sheer, vertical slopes until we reached pavement again, then 100 miles back to the Inn. After a fine dinner, we sat outside with coffee and cognac, the sky's velvet blackness dominated by the fiery white triangle of Comet Hale-Bopp.

As I piece that day together in memory, I still can hardly believe it. But—that's Brutus for you. That's the way he rolls, and that's the way you have to roll when you roll with him. And the habit is contagious.

The same traveling mode came into play on my three-day getaway to Death Valley, every minute and every mile packed with sights and sensations. On the ride home, I took a different route south through Panamint Valley, then skipped between some of the larger desert towns on little-known back roads. From Frazier Park, I picked up the fantastic combination of Lockwood Valley Road and Highway 33 down to Ojai, then across to the Pacific Coast Highway and home. Altogether, I motorcycled over 1,000 miles, hiked eight and a half miles to Wildrose Peak and back, did some thinking, reading, and journal-writing, and mentally "wrote" a good 10,000 words. (And here are more than half of them.)

The Furnace Creek Inn has a pair of outdoor fireplaces beside its spring-fed swimming pool, and they are lighted every evening at sunset. After dinner, on a cold December night, it was a treat to go down there and throw a few logs on one of those fires. I sat and basked in the radiance and warmth, the smell of the pinyon pine logs like incense. Above, a gray plume of smoke streamed from the stone chimney and traced across the starry black sky. While looking through the day's photos on my camera, I started messing with the self-timer, and set up a self-portrait beside the fire—laughing at the very idea.

A Christmas card from Death Valley.

12

A WINTER'S TALE OF SUMMERS PAST

FEBRUARY 2009

This story began as a brief introduction to a book review. At the outset, my modest goal was to relate how the reading of a book sometimes has its own story to tell, outside the book's covers—how I happened to choose a particular book, and the events surrounding its reading.

At the time, I was on my annual "winter retreat" in Quebec, enjoying a couple of weeks of snowy solitude. I spent my mornings writing, and in the afternoons went cross-country skiing or snowshoeing, so there was plenty of time for thinking. The snow was almost five feet deep, and as I glided or strode across its high white cushion, I found it hard to hold onto the notion that I was so far above the ground—elevated on the surface of another element, water-become-earth, a quintessence shaped by both, and by wind, plus reflecting the sun's fire in diamond-dust prisms.

Clearly, I was high on winter.

After a day or two without fresh snow in the woods, other tracks began to appear on my immaculate cloud—a neat line of fox prints;

deer following my packed-down trails to make their own passage easier; the widely spaced impressions like little snow angels left by the snowshoe hares, where they have leapt from one spot to another to feed on the cedars (come spring, those nibbled patches will be five feet off the ground). Their namesake large back feet land in front of the smaller front paws, ready to leap again. Deep in the woods, I might be lucky enough to see a row of holes in the snow the size of salad plates,

Something big, this way went,
crossing something small . . .

where the huge moose, the local monarch, has struggled through. Far from roads and houses, I might also cross the purposeful-looking long strides of wolf tracks, sometimes two or three sets widely separated, where they coursed the woods together.

Standing atop a snow-covered beaver dam, I saw the builder's recent leavings (a brown and yellow territory marker), and the chute where it slid down into a hole in the ice. Otters, too, left a series of sliding chutes across the snow, where they made their playful progress together. The low-slung weasel—ermine in this season, when it turns from brown to white—propelled its body through the snow on tiny feet, a straight line with delicate, parallel indentations. A similar but larger track was probably a fisher, a fearsome little beast I described back in summer '07, in "That's the Way We Roll." Its occasional prey, the porcupine, leaves an unmistakable trail, a deep, curved chute where it has pushed through the snow like a plow, leaving rows of straight lines from its trailing quills.

A circle of feathers, like a nest, showed where a fox had made a meal of a ruffed grouse, leaving only the feathers and a few stains of rusty blood. The fox likely pounced on the bird under the snow, where grouse take refuge in winter, and where they are also sometimes trapped by ice storms that lay a solid blue skin across the surface above.

As I glided along the ski trails, or broke deep tracks in the virgin snow on the snowshoes, I saw all these stories written in the snow, but I seldom spied their elusive authors in the silent woods. Occasional birds flitted by, mostly chickadees, and maybe a hairy woodpecker, a male by the red cockade, tapping at a frozen bare tree. One day I saw a fat brown beaver, down along a frozen streambed, and watched it waddle in alarm from a fresh-cut tree it had been working on. I waddled over myself, on my snowshoes, to examine its work and the well-worn, icy chute leading to its tunnel to safety, a circle of icy water far down at the bottom. Somewhere nearby there would be a domed lodge of branches and mud, accessible only from underwater, where the beaver family dozes in semi-hibernation. (One beaver is assigned to sleep with its tail in the water, to monitor temperature and depth, so they don't become trapped by ice.)

Up to about a hundred years ago, beavers had been hunted and trapped to scarcity in North America (their smaller European cousins long near extirpated) to feed the European beaver hat trend. (Not like those furry bearskin hats, as I used to think; the beaver's short underfur was made into a kind of waterproof felt.) The fur trade that did so much for Canada's growth was largely founded on beaver pelts. Considered a symbol of Canadian industriousness, like the beehive to Utah, the beaver was featured on our first postage stamp and still graces our five-cent coin. Even after fashion switched to silk hats, around the mid-1800s, there were still three million beaver pelts sold in London over the next twenty years.

By the early twentieth century, beavers had become rare in Canada, too, and the animals and their dams were protected. The beaver proved its rodent heritage by being adaptable and prolific—some scientists believe there are more beavers in Canada and the northern U.S. now than even before Europeans arrived, and of course there's not as much room for them (imagine a time when it was said a squirrel could travel from Maine to the Mississippi without touching

A beaver swimming by in summer

the ground, just passing tree to tree). Few predators remain, like wolves, the smaller, fierce wolverine, and bears, which would tear their lodges apart.

Today beavers are often considered a destructive pest, as they take down many more trees than they need for food or dam construction—partly because their characteristic front teeth continue to grow, and must be worn down, but mainly because that's what beavers do. They build dams and alter the landscape around them, with an almost human disregard for collateral damage; the Quebec woods are dotted with shallow swamps fenced and pillared with the bare trunks of dead, drowned trees, where beavers have flooded a low-lying area. Some of my otherwise-gentle, nature-loving neighbors have become virulently anti-beaver after enduring repeatedly flooded driveways, or the loss of every birch tree along their shoreline. If enough complaints are made, government agencies have to hire trappers (which creates jobs, at least).

So I'm gliding along the ski trails, or breaking deep tracks on the snowshoes, and thinking, thinking, thinking. Or more accurately, in the words that came into my mind one day, noting how all my reflections were then chewed over and formed into sentences, I was "writing, writing, writing."

With all that going on, the little tale that was supposed to introduce a book review just kept on growing. Finally it became so long that the management of Bubba's Book Club demanded that I move it over to the story section, where it belonged. (Bubba is so strict.) So here we are.

Back in June 2007, the band and crew were launching our *Snakes and Arrows* tour—a tour that also kept on growing (like this story, or beaver teeth) and would eventually take us into the summer of 2008. (Good thing we didn't know that then, or we would have been frightened.)

The first three shows, in Atlanta, West Palm Beach, and Tampa, were followed by a day off on Sunday, June 17, before the next night's show in Raleigh. On the afternoon of the Tampa show, I was sitting in the front lounge of the bus with maps of the Southeast all around me, thinking about where to go.

In motorcycle and car magazines, I had read of the Biltmore Estate, in Asheville, North Carolina. It seemed to be favored for the introduction of new models to the press because it was an exotic location near some fantastic touring country—the Great Smoky Mountains, the surrounding Appalachians, and the neighboring foothills, with their wonderful little roads, including the famous Blue Ridge Parkway, winding through forested mountains.

It seemed from those magazine stories that you could stay at the actual estate, so I thought that would make a good destination. I chose a drop-off point along I-95 in Georgia (I usually try to keep our after-show drives to around three hours, so by the time driver Dave was looking for a truck stop or rest area to park in, I was ready for a shower and sleep—in a *stationary* bus), then traced a long, complicated route across the back roads of South Carolina, through the mountains, curving back east to Asheville for the night off, then on

Meadows and mountains of North Carolina

to Raleigh—the show-day ride a straight shot of about 250 miles, so we would have time to explore some more back roads that day.

Early that Sunday morning in mid-June, Michael and I unloaded the bikes and zigzagged our way northwest toward the mountains. I had included Deals Gap in the route, because it was there, and because that stretch of U.S. 129 in the southwest corner of North Carolina has become perhaps the most famous motorcycling road in the East ("The Tail of the Dragon," "318 Turns in Eleven Miles," etc.). However, it seemed that little piece of road was getting a little *too* famous.

On our previous visit, in the fall of 2002, Michael and I had stayed overnight at Deals Gap, in the humble motel (foodless, alas—I think we were reduced to microwave pizza that night). A tree in the middle of the parking lot was decorated with smashed pieces of motorcycle bodywork—the "Tree of Shame," for those who had been shaken off the Dragon's Tail. That tree and its decorations told a cautionary tale. Maybe a half-dozen other riders were staying there that night, and in the morning, Michael and I were alone on the Dragon (a dramatic test of riding technique, to be sure, at any velocity).

Four and a half years later, the roads in the surrounding area had been just as enjoyable, but as the two of us rode through the cross-roads at Deals Gap, my eyes bugged out in my helmet—it looked like the circus had come to town. The motel and campground were jammed with hundreds of motorcycles, and sports cars, too (whole clubs of Miatas and Porsches). Tent-marquees had been put up across the road over rows of racks dangling souvenir T-shirts. I had read recently that increasing traffic, and motorcycle crashes (for the Tree of Shame), had led to a reduced speed limit, and its stern enforcement by numerous LEOs (law-enforcement officers—I picked up that useful acronym from a website about Deals Gap).

However, as one who travels so widely on American roads (over 30,000 miles annually in recent years, on two wheels and four), I know that's the story everywhere. In just the last few years zero-tolerance speed enforcement has increased out of all reason, and LEOs have become, perforce, not peacekeepers but predators. Bad economic times raise crime rates in any country, I know, but this increase in police action is not crime fighting, alas, but revenue gathering.

It's a war zone out there—state troopers parking behind bridge abutments and leaning over their car roofs like snipers with high-powered laser guns, and even local cops are casting their nets wider to the state highways, while county sheriffs prowl along handy stretches of interstate, wanting a piece of the action.

But on that busy Sunday in Deals Gap, the traffic alone was enough to slow our progress—we were stuck in a halting parade of Harleys and clones all the way through the 318 sharp turns, switchbacks, and tricky hairpins. That kind of riding was *way* beyond the limited cornering clearance of such "fashion statement" motorcycles, and apparently beyond their riders, too. But at least they'd be able to say they had ridden the Tail of the Dragon. And eventually even those leisurely cruisers drew ahead of us, because we were crawling behind one wobbly neo-biker who looked the look, but most assuredly could not ride the ride. (My Harley-riding friend Dave has a sticker on his helmet that reads "$20,000 and 2,000 Miles Does Not Make You a Biker.") This specimen of fragile masculinity could not bow to letting us by—but at least we would not be having any conversations with the cops in the bushes. (Though they must have been snickering to themselves as we passed.)

Pavement snakes, roadside arrow (and sometimes snakes hiding at the roadside, too . . .)

Witnessing all that, I thought to myself, "Deals Gap is *over*."

This past summer I was introduced to a less well-known area of pavement paradise, just to the south, in the mountains of North Georgia. Ever since the day and night Michael and I spent there in July, I have been wanting to write a story about it, but have put it off for two reasons. One, I wanted to get it all down in a way that would do justice to the experience, and second, I wasn't sure I really *wanted* to tell too many people about it.

But I've had that argument with myself before, and decided it was better to share. And I hate not being able to write about good things.

So, in July 2008, in the last few days of the tour, Michael and I were invited by our friend Wes, guitarist with the excellent band Porcupine Tree (and a fine player and singer as a solo artist), and his wife, Rebecca, to join them at a small resort called Two Wheels Only, in the tiny hamlet of Suches, Georgia. As the name suggests, it is a resort for motorcyclists, with an inn and restaurant surrounded by a campground. On a hot, bright morning, Michael and I rode in from the bus to meet Wes and Rebecca, and the four of us went for a ride.

Wes had "warned" us about Becca—that she was a fast rider, and when they were traveling together he usually just followed her around—so we let her take the lead. Carving through the tight corners between thick forest and rocky cuts, and along meandering streams, she set a fast pace on her little Supermoto-style bike, followed by Wes on his yellow Ducati Monster (dubbed by Michael the "hand banana"), and Michael and me. The challenging, endlessly winding roads were almost empty of other traffic, and we had a fantastic ride on a route they called "To Helen Back," to the small, Bavarian-themed Georgia town (I know—*what?*) called Helen. There we had a Bavarian-themed lunch (the *wurst*, ha ha), then rode back around by way of the summit of Brasstown Bald. Dinner that night at T.W.O. was also unforgettable, hosted by owner G.T., his friend Turbo, and Mimi, a schoolteacher from across the road who helped out around the place.

Two Wheels Only, Suches, Georgia (Note the radiant sky—"silver lining"—used in "Independence Day")

The large main room was comfortably arrayed with dining tables and chairs, sitting areas, and a pool table, the walls plastered with motorcycling posters and memorabilia. Michael and I shot a little pool before dinner, and I attempted a few difficult bank shots that actually went in. Michael expressed his surprise (he's so *competitive*), and I didn't let on that no one was more surprised than me. My streak was soon over, though, and I was back to being . . . a loser. Alas, there is no game or sport that I can actually win at, and of course that's why I am drawn to endurance activities like cross-country skiing or swimming—there's no losing.

A friend once mentioned to me in a conversation about cross-country skiing that after all these years I must be a pretty good skier. I considered the notion, but shook my head and said, "No way, I'm *terrible*—I fall down all the time, I flail and swear. My technique is pathetic. It's just that I can do it for a really long time!"

Endurance is my only salvation—in sports, in work, in life. I was thinking about that one day this past January, in California, when I got up at 5:00 a.m. and drove 350 miles to the Bay Area, then turned around and rode my motorcycle 350 miles back, all in the rain. That day I thought to myself, "That's one thing I can do—I can *endure*."

And that's probably why I enjoyed my stay at Two Wheels Only, and riding the surrounding area. Just, you know, *endured* it.

I don't want the place to get *too* popular. So I don't recommend it—I really don't . . .

And back to the summer before, leaving busy Deals Gap in June 2007, Michael and I continued on, winding through Great Smoky Mountains National Park, which was also awfully busy—mid-June was getting into the height of the tourist season, after all, and it was a Sunday. I have written before about the incredible numbers of people who flock to Pigeon Forge (pun absolutely intended) and nearby Gatlinburg every year, making them the most popular destinations in the Southeast (first most popular is the park itself, though only for driving through—few people actually, you know, go out walking in the *woods*—and the second most popular destination is . . . Dollywood). Growing frustrated by the traffic and our slow progress, Michael and I escaped to I-40 and rode east to Asheville, arriving late in the day at the Biltmore Estate.

I was disappointed to find that the hotel wasn't actually part of the mansion, which we barely glimpsed in the distance. It was a conventional modern hotel on the grounds nearby, but it was a nice enough place, and the restaurant was very good. Our waiter was a tall, bearded man in his forties, who served us with cheerful courtesy. He was reserved and dignified, but good humored, and smiled readily when Michael did his usual routine, giving his order then pointing at me and saying, "And my *father* will have . . ."

Michael, Wes, Rebecca, en route to the Atlanta show

I fired right back, tossing my head and seething out between my teeth, "That's right, baby—who's your daddy?" and the waiter laughed out loud. (In those days Michael was a very old-looking—if boyish-faced—thirty-five, while I was a youthful fifty-four.)

At the end of the meal, when the waiter brought a leatherette folder that appeared to be the bill, and placed it in front of me, I laughed and pointed at Michael, "Oh—that goes to him!" I rolled my eyes and added, with facial italics, "The *Boy*."

The waiter tapped the folder and said quietly, "This is your waiter . . . being discreet." Then he moved away.

Curious, I opened the folder and saw a small note. I put on my reading glasses and opened it. It read: "Rohinton Mistry, *A Fine Balance*—An absolute MUST for Bubba's Book Club!" Below that, "P.S. Atlanta was fantastic!"

I showed the note to Michael, and he nodded and said, "That's pretty cool."

And it was. Throughout the meal, I had picked up no hints that our quiet, dignified server was a fan, and the Atlanta show—the first of the tour—had only been a few days before. Also, Atlanta was much farther away from Asheville than the next day's show, in Raleigh, so apparently he was a pretty *serious* fan, too—as of course he would have to be to know about Bubba's Book Club, and to feel so strongly about a book he thought was "an absolute MUST" for it.

I wrote a little note thanking the waiter for his good service and recommendation, autographed it, and put it in the folder. When he returned to our table, I slid the folder across, saying, "This is Bubba . . . appreciating your discretion."

(That little anecdote was the introduction to the book review I was talking about—the one that started this whole business.)

When Michael and I left the following day, we picked up a stretch of the Blue Ridge Parkway and meandered around for a couple of hours, then surrendered to the interstate—we still had a long way to go to work. And unfortunately, the "anti-destination league" was in full force that day. Both lanes of eastbound I-40 were clogged with slow drivers, and again and again the same pattern was repeated. We'd sit behind a car in the so-called passing lane, wait for the driver to pull over and let us by, and after a few minutes, give up and go around to the right. I hate having to do that, as it immediately puts *me* in the wrong (remembering my cardinal rule: "Whatever happens, it mustn't be my fault"), so when I pulled in front of the offending drivers, sitting there like fat lumps, I couldn't resist sweeping my left arm overhead, and pointing to the inside lane. Nothing obscene—just a suggestion that they "do the right thing."

Passing through Greensboro, the traffic was heavier, in three lanes now, but the drivers were no less inconsiderate, and we were forced to pass on the right so many times that I was getting a little steamed— literally, in the 90° heat, and figuratively, as we were running late and I wanted to get to Raleigh. Suddenly, out of nowhere, there were flashing lights in my mirrors, and Michael and I were pulled over. It was a local cop, and he *claimed* he had been following us, watching us "weave through traffic at high speed," which he said he had clocked at 90 miles per hour.

Well, we knew that was absurd—neither of us had made one pass that was not properly signaled and safely negotiated, and there was no way we were making that kind of speed under those conditions. Plus my radar detector had never made a peep in my earpiece. It seemed obvious that some peevish left-lane squatter had used his cellphone to call Deputy Barney Fife (we were in North Carolina, after all, home of "Mayberry") and report "a couple-a maniac bikers weavin' through traffic at about 90!" And that was all ol' Barney had to hear to swing out onto the interstate and come after us.

But however spurious, it was a serious charge, reckless driving or something, and I had to fight it. And sure, I had the resources to hire a local lawyer, collect documentation and letters-of-reference from LEOs of our acquaintance, and succeed in having those ridiculous charges dropped—but many other people could not have fought such injustice, so it continued to rankle. I hate that kind of stuff. (Like the line in our song "Resist," *I can learn to close my eyes/ To anything but injustice.*")

This image was taken on the fly as I rode solo along the back roads from somewhere in Kansas to Minneapolis, in the summer of 2008. It was one of my favorite photos from the tour, but I never found a place to use it until now. Among the tales this picture tells, there's the pretty, open country, the way I felt riding through it (good), the road shining from the passing rainshower that's fading off to the east, ahead of me (also good), the bug-splattered windscreen, the speedometer showing about 60 mph, the trees reflected in the mirror, and beside it, my guardian radar detector.

South Dakota highway, after a summer rain

Contrary to the shrill ravings of some authorities (like Ontario, Quebec, New York, and Virginia, who ban radar detectors), the proper use of this device is not to allow me to blaze lawlessly through small towns, scattering children and old people, or to weave recklessly through traffic on busy highways. The radar detector is really for a moment like this, when I might be cruising a little faster (without a camera in my hand), maybe at a perfectly safe and reasonable 70 mph, only to be ambushed by a radar gun over the horizon, followed by a boring and costly conversation about the posted limit being 55. That's what a radar detector is for.

So endeth . . . the lesson.

Back on the road to Raleigh, Michael and I arrived at the venue that afternoon, hot and tired. After I cleaned up and got myself organized, I called my wife Carrie and told her about our adventures, and how exhausted I was from traveling.

Now . . . in this reporter's experience, a woman rarely misses an opportunity to try to teach a man a little humility, and Carrie just said, "Well, you didn't *have* to do all that."

Taken aback, I thought for a moment, then blustered, "Sure I did!"

It seemed obvious to me. I had to work in Tampa Saturday night, then in Raleigh on Monday night. So looking at that day between, I could only think, "What's the most *excellent* thing I can do?" If I settled for something less than that, I just wouldn't feel good about myself, or about how I had spent my day.

One time my friend Matt Scannell and I were on a road trip together up around Big Sur, driving in my Aston Martin DB9, on one of the great roads of the world, on a bright winter morning when we had it to ourselves, and we were "in the moment" big time. We talked about how wonderful it was to appreciate an experience while it was happening, and how important it was to make the effort beforehand to *make* that moment—to put yourself into places and situations that might turn out to be that excellent. Appreciating the moment is not a passive endeavor, at least for those who want to appreciate as many moments as possible.

Typically, I tried to frame that sentiment in a line for a rock song, even while I was driving us along that majestic coastline. In an earnest monotone, I sang it to Matt:

> Wake up every morning like you're gonna live forever
> Go to sleep at night like it's the last day of your life.

Matt nodded and smiled, and said, "Remember that line—it's good." I said, "Dibs!," and he laughed. "You know, I think when you say something, it's kind of automatically 'dibs.'"

Oh, yeah. Right.

Later it occurred to me that maybe the reverse was even better:

> Wake up every morning like it's the last day of your life
> Go to sleep at night like you're gonna live forever.

It's funny how Matt and I so often think and talk in terms of *songs*—whether finding the right words to express a feeling or experience, collaborating on a couple of songs that pleased us, or dreaming up elaborate stage musicals like last year's "Snowdance" (see "The Best February Ever"), or more recently, a couple of massive conceptions that we have discussed back and forth in arch seriousness, and outlined in great detail. One is a kind of California cars-and-guitars surf opera, based on a fictional surf group called Lola and the GTs, with fast cars and faster women. Or an R&B musical extravaganza called "Supernatural Lover," which will recount the adventures of a teenage Casanova, but on a mythic plane. Drawing upon musical moods from the likes of Marvin Gaye, Isaac Hayes, and Barry White, the curtain opens on a dramatically lit stage lined with ranks of angelic, white-robed maidens, then builds through time-honored themes like Stained Innocence, Young Conqueror Rampant, and the Unattainable One. (Obviously based on the adolescent exploits of the younger, cuter one of us.)

But back to "the moment" (the generic one).

It's important to stress that such an approach to life doesn't have be all *exigent* or anything—it's not like you always have to be *doing* something. Sometimes there is definitely "excellence," and satisfaction, in doing nothing at all.

When I first arrive at my refuge in the Quebec woods, for example, I am more than content to hibernate for a few days (or "estivate," in summer), doing nothing, with nobody. Just keep the fire going, enjoy the silence, and open a good, long book.

As to whether I "have" to do any particular thing—like after a few days in Quebec, when I'll be out skiing and snowshoeing in winter, or rowing and swimming in summer—my answer is yes, I do. I have to do things. Sometimes hard things. That is a conversation I have obviously thought back to many times, and "written about" in my head.

Similarly, there's another comment I've heard a few times, when I might mention to someone that a particular activity or journey I had undertaken had been grueling, and how sore and tired, and maybe ill (thinking of bicycling in Africa) it left me, and I'll hear in response, "Well, that's what you wanted to do."

Yes . . . but my desire to attempt a challenge certainly doesn't diminish its difficulty—the opposite, usually—and doesn't mean it would be any easier if I *hadn't* wanted to do it.

So the most excellent thing I could do on Sunday, June 17, 2007, was ride across South Carolina to Deals Gap, then east to Asheville, and the next day make it to the show in Raleigh. The little note from our waiter at the Biltmore Estate became a bookmark at the back of my journal, marking the "bike service needs" page, for the rest of the tour, and I still have it. Of course I remembered that book recommendation anyway, and it happened that at home, we already had a copy of that dauntingly thick novel (700 pages) in our bookshelves, given to Carrie by her Toronto photographic printer, Bob Carnie.

This February, I brought that book with me to Quebec. In those first couple of "hibernation" days, I settled in on the sofa, fire blazing, warm and radiant, snow falling in slanting curtains outside, the birds flocking around my feeding station, Bubba's Birdbrain Café. Chickadees, woodpeckers, jays, redpolls, nuthatches, and a rare and striking visitor, the pine grosbeak—large in size, and richly colored, the males rosy-gray, the females olive-gold, both with delicate black and white patterns on their folded wings. The pine grosbeaks usually winter farther north, but are sometimes driven south by harsh weather.

The birds made me smile, especially the perky chickadees flitting around ten or twelve at a time. (If I go outside to fill the feeder, they will fly up close beside my head, in a whir of wings, and land inches away from me and continue feeding. With a little patient stillness, they will even eat right out of your hand.)

The silence was perfect, the day was perfect, and there was nothing more important to do than watch the birds for a little while, then open my book and start reading.

Bubba's Birdbrain Café
(Left to right: nuthatch, redpoll, chickadee)

13

THE QUEST FOR THE PHANTOM TOWER

MARCH 2009

Out of nowhere, it appeared in the night sky last summer. Since time immemorial, nights in the Laurentian Mountains of Quebec had been utterly dark, speckled with stars, planets, and occasional meteor showers, while the moon in its shifting phases ruled over all. Then suddenly, literally overnight, there was a bright red beacon hanging above the wooded hills to the north, across the lake, all night, every night, unnatural, unblinking, and . . . unignorable.

With no other man-made light in view, save perhaps the yellow glow from the windows of a neighbor's cottage across the lake—and even that usually only on weekends, when people came up from their homes in Montreal—the nights there are still very dark. But from that fateful night on, that piercing, alien red light ruled the darkness, like the Eye of Sauron in *The Lord of the Rings*. I guessed it was an aircraft beacon on some kind of tower, but its scarlet laser eye was brighter than the stars, brighter than the planets, brighter even than the full moon, and worst of all, I could see it from every room in my house. Every night my eyes were drawn to that dot of red light above the northern horizon, glaring balefully, like a perpetual, malevolent warning. It was a symbol of everything I go to that place to get away from, and I was soon calling it the Eye of Satan.

The bedroom windows in my house were designed to reach down to the level of my bed, so I can sleep with my head beside the window, as near as possible to the outdoors. In summer I keep the windows raised high, screened from insects, but open to the night breezes and the sounds of the wild, like the stirring call of the loons echoing across the lake. In winter, I leave the curtains open (at least when I'm alone, free from spousal objections), so I can look up at the stars, or falling snow, and awaken at first light to see the new day. However, now if I even briefly open my eyes during the night and look outside, I look straight into the Eye of Satan.

Scanning through binoculars at twilight, just as the Eye became visible, the tower itself was noticeable among the tree branches for its *straightness*—as my drum teacher, Freddie Gruber, pointed out years ago, "There are no straight lines in nature." When the daylight faded into darkness, the Eye glowed brighter.

As a symbol, it is rather too obvious, and a red light bulb in the sky is not the world's biggest problem, I know. Given that most people in the western world dwell in a sea of artificial light anyway, they might not even comprehend the problem. But it's different for those of us who choose to live in the woods, and that man-made intrusion was a serious blight on my personal soulscape. I can't help but wonder why it is possible for some corporation, and some cooperating government agency, to commit such an invasion of a person's night sky—of so *many* people's night sky. In those low, glacier-raked mountains of forests and lakes, that beacon was surely visible for hundreds of square miles—which would be its *purpose*, of course, but considered as a first-class felony of "light pollution," it was pretty heinous.

Shouldn't they have had to ask us?

Warn us?

Shouldn't we have been able to say, "No thank you!"?

Well, obviously not, because there it is, and there it will remain, through every night I spend in that house, smack in the middle of my horizon.

The Eye of Satan was soon identified as a beacon on a telecommunications tower, because it brought another unasked-for change to our local atmosphere: cellular telephone service. For sixteen years I had been contentedly living in an area without cell coverage—kind of liked it, really—but one afternoon last summer I was standing in the kitchen with my property manager, Keith, and his cell phone rang. We looked at each other, then at the phone, and sure enough—suddenly we had cell service. Thank you, Satan.

All through my time in Quebec last summer, that bright red night-light haunted me, stabbing my eyes every time I looked out toward the dark lake, and it was the same again this winter. Acts of sabotage were contemplated, of course, involving plastic explosives, a high-powered sniper rifle, or, as one neighbor suggested with a smile, "Just go over there and unscrew the light bulb!" I knew well enough there was nothing to be done about it— "What cannot be altered, must be endured"—but it loomed large in my night-thoughts, and I decided I had to go there, hike to that tower. Just to see where it was—and maybe stand beneath it and shake my fist at the Eye of Satan.

This February I recruited a willing accomplice in my neighbor, Charles (silent "s," *à la française*), a good-humored, nature-loving French-Canadian. I have liked Charles since we first met many years ago at local association meetings, which could sometimes generate controversy, demonstrating the contrasts in my neighbors' reasons for building a house on a lake in the woods— basically the difference between pioneers and suburbanites. Charles would often be the voice of cool, wry reason, and made some good jokes. His wife, Marthe, was quiet, pretty, and, I learned later, an excellent painter.

But what really won my lifelong affection for Charles was an act of compassionate, impetuous generosity, so typical of that quality of open warmth, *chaleur*, I have always admired in French-Canadians. One afternoon in the summer of 1998, when I was hiding out in the woods after the loss of my family, I was on the lake in my rowboat— as always back then, vainly trying to escape, somehow, somewhere, by any kind of *motion*.

That day I was having trouble with one of my oarlocks, and when it came undone far from my dock, I sat floating on the still water with one long oar across my legs while I tried to repair it. Across the bay I recognized Charles and Marthe in their canoe, and I saw them start to steer in my direction.

Charles, under a heron's nest,
in his "hunter-resistant" jacket

To describe my state of mind that summer, without getting "all into it" too much, I was awfully fragile. That day in particular, I was already disproportionately upset over the momentary crisis of a broken oarlock, and in general, I was pretty shy of contact with people I didn't know well. So, to be frank, I really didn't want to talk to anybody.

When their boat drew near, Charles, in his perfect English, and perfect French-Canadian accent, made me a speech I will never forget.

"Every night I see your light across the lake," he said, then lowered his eyes and shook his head. "And . . . I think about you."

He went on, and though I was getting teary (other people's emotion could so easily trigger my own), what Charles said was so right, so beautiful. The gist of it was "If there's ever anything I can do for you, or just be there for you, you have only to call, or knock on my door, anytime."

Moved, I nodded and said, "Thank you, I appreciate that." And I meant it.

As I wrote in *Ghost Rider*, it was impossible for anyone to really *relate* to me at that time, and I was aware that facing me could be difficult, even for my friends and loved ones. My reading of what some good people offered me was a simple statement: "I don't know what to say—but here's my heart."

That was a message I could receive, even then, and that's what Charles was saying. The feeling was repeated in Marthe's dark eyes, brimming with deep sympathy.

So when I moved across the lake a couple of years ago, next door to Charles and Marthe, I was glad to get to know them better. One day last winter Charles invited me to go snowshoeing with him, and he guided me through the woods to a trail he knew that led to an uninhabited lake where great blue herons nested. Their huge nests of woven sticks, abandoned in winter, formed a colony, in a line of dead trees along the shore.

Like many of my neighbors, Charles lives and works in Montreal most of the week, and spends his weekends in the Laurentians, just an hour or so north. This winter he and I have been snowshoeing together every Saturday, exploring the wooded backlands around us, and introducing each other to hidden trails we have discovered on our solitary ramblings.

Charles's knowledge of nature, and his *love* for nature, gave us an immediate bond, and we are both entirely happy to be tramping through the winter woods for hours. While we hike, Charles and I trade the names of trees and animals in English and French—the hemlock is *la pruche*; the fir is *le sapin*; the hare is *le lièvre* (Charles is amused by the English word, and when we cross their tracks, he always has to spell it out, "That's a hare, h-a-r-e"); the ruffed grouse is *la gélinotte huppée*; the moose is *l'orignal*.

As with all of my French-Canadian friends, I always regret that our conversations have to be in English, but my French is just not up to that challenge. My reading *en français* is workable (at least to the level of Tintin books, like a ten-year-old), and sometimes I can say what I want, but I won't understand the rapid-fire response, especially in a Québécois accent. As I tell them, *"J'ai le vocabulaire, mais je n'ai pas l'habitude."* I just haven't spent enough time among francophones to develop the facility, and the "ear."

Charles could see the Eye of Satan, *l'Oeil du Diable*, from his house, too, and was likewise curious about it, so as a "conceit" for one weekend snowshoe hike this winter, I suggested we go in search of that tower. We took a compass bearing from our houses, and set off across the frozen lake, buried in deep snow. We guessed it might be a couple of miles.

The surface of the snow was hard that day, because earlier in the week there had been a brief thaw with some rain. The temperature had dropped again, and the deep snow refroze with an icy crust, so traveling was relatively easy. On the open lake, swept by frigid winds that further toughened its skin of snow and ice, you could even get by without snowshoes, and though the snow was softer in the woods, it was still easier going than breaking trail through deep powder.

On my solo wanderings in the winter woods, I have been musing over a theory of the Geology of Snow—how over the course of a winter the snow resembles a high-speed demonstration of the shaping of a landscape, by wind, water, temperature, and pressure. Mountains rise and fall; mesas, cliffs, and dunes are shaped; blocks and faults crack and shift beneath the surface; watercourses are carved; and always there is *change*.

One good example can be seen where an animal has crossed the snow, pressing down a line of tracks. The air temperature rises a few degrees above freezing, a little rain falls, and the surface recedes—now the pressed-down tracks are left *higher*, embossed on the surface like a row of tiny mesas. Because the circles of compacted snow had been made harder, like the capstone of a mesa, they resisted the erosion that cut away around them. In just this way the pillared rock towers of the American West, like Monument Valley, were formed—though that took

a few million years, rather than a day or two (a winter's creation-myth, perhaps, as well as high-speed science).

Across that day's Geology of Snow, Charles and I headed into the woods north of the lake, where there were no trails. But with five feet of frozen whiteness smoothing over the underbrush, roots, rocks, and marshes, and the trees bare of leaves, one of the great advantages of snowshoes is that we could pretty much walk anywhere we wanted.

Taking turns breaking trail, or walking beside each other, we left a winding pair of tracks that meandered around low-hanging branches or between dense thickets of scrub, but we tried to keep to our bearing, just west of north. The trees were relatively small in those third-growth woods, because—as in pretty well all of Eastern Canada and the United States—the Laurentian forests have been clear-cut twice over, once around the turn of the twentieth century, and again in the 1950s. The great oak and white pine forests that once shaded that land with a canopy as high as 200 feet would never grow back, crowded out by faster-growing poplar, birch, spruce, beech, and fir. Charles and I always pointed out the rarities, like good-sized hemlocks (*les pruches*), wondering how they came to be spared by the loggers (sometimes, I have learned, to make shade for their camps). Generally, the bigger trees these days were bushy cedars in damp lowlands, short-lived poplars and birches, and vanishingly few remnant pines.

Originally, most of the huge white pines went to build British warships, thus constructing the world's most powerful navy in the eighteenth and nineteenth centuries. In the time of the Napoleonic wars, the ports around the Baltic Sea—and thus alternative sources of pine—were blockaded, and the largest white pines in Canada, three feet or more in diameter, were reserved for the British navy.

After the loggers came the settlers. The earliest Europeans to homestead in the Laurentians were French Catholics and Scots-Irish Protestants. The modern-day villages mostly had names commemorating Catholic saints, but the old-time township names told a different tale—Kilkenny, Kildare, Derry, Suffolk, Harrington, and Wentworth. Many of those were "Frenchified" in the 1960s and '70s, but some remain.

The early settlers faced an insurmountable challenge, for after clearing the forests and rocks with axes and stoneboats, they soon learned that the glacier-scraped soil was thin, rocky, and impoverished, while the growing season was dangerously short. Still, despite that reality, in the later 1800s a Catholic priest, the famous (should be infamous) Curé Labelle (*le Roi du Nord*, the King of the North), a huge man for his day, over six feet tall and 300 pounds, had a vision. When he was posted to the remote *Pays d'en Haut* (high country) north of Montreal, he was determined to bring in more Catholic settlers. Many had been fleeing south to work in the mills of New England, not surprisingly, and he wanted to increase their numbers against the Protestants—and not incidentally, increase his own power and influence. Curé Labelle promoted the agricultural potential in the Laurentians, and like the American hucksters who lured settlers to the arid West by assuring them, "Rain follows the plow," his misguided efforts were successful, temporarily.

The persuasive curé even convinced the Montreal authorities to bring in a railroad, *le Petit Train du Nord*, by 1876, but the new arrivals it brought had no more success at farming. Many families suffered terribly, through harsh winters, fierce mosquitoes, unproductive land, and desperate need. Eventually some of them just gave up, leaving behind abandoned farms and full graveyards. Others survived by hiring out as lumberjacks in winter, and by burning vast amounts of hardwood to make potash—rendering the ashes of maple and beech into a distillate used in the making of glass, soap, fertilizer, and fabrics. Apart from a little maple syrup, potash was their only cash crop, but it took a lot of work, and a lot of trees—in a one-time-only, slash-and-burn harvest.

The Eye of Satan watches over all

As demand for construction lumber rose in the United States, water-driven sawmills were built on every river and stream of any force, and villages grew around them. The sawmills were insatiably hungry for trees, too.

The final blow to the Eastern Canadian forests was a blight, introduced from Europe, that attacked white pines, killing them from the top down. Because Canadian white pines would not grow in Europe, the British raised crops of seedlings there, then shipped them back to Canada for transplanting. Result: disaster.

When all of the big trees were gone, the remaining scrub was harvested for pulp, to feed the twentieth century's demand for paper. In that connection, a Winston Churchill quote comes to mind, one I cited in *Roadshow*. In 1929, the future British leader and wartime hero visited Western Canada, and remarked, "Fancy cutting down all those beautiful trees to make pulp for those bloody newspapers, and calling it civilization."

Photographs of the Laurentians taken in the early twentieth century show bald hills and empty fields—though sometimes dotted with summer vacationers, or winter skiers. These people would be the "cash crop" in later years, filling Curé Labelle's *Petit Train du Nord* and the many hotels and boarding houses that sprang up to lodge them.

(My appreciation to Joseph Graham's fine book, *Naming the Laurentians*, for some of this historical background.)

When I was a boy, growing up in Southern Ontario, our family sometimes traveled "Up North," to a campground or rented cottage. When I walked into the shadows of the rich-smelling northern woods, through pine needles, ferns, and arbors of sumac, I always imagined I was entering the *primeval* forest—thrilled to think that where I stepped, perhaps no human had ever set foot before. Eventually coming to understand the reality of the wholesale logging that had stripped that

Old tracks, young trees

land again and again, and that only a scrubby imitation of its former majesty had regrown, was one of those poignant surrenders of illusion for reality, of innocence for knowledge. That exchange is sometimes difficult, even painful. As I wrote in a song long ago, *"Illusions are painfully shattered/ Right where discovery starts."* Ain't it the truth.

For myself, I would always rather know than not, would rather pay that price for the apple of knowledge—because painful truth seems preferable to blissful ignorance.

But I would sure give a lot to see the forests of Quebec as they once were.

Charles and I followed the rolling contours of those ancient, glaciated hills, working up and down through the scrubby young trees for a couple of miles, all the way over to the giant hydro-electric lines.

There we stood beneath another satanic construction, an electro-mechanical network of immense scale that beggared belief. Gigantic, robotic-looking metal towers, with thick cables sagging between their upright trusses, marched along a treeless gash (kept clear by herbicides), a naked "corridor" that was 450 feet wide (one and a half football fields). That monstrous procession stretched all the way from James Bay, hundreds of miles north, down to the population centers of southern Quebec and into the Northeast United States. The source, the dams and turbines of Hydro-Québec on La Grande River, were 1,000 kilometers by air north of Montreal, and with the occasional zigzag angles the corridor took to avoid lakes and higher mountains ("no straight lines in nature"), the entire electrical superhighway was probably nearer 1,000 *miles* long.

The silhouettes of those immense towers, and even the heavy wires shining silver in the sun, could be seen from many parts of our lake (such as from my kitchen window, alas). Like the Eye of Satan, they made another unfortunate intrusion into our scenery and sense of wilderness, but there must surely be yet a bigger story behind that massive scar across the Earth. If I were an investigative reporter, rather than merely a cranky observer, I would want to find out what that project *really* cost, in billions of dollars and in immeasurable, permanent environmental devastation—especially the dams and infrastructure in the Far North, for example, where no one can see the mess they made.

That massive Hydro-Québec project was conceived in the 1970s, before such barriers as environmental regulations and reviews were in place. Construction began without even *informing* the people who would be affected most—the Cree and Inuit natives who lived and hunted in the region. The project swallowed an area larger than New York State, and like the long-lost Laurentian forests, which no one alive or unborn will ever see, the North is a deceptively fragile landscape. *It does not grow back.*

And when (not if) those mighty towers are struck down by an ice storm, as happened in the winter of 1998, vast numbers of people will be left without electricity through many frigid days and nights—as long as two weeks, that time. And what unimaginable millions must it have cost to fix *that* disaster?

Of course, hydro-electric power seems preferable to, say, burning coal, as the United States relies upon for more than half of its electricity (for complicated political reasons that we needn't get into right now, thank you), but still—hydro projects make a heck of a mess, too. In recent years, even in countries like China and Brazil, such enormous enterprises of damming and flooding are resisted—if not actually prevented.

At home, nowadays the simple "eyesore" argument is gaining traction, and even seemingly benign wind farms are banished by people

who treasure their natural landscape, like the residents of Cape Cod. In otherwise aesthetically sensitive Quebec, alas, that was not a consideration in the bad old 1970s.

This photograph, taken from a high hill to the south, encapsulates the dynamics of the modern Laurentians: young trees in the foreground are growing back after a recent clearcut; the lakeside cottages in the middle ground form an imagined Eden; on the horizon, the Tower of Satan to the left, and to the right, the bare white patch under the power lines, and the silhouettes of their towers.

In principle, those Hydro-Québec power lines are like the aqueducts in the American West, which also slice for hundreds of miles across uninhabited wilderness, deserts, and even mountains. But water is, by nature, prettier than metal towers. In the same way that a significant amount of water in those aqueducts is lost to evaporation, so the hydro lines suffer leakage, too. The old-time fear that the electro-magnetic energy they radiate caused brain tumors in people who lived under them has been discredited, but still, I once stood beneath those Hydro-Québec power lines during an icy rain, and heard the wires crackling and buzzing, like static electricity.

Charles and I emerged from the woods into the cleared area under the towers, the snow solid white across the bare, heaving landscape—a shroud laid across a skeleton. We climbed a steep, high ridge, hoping to get a view of Satan's Tower, but saw nothing but bare trees all around. We paused in the open sunshine to drink some water and share the goodies in our packs (including some delicious nuts roasted in curry powder, sent by Marthe, an artist in the kitchen as well as on canvas).

The hydro-line corridor had long been a popular snowmobile and ATV route, which seemed a suitable match, and as a motorcyclist myself, I could hardly resent these recreational "cousins"—as long as they weren't ruining my cross-country ski trails. As Charles and I stood in the sun, contemplating our next move, we heard the buzz of engines in the distance, quickly drawing nearer, and louder. Three snowmobiles crested the ridge and headed north in a steady, metallic snarl, and after they passed, their exhaust smell hung in the thin winter air for a long time.

We struck off into the woods in the direction we thought the tower should be, but even the crowns of the hills were thickly wooded, and obstructed our view of anything higher. We tried to keep tending upward, and northward, with frequent checks of our compasses (*boussoles*). At the summit of every hill (*colline*), we would hope to see the object of our quest, *la Maudite Tour du Diable*, but there was no sign of the phantom tower. We headed down into a long, narrow valley and across a small lake, level, white and open to the sun again. We paused on the far shore beside an abandoned hunting cabin, its roof collapsed beneath the snow. A snowmobile trail led up through the trees to the north, and we agreed to follow it for a while, and try to make it up one last hill, then call it a day.

We had been laboring up and down over the deep snow for more than two hours, and it was time to be heading back, while we still had enough daylight, and at least an hour to spare (call it "trailcraft"). It

Shadow of the explorer

was early afternoon, and winter days are short. Giving up on a mission is always difficult, but when you are far from home in the winter woods, you have to be—well, as Charles said to me, "I am glad you are . . . *sensible*."

And thus did the First Expedition end in failure. But as I said to Charles, "For me, the exploring is worthwhile for its own sake. Like the saying I once heard about fishing, 'Only a fool thinks he goes fishing to catch fish.'"

In *Ghost Rider*, I described the kind of exploring Charles and I were doing as "disorienteering," and in guessing the distance to that tower to be only a couple of miles, it would turn out that we had "misunderestimated" that distance by a factor of about three. The Eye of Satan was much farther away than we thought . . .

Looping back toward the power lines, we were excited to come across the unmistakably huge tracks of a pair of moose, most likely a female and her yearling calf, as the males are solitary (and ornery). We followed the deep troughs where the two had struggled through snow up to their great bodies, and saw the hollows where they had rested overnight, and their truffle-sized droppings. Moose are rare and elusive in our area, and hunters take a few of them every fall, so we were always glad to see what Charles called "signs of moose activity."

Back home that night, I pored over maps, and studied the aerial photographs on Google Earth. The tower had only existed for seven months, so wouldn't appear on maps, or even on satellite images that might be years old (some of them low-res, too, in that backwoods area), but I was searching for some clue of where to look next—an access road, perhaps, that a tower would require for construction and maintenance.

Then I had an inspiration: Who would have to know about an aircraft beacon?

A *pilot*, of course!

I sent an email to my old friend Brian Laski, "Vings," who flew for Air Canada, and asked if he could help. He made some calls to aviation and associated government agencies, ordered a relevant chart, and came up with a few suggestions.

Most of them were too far away, or in the wrong direction, but one set of coordinates looked promising—a little farther away than Charles and I had thought it must be, but on the right compass bearing. On Google Earth I picked out a small, square structure on the site—possibly the tower's utility building?

The next Saturday, Charles and I launched what history would come to know as the Second Expedition. We drove to a trailhead farther north, and snowshoed into the woods along the old railway alignment. Abandoned in the '60s, the tracks had long ago been taken up, the roadbed now devoted to cross-country skiing, snowmobiling, snowshoeing, and, in summer, bicycling and hiking. ("Rails to trails," one of the better devolutions of modern times.)

I was familiar with that part of the so-called Aerobic Corridor from a couple of mountain-bike rides out that way years ago, and on Google Earth, I had spied a small logging road that would take us to where the tower was supposed to be. The clues all added up.

Once again, the snowshoeing was easy that day, especially where a snowmobile had packed down the trail, but the structure I had seen from space turned out to be an abandoned cabin, perched lopsidedly on an old flatbed trailer.

I was disappointed—and *puzzled*. Those coordinates were supposed to be official aviation data, and I had to wonder, wouldn't pilots need to have, you know, *accurate* information? Mysteries abounded on this quest.

Charles and I continued west along that logging road, unplowed and untracked, scanning the treetops all around for a glimpse of that cursèd tower. The road ended at a good-sized lake, with only one tiny cabin on its far shore. We headed out to the middle, hoping for a more open view, and *voilà*—there it was, rising above the trees to the north: the Tower of Satan. However, Charles figured it was still a few kilometers away, and his photo, taken on full 5X zoom, seemed to bear out his guess.

We took a bearing on our *boussoles*, and tramped off into the scrubby bush. We could tell that area had been clear-cut only ten or fifteen years before, as all the trees were skinny saplings, and their density made for heavy going. We meandered along for another hour, trying to keep to our compass bearing, and to the high ground, where we might catch another glimpse of *la Maudite Tour du Diable*. But once again we were forced to turn back—by the lateness of the hour, and by good sense. The Second Expedition, alas, would also end in failure.

My determination was only reinforced, though, and the next day I had another inspiration. Charles had mentioned that elevations were shown on Google Earth, and once I figured out where that information was displayed, I scrolled over the "area of interest," looking for the highest peaks. If dead-reckoning navigation and high-tech information had failed, perhaps old-fashioned *deduction* would succeed. I thought of the Sherlock Holmes maxim: "Once you eliminate the impossible, whatever remains, no matter how improbable, must be the truth."

I identified a few higher peaks, and marked them by their elevations in meters: Peak 500, Peak 526, and so on. One of them was near a two-lane highway north of us, and although it seemed too far away, I took a drive along there to have a look, and *bang*—there it was.

Fittingly, I glimpsed it this time through the thick cables of the James Bay powerlines, just where they crossed that road. The steely gray tower rose starkly above the winter woods, straighter than nature, and a few hundred feet taller. Its satanic eye was not visible in daylight, but through my binoculars I scanned the heavy trusswork barbed with angular antennas and a drum-shaped reflector, and saw that the tower's great height was anchored with huge guywires. It was indeed a *monster*.

Measured on the satellite map back home, I was amazed to learn that it was almost nine kilometers, more than five miles, from my house—that diabolical light was so bright, and the tower itself, in twilight, was as visible through binoculars from my balcony as it is in this photo. Not as close, of course, but in proportion, just as big.

Well, obviously, there was still one step remaining on this quest, one more peak to climb. Like Frodo and Sam in the mountains of Mordor, Charles and I would have to travel to the very Tower of Sauron. We had no Ring of Power, nor even a lump of gelignite or a high-powered rifle, but . . . I could shake my fist at it, maybe throw a few snowballs.

The following Saturday, Charles and I drove to the area and parked at the foot of a small, unplowed road. We strapped on our snowshoes, and headed up the steep grade. On one side, wooden utility poles, obviously fairly new, carried electrical wires upward, and in the middle, a single snowmobile had passed up and down just before the previous day's light snowfall.

The day was gray and mild, a couple of degrees above freezing, and we were soon feeling warm—and winded. We paused for a breather, and Charles smiled and tapped his chest, saying, "My heart needs to readjust its rhythm!"

Climbing onward, looping around the peak among the dense young trees, bare and spindly, eventually the tower's trusswork and antennas came into view. We knew we were getting close.

And finally we stood before that tower, amazed at the sheer *immensity* of its construction—Charles counted the meter-high triangular trusses all the way to the top, and guessed it was close to 300 feet. Even the three bases anchoring the thick guywires were protected by chain-link fences (we wondered from *what?*), which were presently almost completely buried in snow, and a larger enclosure surrounded a metal building and the tower itself. We could see that the snowmobile had stopped there, and the gate had been opened by a maintenance inspector, who had then circled back down. Reading the snow, Charles and I figured that visit had only been two days before.

The domed red light at the top, the veritable Eye of Satan, glowed with an inner fire—apparently lighted in daylight hours as well—and even up close, it really did look evil. We lined up our *boussoles* toward home, guessing where our lake lay, far to the south among the rounded, receding hills. Scanning around the horizon with our binoculars, we saw northward all the way to the ski slopes of Mont Tremblant—twenty miles away. We took a few commemorative photographs (as if at the summit of Everest), and headed down again.

The Third Expedition had finally achieved the goal of our quest.

However, as has been observed by many another quester, a holy grail, or a satanic light, may launch a quest, but is not really the object. The *quest* is the object, and the journey itself is the real reward—"Only a fool thinks he goes fishing to catch fish."

For me to finally stand at the foot of that tower and shake my fist at it didn't change a single thing, of course, but taking part in those three expeditions, tracking the Eye of Satan to its lair, had been fun for Charles and me, and taught and showed us many things. The natural world, and the electro-mechanical world, had yielded a few mysteries.

My night sky will continue to be ruled by that bright red Eye on the northern horizon, no doubt for the rest of my days, but I feel better about it now.

I know where it lives.

14

UNDER THE MARINE LAYER

JUNE 2009

The obvious "marine layer" here is the surface of the Pacific Ocean, about ten miles out in the Santa Barbara Channel, off the coast of Southern California. Early one Saturday morning in May, the tour boat was on its scheduled run from Ventura to Santa Cruz Island, the largest island in the Channel Islands National Park, with a cargo of hikers, campers, kayakers, and birdwatchers. The captain shut down the engine, and the boat drifted silently in the middle of an enormous pod of dolphins—*hundreds* of dolphins, all around us, cutting the calm gray surface in every direction. Groups of six or eight at a time rose in synchronized arcs, a pattern repeated near and far and all around, like some fantastic water ballet. Raising cameras and binoculars, people moved slowly around the deck, in a kind of quiet reverence broken only by occasional half-whispers along the lines of "Wow!" and "Look at that!"

The only comparable wildlife spectacle I have witnessed would be the teeming herds of antelopes, zebras, and wildebeest in the Serengeti, or the huge flocks of sandhill cranes and snow geese in

Alaska, massing for their southward migration. Wildlife in such numbers are rarely seen in these times, and a sight like that catches the breath of a nature lover like me, or my friend Craiggie.

Craiggie is a keen and artful amateur photographer (his credit in these pages, "*Dunkelkammer*," is German for "darkroom"), and his opening portrait of a few of those dolphins is an evocative, luminous image—surely worth a thousand words. However, it is also true that bringing Craiggie and me to that boat off the coast of Southern California—painting the frame around that portrait—might take *two* thousand words.

The graceful dolphins and calm water were textured by the misty gray air over the ocean that morning—the true "marine layer." The term is often heard in Southern California weather reports, and refers to a "sandwich" of cool, moist air above the cold water, held down by a warmer layer above it. Despite Southern California's stereotype of sun, sand, surf, and endless summer, the water along the California coast flows south from the cold Northern Pacific, and can be up to thirty degrees colder than the same latitude on the Atlantic shore, warmed by the Gulf Stream. Over land, the marine layer phenomenon becomes a "thermal inversion," a stagnant weather pattern that presses down a smoggy bubble over unlucky valleys like the Los Angeles Basin or Mexico City.

Along the coast, though, the marine layer is fresh ocean air, but it can linger for days, even weeks. Some residents disparage this weather pattern, calling it "May Gray" or "June Gloom," and they pine for the California sun to emerge in all its glory. Others among us are *grateful* for the relief offered by that marine layer. The misty air attenuates the heat that can become oppressive in late summer and fall, yet the thin overcast is not like the dark and gloomy fogs of, say, the Pacific Northwest. With no heavy clouds above, sunlight permeates the marine layer with a soft, pearly glow that often remains bright enough to make you squint and reach for your sunglasses.

Vivid colors seem to jump out in that muted light—the pink and magenta bougainvillea on the walls of our house; a high tunnel of purple flowers on the jacaranda trees arching over the streets of Santa Monica; the yellow blossoms of the chaparral along the mountain roadsides. Distant sounds are dampened, making backyard birdsongs clear of ambient noise, and dry of any reverberation.

The song those birds are singing must be "In Praise of June Gloom," for it is a busy season in birdland: mating, nest-building, incubating, and baby-feeding. I would join the birds in that song of praise, for in

Garden in the June Gloom,
full of singing birds

2009 I have been able to experience that time of year for almost the first time in the nine years I have lived in Southern California (I'm usually away touring or recording in spring and early summer), and it has become my favorite season there.

And "season" is by no means an exaggeration, once you become attuned to the subtle, but no less far-reaching rhythms of this Mediterranean-like climate. If a desert is defined by receiving less than ten inches of rainfall per year, the Los Angeles area, a true semi-desert, averages less than fifteen inches. More than half of that rain falls in January, February, and March, while almost *none* of it falls in June, July, and August—thus May Gray and June Gloom come after the rains and before the drought, and so are the greenest months of the year. Even apart from the lush subtropical gardens, which of course are irrigated by distant rivers, the naturally arid chaparral hills are blooming in rich colors of green with delicate blossoms of yellow and blue. The tall white spears of a succulent aptly named Our Lord's Candle stand out on the hillsides like huge white flames, blooming only once, in a true blaze of glory, before they die. According to a local botanist who studies our hiking trails, in winter only about ten or twenty species of plants are blooming, while in May there can be up to 200 varieties of flowers.

The marine layer's cool and shady weather pattern favors the hiker, the birdwatcher, the dogwalker, the bicyclist, the protectively dressed motorcyclist, the top-down motorist, or the driver of an old car with no air-conditioning. People like that—me—prefer cooler, hazy days to the hot, dry frying pan of August and September, or worse, the gritty rasp of the Santa Ana winds blowing from the inland deserts and through the congested suburbs of the Los Angeles Basin.

Yet those congested suburbs are broken up and surrounded by an unparalleled network of parks, from the San Gabriel Mountains to the northeast, to Griffith Park above Hollywood (which begins a chain of parkland that stretches west for many miles through the Santa Monica Mountains, including Topanga State Park) to the undeveloped coast north of Malibu and out to the eight islands of the Channel Islands National Park. Inland, the Santa Monica Mountains Conservancy protects more than 60,000 acres of chaparral woodlands, with miles of hiking trails, campgrounds, and picnic areas, and a rich variety of wildlife, including deer, rabbits, coyotes, many kinds of birds and reptiles, even a few mountain lions.

With a nice long stretch of time at home in Southern California this year, I have been able to work on a good flow of prose writing, especially for the new cooking department, Bubba's Bar 'n' Grill. In addition, I have made it my mission to explore more of our local hiking trails, and found a good partner in my website designer and collaborator, Greg Russell. Greg and I first hiked together back in January, meeting in Topanga State Park and hiking to Skull Rock, a prominent outlook of sandstone eroded into the shape of its name. The view from there was a sweeping panorama of rounded mountains and fingered canyons carpeted in low shrubs, grasses, and live oaks (also called "evergreen oaks," as they don't drop their leaves in winter), all rich green after the early winter rains.

Through the eyes of Skull Rock, Topanga State Park

Fittingly, on that hike I was wearing my "skulls and roses" bandana (stage clothes from the *Roll the Bones* tour in 1992).

Greg and I are both avid motorcyclists, and we decided to develop a new sport called "motor-hiking," to combine the world-class motorcycling roads of the Santa Monica Mountains with access to various trailheads for scenic hikes. Over lunch in Topanga Canyon one day in March, Greg and I were discussing our next hike, and I wondered where the highest peak in those mountains was, and how we could get to it.

I did a little online research, and one foggy day in April—advance notice of the coming May Gray—Greg and I met at a trailhead on Yerba Buena Road, way north in Ventura County, to make that ascent. It was called Sandstone Peak, though the name was mysterious, because there was no sandstone on that mountain—it was a *volcano*. Just when I thought I had the geology around there figured out, I learned something new that turned it upside down—like the notion of volcanoes. I had thought those mountains were all sedimentary rock, ancient seabed pushed up by the collision of the Pacific plate with the North American plate— which continues to create the majestic Sierra Nevada to the east, as well as the area's frequent earthquakes—but apparently primordial volcanoes had contributed some igneous rock, too.

Sandstone Peak summit, laughing at the "view"

The mountain's name was another story. The area around Sandstone Peak was originally given to the Boy Scouts by a rancher, and the Scouts named the mountain after him, Mount Allen. However, the U.S. government's Board on Geographic Names did not allow a natural feature to be named for a living person, so the government gave it another name— after a kind of rock not found there. The Boy Scouts did put up a bronze plaque at the summit in honor of Mr. Allen.

Truth to tell, Sandstone Peak wasn't that impressive a summit—just over 3,000 feet—but it was the highest in the range, and that's what counted. Poring over trail maps and Google Earth (how nice to tilt the horizon on a hiking trail and see what the *elevations* look like), we planned an eight-mile loop that would take us to the summit, where the views were said to be spectacular—with the spread of the San Fernando Valley and the San Gabriels to the northeast and the wide blue Pacific and the Channel Islands to the west.

But therein lay the one flaw in the atmosphere of May Gray and June Gloom: it's not great for views. That day was so foggy we could barely see thirty feet in front of us, and those expansive vistas were only hinted at by occasional rents in the clouds.

But again, the marine layer made for cool walking, especially uphill, and the soft pearly light had its own magic. The closed-in circle of the visible world drew us inward as we hiked along, and our conversation seemed more open and unguarded. Someday Greg and I will

do that hike again, maybe in winter, which is also nice hiking weather, and more likely to be clear.

But having "conquered" the highest peak in the Santa Monica Mountains, and learned about the volcanic history of some of those peaks, I now knew that they stretched westward not only to the shore of the Pacific, but continued under the ocean all the way out to the Channel Islands, which were also volcanoes. In my season of local exploration, and a newly discovered ambition to be what I might define as a "nature writer," I was more than ever eager to visit those islands—an official national park, after all, and one of the very few in the United States I hadn't explored.

Yet it took a bird, the island scrub jay, to clinch the deal, and inspire Craiggie and me to plan that expedition—the boat trip to Santa Cruz Island that began this wandering tale.

From now on, it's all about Craiggie and me.

Craiggie and I had first met almost forty years before, back in our hometown of St. Catharines, Ontario. By chance, we were reacquainted earlier this decade, in Southern California, where Craiggie worked for the mighty Fox empire, in the "music legal" department. He had some dealings with Pegi at Rush's office about licensing one of our songs for a Fox show, and Pegi put Craiggie and me back in touch.

Craiggie lives with his wife and two daughters in a rambling old house, designed in the native Craftsman style I have long admired, in Pasadena. There Farmer Craiggie tends an impressive vegetable garden, as well as hosting large numbers of birds, both domestic and wild. For a long time, just about every Sunday Craiggie would email me a photograph (to "Dr. O," for "ornithologist") of some bird that had visited his garden (or eaten one of his doves, like the peregrine falcon or the Cooper's hawk), wanting me to identify it. Those exchanges were amusing for both of us, but I encouraged Craiggie to get his own field guide, so he could enjoy looking up those birds for himself. He started sharing some of the bird sightings and identifications with his eleven-year-old daughter, Selena, and she developed an "eye for the birds," too. When I discovered a hummingbird nest in my backyard in May, I sent over a photo to Craiggie and Selena.

She's called an Anna's hummingbird (named by a French naturalist after Anna Masséna, Duchess of Rivoli—perhaps a patron, perhaps a lover; it suggests a romantic story), and here she is building her nest, shaping it by moving her body around ("frolicking," as I once described the behavior to my mother—to her great amusement) in the egg cup–sized interior. The tiny woven bowl of grasses, small leaves, and dried flower petals is bound together with spider webs—an exquisite thing, though precarious looking on its thin branch of bougainvillea (to protect it from heavier predators, like snakes or bigger birds). As I spied on her from day to day, now calling her Anna and trying not to disturb her too much, I saw that she had laid two pea-sized white eggs.

Around our house, there was a lot of nesting going on under the marine layer. A pair of black phoebes had moved in under the eaves, as they did every year, and constantly relayed bugs to feed their hatchlings; a pair of California towhees (perhaps the plainest, brownest birds ever) had a nest hidden deep in the bougainvillea; white-crowned sparrows built theirs in the hedge; and on the downhill side of the house, a pair of cliff swallows soared out over the canyon in long swooping forays for their insect baby food.

At the same time, under that same marine layer, my wife Carrie was seven months pregnant. [Pause for sharp intake of breath and shiver of apprehension.] Our baby was growing and kicking, protected and insulated in its own oceanic fluid, its own marine layer. The anxious (not to say *terrified*) father kind of wished the baby could stay there, safe from harm, and not have to embark upon a life of menace and potential tragedy. He had lost before, and probably couldn't stand to lose again. People kept saying it was going to be all right, and he tried to keep telling himself that. Even in the June Gloom.

But like I said, there was a lot of nesting going on around our house . . .

Back in February, when I was in Quebec—enjoying what might be my last long stay there for quite a while, as we await the Blessèd Event—Craiggie wrote from Pasadena and told me Selena was doing a school project on a bird called the island scrub jay, and they wondered if I had anything to contribute. I'm still not sure how Selena came to pick that bird—a larger species of the common blue and gray California scrub jay, the island scrub jay is found only on the island of Santa Cruz, in the Channel Islands. I told Craiggie that I had never even seen one and, in fact, had never been to Channel Islands National Park. We decided to plan an expedition when I got back.

The females in our nests, mates and hatchlings alike, seemed to think there were better ways to spend a whole Saturday than taking a long boat ride to an uninhabited island and hiking around it for a few hours—so our plan didn't come together until May, and then it would just be Craiggie and me.

After I had checked out the schedules, Craiggie made the boat reservations for the next Saturday, May 16. We agreed to meet at the harbor, and a little before 6:00 a.m. that day I set out on my motorcycle, cruising north along the Pacific Coast Highway with the early morning soft and cool in pearly shades of May Gray. We met at Ventura Harbor before 7:00 to check in, and at 8:00, boarded the tour boat with about thirty other people—campers, kayakers, a few families, and a small troop of Boy Scouts.

The marine layer seemed to suit these sea lions, too, lounging on

a navigation marker as we motored toward Santa Cruz Island. Other sea lions and harbor seals frequently popped their canine heads out of the ocean beside us, singly or in pairs. In shallower water, massive kelp beds waved in the currents, part of an undersea forest that provided havens for multitudes of fish and crustaceans. Great numbers of seabirds filled the pale gray sky, wheeling around the boat in graceful flight, or floated on the still, almost oily looking dark gray water—cormorants, pelicans, ducks, shearwaters, terns, and gulls. Few sights in nature are more fetching than a flock of pelicans gliding inches above the water, in perfect symmetry, and without apparent effort. With all that, and the splendid vision of that dolphin ballet about halfway through the one-hour crossing, Craiggie and I were delighted, and encouraged, to see so much natural abundance, in an apparently healthy and productive environment.

We observed it all from our bench on the port side of the boat, a location I had recommended to put us on the landward side as we approached the islands. Craiggie was amused by my story of where the word "posh" came from: In the days of British aristocrats traveling by sea to the Mediterranean, the prime cabin choice for views toward land was "port out, starboard home." We too would be traveling "posh."

Santa Cruz Island is three times the size of Manhattan and is the largest of the eight Channel Islands. Stories from its modern history are suggested by some of the place-names, straight out of a Hardy Boys or Tintin book—Scorpion Ranch, Prisoners Harbor, Smugglers Cove, and Chinese Harbor. The first settlers were the Chumash Indians, but like elsewhere in coastal Southern California, they were displaced by Spanish ranchers, then nascent Americans. All of the islands were privately owned for many decades, mainly for ranching, and their landscapes were altered forever by great herds of cattle and sheep that nibbled away the vegetation in a devastating cycle of over-grazing and erosion.

Like other islands where pigs were introduced, from Hawaii to the Caribbean, the Channel Islands became overrun with escaped feral pigs, among the most destructive of animals. Being *pigs*, after all, they root around everywhere like ravenous bulldozers, tearing up the land-scape and devouring eggs, young birds, and delicate plants—which were also decimated by the introduction of rabbits, feeding and breed-ing in their tireless, prolific way.

The native flora was further transformed by the introduction of range grasses and this-tles, eucalyptus trees, and an unexpectedly virulent "invasive species," fennel. Also found in some of the mainland canyons where I hike, the feathery green clumps of fennel are pretty, and have a delicious licorice perfume, but they crowd out the native plants—just as the fra-grant yellow flowers of the Spanish broom along mountain roadsides in California, a sight and smell I love so much, are a threat to their native neighbors.

The guano-covered sea stacks around Santa Cruz Island came looming out of the fog, and the boat pulled up to the pier at Scorpion Ranch, where many of the passengers debarked. Craiggie and I stayed aboard until the next stop, Prisoners Harbor. (I have written before about the U.S. government's Board on Geographic Names hating not only the names of living persons, but apostrophes; this is no excep-tion.) The name comes from a story that in the days of Spanish empire, a ship sailed north from Mexico to California with a cargo of convicts. None of the coastal communities would take them, so the captain ma-rooned them on Santa Cruz Island, with a good supply of food and hunting and fishing equipment. When he returned at some later date (accounts vary), the convicts had disappeared (my original phrase was "he found them gone"), and it was never determined if they had died there, or escaped by raft to the mainland.

As soon as our boat tied up at the pier and we climbed the ladder to the dock, I started looking through the gray mist at the eucalyptus trees and semi-desert shrubs, watching for an island scrub jay. By all accounts, the Prisoners Harbor area was the most likely location to see them, but—not to puncture any suspense this June Gloom Love Song may accidentally contain—ours would be the Quest for the Phantom Jay, and we never did see an island scrub jay. It didn't matter to Craiggie and me, but for Selena's sake, in commemoration of her school project, we would like to have seen one for her.

We shouldered our packs and headed uphill through a rounded landscape of low, grassy vegetation, punctuated by occasional live

oaks in sheltered draws. The climb was steep and steady, following a dirt and gravel track called the Navy Road (hints at other uses those islands had been put to by the U.S. military, as bombing and shooting ranges). The marine layer still ruled the day, creating an ever-changing cloud of moist air that occasionally thickened to fog, or thinned to a curtain of mist that parted to admit brief patches of pale blue sky and stronger sunshine. Feeling the heat of that sun even for those short intervals, we appreciated the coolness of the mist when it returned. We agreed, "The marine layer rules!"

The road climbed for a mile or so, and continued very steeply.

Craiggie was an unpracticed hiker—his usual physical recreation was yoga and meditation—so under the unfamiliar aerobic strain, he began to fall behind. When climbing hills, whether on foot, cross-country skis, or even on a bicycle, every climber has to settle into their own pace, and slog along as best they can. I waited for Craiggie whenever the grade leveled out, or when we turned off onto the narrower Del Norte trail, and made sure he caught his breath and took a drink.

Craiggie gives the secret distress signal

I told him, "When I'm on a motorcycle ride with someone who doesn't ride as . . . 'enthusiastically' as I do, I always tell them the same thing: 'Look, I never mind stopping to *wait* for people—I only hate turning back, because that means I'm worried.'"

We agreed that I would watch behind me, in case Craiggie had to give the "secret distress signal" (from *Team America: World Police*—you raise your hands in the air and wave them around in wide-eyed, open-mouthed panic). I promised I would keep an eye on the time and distance, wait for him often, and watch for a nice shady place to have lunch.

Just at the point where the distress signal was received, I had spotted a grove of oaks with a shady patch of grass beneath. I waved Craiggie onward, trying to point to the shady grove where I would wait for him.

But he didn't come. Long minutes passed, until finally I went back down the trail (I mentioned how I hate that—because I *worry*), and found him gasping uphill from the last gully.

He looked up and said, "I think I've about reached . . . that point."

I told him about the cool picnic spot just ahead, where we could take it easy and "have some lunchy-wunchy."

And oh, did we have some lunchy-wunchy. Farmer Craiggie unpacked and mixed a salad almost entirely from his garden, and also brought double chocolate brownies, Fig Newtons, trail mix, granola bars, and mixed fruit. From my pack came bottles of pink lemonade, sourdough rolls, Black Forest ham, havarti cheese, Grey Poupon mustard, mayonnaise, butter lettuce, and vine-ripened tomatoes, and I made a sandwich for each of us with my Swiss Army knife. As we spread our feast around us on the grass, I said, "I don't think we'll starve."

"Not for a few days, anyway," Craiggie replied.

And indeed, I had been thinking of what we would do if we were caught overnight on the island. I had never been on a hike that had to finish at a certain time, and it was a different, more *pressured* feeling. The one and only boat back to the mainland left at 3:00 p.m., and we were several miles from Prisoners Harbor now. If we happened to get lost, or even just twist an ankle to delay our return, what would happen?

We decided they'd probably send a helicopter for us, or at least a special park ranger boat. That sounded like fun, and we argued over which of us was going to throw himself down a cliff.

But when I glanced at my watch and saw that it was already nearly 1:30, I felt a little real concern. We were supposed to return to Prisoners Harbor by 2:45, and we had hiked over an hour, so we might be a little tight for time now. We repacked the remains of our lunch, and set off again. The clouds began to lift occasionally, letting the hot sun radiate across the magnificent views, and blaze on the shadeless trails, then they would close again and give us some relief.

Craiggie was still struggling, and I was trying to wait patiently, though struggling myself—against the urgency of getting to the dock in plenty of time. I kept him in sight, kept an eye on my watch, and was continually surprised at how long the Del Norte trail went on before we got back to the Navy Road. I'm sure Craiggie was, too.

Finally reaching that junction, we knew it was an easy downhill curve back to Prisoners Harbor, so we could relax and enjoy the experience again. Craiggie and I fell into step on the descent, making jokes from old episodes of Canada's *SCTV* (it's always nice for us ex-pats to share our comedic roots).

I watched the birds more closely, spotting towhees, sparrows, and swallows, but still no jays. With the harbor in sight at last, and a few minutes to spare, we paused in the shade of a eucalyptus grove, leaning on an old fence and looking around. No jays.

Even back on the rounded stones of the beach, while we waited to board the boat, I studied the trees and brush all around, hoping for a glimpse—just to say we saw them.

But, we didn't.

And it was all right.

Everything was all right, under the marine layer. The dolphins and sea lions in the ocean; the hummingbirds, towhees, sparrows, phoebes and their babies in my backyard; and the little baby growing inside Carrie. It was all going to be all right.

People kept telling me that, and I kept telling myself.

Never mind the June Gloom.

A LITTLE YELLOW CABIN ON YELLOWSTONE LAKE

AUGUST 2009

First I thought of Utah. (And when you've got an opening line like that, you almost want to stop and let the reader take it from there.)

I had five days in early June to travel somewhere on my motorcycle, to make my Last Getaway before settling in with my wife Carrie to await the Blessèd Event—the birth of our baby in August. After that, I wouldn't be going anywhere for a while.

So I thought of Utah. Do some motorcycle touring and hiking in the national parks like Zion, Bryce Canyon, Arches, and Canyonlands, and maybe stay a couple of nights in one of my favorite Western towns, Moab.

But as my eyes wandered through the road atlas (the Book of Dreams), they were drawn to a corner of Wyoming, an area colored in green that bordered Montana and Idaho—Yellowstone National Park. It was the only major park in the American West I hadn't visited, and one of the few in the whole country. (Those two in northern Alaska are going to be *really* hard to get to!)

I had tried to visit the Yellowstone area on my *Ghost Rider* travels in October 1998, but was turned back by early snow in Utah, and headed south instead. Since then, I had just never made it that way. Motorcycling on Rush tours had taken me all over the country several times, but Yellowstone was far from any cities with sizable concert venues (the only possible scenario would be a day off between Salt Lake City and, say, Boise, but that rare combination had never occurred).

So yes, I wanted to go to Yellowstone all right. I looked up its distance by road from my Southern California home, and frowned when I saw that it was over 1,000 miles. Hmm. That's far. With only five days to get there and back, and wanting to spend some time in the park, it was a bit much, really. But . . . I *had* ridden 1,000 miles in a day before, and anything close to that would make a good start on the first day. Maybe I could do it.

Grand Teton National Park was right on the way, too—adding the possibility of *two* new national park passport stamps for the growing collection.

The more I thought about it, the more I wanted it.

So after some feverish planning and packing, I set off on Monday, the first of June, at a little before 5:00 a.m.—a time when it is usually possible to get on Interstate 10 and make it across the width of Los Angeles before the Monday morning gridlock sets in. I turned northeast on I-15, across the Mojave Desert, and those long empty miles passed pleasantly and easily.

Only the cities loomed as potential interruptions to my rapid progress—after escaping L.A. so early, I would hit Vegas by 9:00, with its heavy traffic and ceaseless construction. And though Las Vegas can be a dramatic sight by night, it does not look its best in the morning (I guess few cities do).

Straight four-lane highway arrowed for hundreds of miles across the open desert, up past Mesquite, Nevada, to the northwest corner of Arizona, where it suddenly curved up into the Virgin River Gorge. That spectacle ought to be more celebrated, though admittedly, the rocky majesty is somewhat marred by having an interstate hacked and blasted through the middle of it!

Running north now, up into Utah, the creosote and Joshua trees of the Mojave gave way to the sage and juniper of the Great Basin. Snow rimmed the higher peaks and dark cumulonimbus clouds bulged in every direction. Black veils of rain trailed below the clouds, slanting to windward, and often disappearing into thin air—the so-called *virgas* that evaporate before they reach the parched land below. Only a few scattered drops struck my face shield.

As the miles and hours went by, with occasional breaks for gas and water (in and out), I was starting to think about stopping to eat. On shorter riding days I will often forgo lunch, and just keep moving toward the "somewhere" I'm trying to reach, but on a deliberate marathon like this I wanted to make sure I felt as good, and as sharp, as possible. With few dining options in those far-flung Western service areas, I had brought a couple of bottles of water, and some ham, cheese, and bread to make my own sandwich. I planned to stop at a roadside rest area and relax at a shady picnic table, having the best lunch I could, yet in the shortest amount of time.

From passing through southern Utah on my way cross-country a few years previously, I remembered some nice rest areas along that part of I-15, but I wanted to hold out until I got closer to Salt Lake City—the next obstacle of potential traffic and endless road construction. Unfortunately, in central Utah the department of highways seemed to be experimenting with an ill-advised "partnership" between the public and private sectors—at least that's what the signs called it. When I pulled off at a couple of different places signed as "rest areas," there was a truck stop and a fast food outlet with big paved parking lots, and one cruddy metal picnic table beside a dusty offramp, without even any shade. Phooey on that.

In Utah I had crossed into the Mountain Time Zone, and lost an hour, so it was close to 2:00 when I gave up on the "rest areas" and took a random offramp, pulling up beside a boarded-up family restaurant (always a sad sight—as I have described it before, "the death of a dream"). I had covered 600 miles in eight hours (averaging 75 mph, even with gas stops and such—a good pace). My radar detector's earpiece defended me against overzealous law enforcement, though Western highways are generally posted at a reasonable 70 or 75 mph anyway, and a couple of stretches of Utah interstate offered an "experimental" 80 mph limit. So I didn't really need to exceed the "eight-over-the-limit" formula to make good time. Sometimes I just wanted to.

Pulling the bike back on the centerstand, I unpacked my lunch supplies, then sat on the crumbling steps in the shade of some scruffy cottonwoods. I struggled out of the inner layer of my riding clothes— the temperature had climbed from the pre-dawn 50s to the 90s in Nevada, then down to the 60s again as the elevation rose, then up to the 80s by that offramp in central Utah. It's hard to dress for that range, but by overdoing the layers, then peeling off the plastic rainsuit when it was warmer, I had felt pretty comfortable most of the time. It felt good to strip down to the basic leathers and T-shirt, then assemble my ham and cheese sandwich. I ate it slowly, letting my eyes go out of focus for a few minutes.

My nominal goal for the day was Logan, Utah, as that would represent the end of the interstate riding, and put me in easy reach of Yellowstone for the following day. And at 790 miles, it was plenty far enough. I cruised the neat-looking Main Street, and consulted my GPS screen to compare the options, then decided on the Best Western. I swung a weary leg over the saddle and went inside to register, then parked in front of my room. After carrying my luggage inside, I poured a Macallan on ice into a Best Western cup of finest plastic, then took a self-portrait of my weary, saggy face. It was not a pretty sight, and won't be shared with others—but I wanted to remember.

Following the desk clerk's recommendation, I walked down Main Street to the Bluebird Restaurant, and sat down to catch up on the day. My first journal entry, after noting the location and mileage, was, "Every detail I think of putting down seems inconsequential, yet it is the sum of those details that made the day." Well, ain't *that* the truth!

Logan, Utah, sits at 4,535 feet, surrounded by the high rounded mountains of the Bear River Range, their peaks still streaked with snow. Behind the motel a roaring stream strained at its banks, a loud torrent swollen with that same snow, slowly thawing. Ever since I had turned off the interstate and into the mountains, the greenery had overwhelmed me—because once again, as I described in *Roadshow*, I had become used to the arid economy of Southern California's semi-desert climate; my eyes were accustomed to what nature writer Mary Austin called "The Land of Little Rain." Whenever I re-encounter lush green fields and woodlands of dense leafy trees, they take me back to the surroundings of my childhood in Southern Ontario, and I feel it deep in my being.

Mountain towns have a special character, at least partly from being dwarfed by their surroundings, the modest buildings huddling together as if for protection beneath a rising landscape, and partly from the weather—they tend to get a lot of snow in winter, and fierce thunderstorms in summer. Being nestled in a valley, closed to the natural sprawl of desert or prairie towns, plus inhospitable weather and isolation, tends to keep such towns smaller, so the lodgings and restaurants are more often central, a pleasant walk apart. A few North American examples would be Banff, Alberta; Nelson, British Columbia; Littleton, New Hampshire; Gunnison, Colorado; Taos, New Mexico; Ketchum, Idaho; and Creel, Mexico, on the rim of the Copper

Canyon—all those places, and many more, share a certain "splendid isolation," and a bracing edge to the thinner air of higher elevations. I have long wanted to live for a while in one of those mountain towns. Maybe someday.

Mormon towns have a special character, too—neat and well tended, centered on a spectacular temple (I can't help but admire their sacred architecture), and the small family businesses apparently thriving, unlike the main streets of so many other American towns. The storefronts look quaint, and sometimes a generation or two out of time: a sub shop called "Logan's Heroes," a clothing store selling prom dresses, formal wear, and "missionary attire" (suits for the young Mormon males who are sent away to proselytize, then return as so-called elders—all over Mormon country I would see homemade signs like, "Welcome Home, Elder Berry"). Along the Utah interstate that day, I had laughed out loud in my helmet as I passed a pickup, its rear window decorated with one of those oval, black-on-white "destination" stickers that commonly read "YNP," for Yosemite National Park, or "OBX" for the Outer Banks of North Carolina. This one read "Gentile."

Apart from a couple of old cinemas, still apparently operating, the bright spot on Main Street was the Bluebird, an old diner-style family restaurant. True to the Mormon proscriptions of alcohol, tobacco, and coffee (a prescription, to this gentile), the Bluebird offered a decent American menu, but served nothing stronger than lemonade.

The décor was fantastic, though: high ceiling, mosaic tile floor, marble-and-mirrored soda fountain with a long row of stools, wood paneling, wooden chairs and tables. The customers were well-scrubbed families, or groups of neatly groomed youths, all Caucasian, probably mostly Mormons. With all that Norman Rockwell Americana, and the all-American menu, I was amused to read in the menu's "historical notes" that the Bluebird was now owned by the Xu family. Truly, America is the land of *plus ça change, plus c'est la même chose*—the more things change, the more they stay the same.

The lighted sign and neon trim outside the Bluebird were especially impressive to me, as I had just been working with Hugh Syme on the logo for my online cooking department, Bubba's Bar 'n' Grill. So around that time I was looking at vintage restaurant signs with new eyes. As I stepped out of the Bluebird, into the long slow twilight of June in the mountains, I noticed the neon bluebirds that decorated the underside of the entrance.

Strolling along Main Street, and across the tree-shaded lawns around the temple, I looked along the storefronts, mostly dark in the evening but for the brightly lit beacon of the Bluebird. I imagined all of the businesses my alter-ego Bubba could open there: Right beside Bubba's Bar 'n' Grill could be Bubba's bookstore, then Bubba's liquor store, Bubba's groceries, Bubba's Best Western, Bubba's motorcycles and classic cars, Bubba's gym and yoga studio, Bubba's music store, Bubba's outdoor shop (bicycles, cross-country skis, snowshoes, hiking boots, binoculars, bird books), Bubba's bank, and Bubba's farm equipment.

Back at the motel, I was soon asleep, dreaming of Bubbatown . . .

Rain came in overnight, and the morning downpour and gloomy light looked as though they would be staying for a while. After the "free breakfast" (getting better these days, I must say, offering fruit and hard-boiled eggs with the usual dry cereal and gooey pastries), I dressed in all my foul-weather gear—not only for the rain, but because where I was headed, to the higher elevations of Wyoming, overnight temperatures were down in the low 30s, and the days only creeping into the 50s. As I had learned the previous year (see "When the Road Ends"), in the higher-elevation areas, early June was still late winter.

I have often described the stately, meditative mood that riding in the rain can evoke. With diminished visibility from mist, rain, and splash-back off the pavement, especially through a wiperless face shield, and uncertain traction on wet shiny pavement, you naturally choose a slower pace. I was away from the interstates now, following a winding two-lane into forested canyons, often meandering beside turbulent rivers bursting with snowmelt.

Wisps and shrouds of fog and cloud draped across the distant mountaintops, darker than the snowy peaks peering through behind them—the Salt River Range and the Caribou Range. The ribbon of sodden pavement led me past ranches and forests, and through occasional small settlements, north to the busier town of Jackson, Wyoming, at over 6,000 feet now, in the valley called Jackson Hole. I had long been curious about that much-admired mountain town and its surroundings, and had heard stories about people who had settled there happily, but the teeming rain "dampened" my experience of it that day.

Turning off at Moose Junction, I entered Grand Teton National Park (in French "vulgar slang," *grand téton* means, to put it politely, "big bust"—describing the shape of the mountains as they appeared to lonely trappers). I stopped at the Visitors Center, which was *jammed* with people, many of them on bus tours, and got my passport stamp. The road through the park was marked "Closed in Winter" (which, again, can mean well into June in those parts), but the ranger lady told me it was open.

I set off into the rain again, catching glimpses of the high, rugged, snow-capped Tetons to the left, and to the right, sweeping sagebrush, meadows, and wetlands—sometimes dotted with small herds of elk, displaying the characteristic buff patch on the butts of their dark brown bodies. Just from passing through Grand Teton so briefly, I saw that it would make a great destination on its own—the park brochure showed the majestic scenery as it would appear on a brighter day, and there were plenty of interesting hiking opportunities.

But Yellowstone was still ahead, and not far now.

One common summer obstacle in high-mountain areas is road construction—repairing the damage left by harsh winters and violent thaws. Typically, one lane will be closed, sometimes for a considerable distance, and flaggers and pilot cars control the flow of traffic in one direction at a time. A few times I straddled the bike and waited in a line of RVs and cars, but was soon moving again—and climbing ever higher, into the 7,000-foot level now, and the snowdrifts were deep at the roadside and in the woods.

The ravages of the great forest fires of 1988 were visible around me, as in the above photograph, the hills spiked with young lodgepole pines and rotting trunks. In that dry summer of 1988, several smaller fires had swept out of control, then combined into larger firestorms, and burned for several *months* across the park's nearly 3,500 square miles. As many as 9,000 firefighters and 4,000 military personnel battled the fire (incredibly, without loss of life), and the conflagration ended up devouring almost 750,000 acres.

However, perhaps the most important fact about Yellowstone National Park is that it is the oldest national park in the United States—founded in 1872—and the oldest national park in the *world*.

A writer I have long admired and often quoted, Wallace Stegner, wrote that national parks were "the best idea we ever had. Absolutely American, absolutely democratic, they reflect us at our best rather than our worst." America's only other comparable idea, perhaps, was philanthropy—another great invention that was unknown to wealthy Europeans (reluctant alms-givers at best, and their only "parks" were private hunting estates, where the entry fee for commoners was, oh, *death*). Europe had the Quakers to protest slavery, and the suffragettes to demand the vote for women, but the United States led the way in every cause you can think of where rich people helped poor people, willingly and generously. The roots of the word philanthropy are "love" and "mankind," and the concept also reflected a "morality of wealth," as expressed by perhaps the first and greatest of philanthropists, Andrew Carnegie: "To die rich is to die disgraced."

National parks and philanthropy are certainly grand visions that speak eloquently of the magnanimity of America—its greatness of spirit. As agents for change, Americans set an example that the rest of the world, to a greater or lesser extent, has followed. We could always use more philanthropists, but today there are national parks in England, Tanzania, Switzerland, South Africa, Great Britain, Australia, Canada, and many other countries.

In the nineteenth century, when President Ulysses S. Grant signed the bill to establish Yellowstone National Park, the preservation of natural habitat and wildlife wasn't yet a priority. Back then the intention was to preserve the unique thermal attractions—the geysers, hot springs, steaming mudholes, and fumaroles. The park is basically one big volcano, a collapsed caldera, and its active state is well demonstrated all over, even along the roadside.

By early afternoon I had entered the park, content to cruise along the wet road at the posted limit of 45 mph, between dense forests of lodgepole pine—which cover eighty percent of the park, the name describing the aboriginal use of their tall, straight trunks. The rain continued, but I was used to it by then, and just kept riding, sightseeing

as much as I could, and pausing at occasional overlooks to spend more time taking in the views. Around the West Thumb Geyser Basin, plumes of steam gushed into the air, amid the unmistakable smell of sulfur (probably the origin of "yellowstone," I'm guessing).

What looked like smoky fires along the shore of Yellowstone Lake were actually hot springs meeting the cold water and creating steam. The sulfurous, rotten-egg smell reminded me of a few other living volcanoes I had experienced—on Sicily, the Big Island of Hawaii, and especially, on the Caribbean island of Montserrat, just a few years before its volcano became seriously active and destroyed most of the island. No wonder early humans associated the smell of sulfur ("brimstone") with various devils.

Yellowstone Lake is the largest mountain lake (above 7,000 feet) in North America, and as I cruised along the northwest shore, I was surprised not to see any boats, even canoes. Later I learned from the park brochure that despite all the warnings about the park's many other dangers (such as bison, black and grizzly bears, thermal hotspots, and crashing into large animals on the roads), the most lethal activity in the park was probably boating—the water was so cold that if you fell in, you wouldn't survive more than a few minutes.

In mid-afternoon I pulled under the wide portico in front of the Yellowstone Lake Hotel, a massive edifice of wooden siding painted in pale yellow with white trim. Originally built in 1891, it sported a few colonial-style add-ons from the 1920s, like the tall white columns on the façade. The hotel offered rooms in the main building, the large Annex, or separate little quarters they referred to as "frontier cabins." Well, with plumbing and electricity, they were hardly primitive, and I always prefer those cozy, private kind of accommodations to being crammed into a big warren. Plus you can generally park in front of your door, making unloading and loading much easier. Soon I was parking my wet motorcycle in front of a little yellow cabin on Yellowstone Lake.

The phrase had an irresistible rhythm, like a song lyric (in iambic tetrameter, to be technical). I couldn't imagine that line in any rock song, but it might work for a country singer—a Montana cowboy could escape his cheating woman by driving away in his pickup truck, then wind up drunk and broken-hearted, in a little yellow cabin on Yellowstone Lake.

Not too far north of that little yellow cabin on Yellowstone Lake, back in the fall of 1998, I had been hiking in Waterton Lakes National Park, in Alberta, and while pausing beside a waterfall, I noticed two birds perched above me. They inspired another unlikely line of iambic tetrameter, "Two gray jays in a lodgepole pine."

After just over 1,000 miles of riding, it was great to feel myself slow down, as I carried in my luggage piece by piece, changed into walking-around clothes (and my rain jacket), and took a stroll around the grounds. I ducked through the rain, keeping to the shelter of the lodgepole pines when I could, noting many large "cow pies" (probably buffalo—properly bison—though I hadn't seen any yet). Deep mounds

of snow remained here and there in sheltered areas, and one resourceful traveler in a neighboring cabin had stuck six bottles of beer into
one of them.

The nearby general store was a big old barn of a place, built in
1919, centered on an octagonal building of brown logs and shingles. It
had an old soda fountain inside, and I took a stool and ordered a
"Chicago-style" hot dog and a chocolate milkshake. Both were the best
of their kind I had experienced in a long time.

The big yellow lodge itself was massive inside, the lobby open to a
vast seating area of sofas and tables, with a bar and restaurant, souvenir shop, and tall windows looking out on the misty gray lake, the
snow-dappled mountains beyond, and the overcast sky. The lodge was
filled with enough people to be lively, but not to be crowded. The Lake
Yellowstone Hotel is closed in winter, not opening until late May (the
reason hinted at by those slowly melting snowdrifts still lingering on
June 2), so I had made it there about as early in the season as possible.

All of which meant that it was still *cold* in those parts, and the
weather forecast showed mornings in the low 30s, and the possibility
of snow showers. My little yellow cabin was a cozy refuge in the night,
and I took my time in the morning—walking up to the hotel in the
rain to enjoy a full breakfast, then slowly climbing into my riding gear.

With only one day to tour around the park, before beginning the
long ride back home, I wanted to see as much as I could. The day's
first goal was Old Faithful—apparently not so "faithful" these days, as
each eruption can only be predicted by the previous one. Depending
on its height and duration, the next eruption can be anything from
one hour to two hours later. As I browsed in the visitor center bookstore and collected my passport stamp, I saw that the next eruption
was predicted in about forty minutes, so I joined the crowd gathering
in a circle around the boardwalk that represented the "safe area." (One
nearby warning sign had been erected by a couple to the memory of
their son, aged nine, who had been scalded to death by falling into a
thermal hotspot.) Under an intermittent drizzle, the crowd grew to
several hundred, all eyes on a mound of clayey-looking sediment,
from which a plume of steam emanated steadily, drifting away on the
damp breeze. Every short belch of increased activity heightened the
crowd's anticipation, murmurs spreading and cameras raised, until
at last the tower of white steam burst up, over 100 feet high, with a
power and sound that were truly awe-inspiring.

Back on the rainy highway, I soon encountered another equally
stirring sight—a large herd of bison crossing the road, blocking traffic

in both directions while they made their leisurely way from one stretch of riverbank to another.

Earlier that morning I had encountered my first bison, feeding at the roadside, and I had turned around and nervously paused to take its photograph. Bison, like the African buffalo (one of the "big five" on African safaris, for their deadliness to humans, along with lion, rhino, leopard, and another unexpectedly homicidal animal, the hippo), are famously ill-tempered and unpredictable, and can weigh up to two tons, so as I straddled my motorcycle on the wet road, I felt a little vulnerable. In my most recent encounter, I was hemmed in by traffic and the bridge railings as a mother and her calf passed right alongside me, but without haste or paying me the slightest attention.

I knew I couldn't expect to see much of Yellowstone National Park's vastness in that one day, but all the same, despite the rain and cold, it was a pretty amazing day. A road circled the park's interior, and a few signs along the way sketch a picture: Fountain Paint Pot, Firehole Lake, Steamboat Geyser, Obsidian Cliff, and Mammoth Hot Springs—an immense array of stepped travertine pools, sculptured circles brimming with steaming water and mud. From there I turned east, then south

through a more open, prairie landscape and the lush green meadows framing the Yellowstone River, where I saw many more herds of bison, near and far, and occasional elk, feeding among the pines.

Unexpectedly, the star attraction to me was the Grand Canyon of the Yellowstone, where two mighty waterfalls plunged in white sheets between jagged walls of yellow and red rock. I followed the spur road to the lookout points on the north side, parking to take in the incredible views, then traveled to the south side, which was even more spectacular, especially from the aptly named Artist Point. On a U.S. Geological Survey expedition in 1871, the great landscape painter Thomas Moran had painted the Yellowstone Falls from a spot near

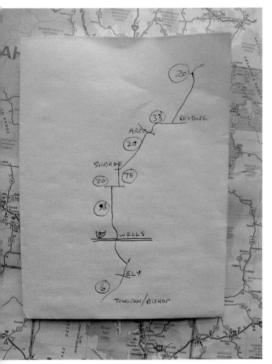

there, and it had been his paintings, and William Henry Jackson's photographs from the same expedition, that had helped to influence Congress to declare the area the world's first national park the following year.

With my binoculars, I followed the angle of a birdwatcher's powerful scope, and saw that it was trained on an osprey's nest, a huge jumble of sticks perched on the pinnacle of an isolated crag. Two scruffy-looking chicks sat hunched against the chill and rain.

By the time I circled back to Yellowstone Lake, my eyes felt prickly with fatigue—overwhelmed by an excess of beauty (like the feeling I get in art museums, worn out after an hour or so of really *looking*), I stopped by the general store's soda fountain for another bratwurst and chocolate shake, while I caught up on my notes and reviewed my photographs. Two of the employees, an elderly waitress and a white-haired old man at the cash register, recognized me from the day before, and both of them, separately, asked me if I was working around there—I wonder what I looked like to them? "Outdoorsy," I guess.

It made me smile to think that apparently I looked, spoke, and acted like the kind of guy who would work in a national park. But after all, my first childhood ambition was to be a forest ranger—until I decided to become a professional birdwatcher, then a lighthouse keeper, then a history teacher. When it finally became clear that I couldn't actually *do* anything else, Fate let me be the drummer . . .

That night I got out the maps and charted my route home. My navigation tools were primitive, but effective—a paper map of the Western states, a blank sheet of paper from the typing tablet I always carry in my bike bags (as recounted in *Ghost Rider*, they started to become scarce with the decline of typewriters), and my Montblanc pen. I studied the map for a while, my finger tracing high desert roads, and eventually I nodded decisively—I would take a two-lane route home. Cutting down through Nevada, I should be able to make good time on those long, straight, empty roads. I drew a map of my route, showing the highway numbers, general directions, and town names (especially as refueling reminders, in that part of the country, where opportunities can be widely separated).

Once again, I was planning a marathon day—to get as close to home as I could, and to make the following day more enjoyable (and so I wouldn't arrive home exhausted; wives seem to hate it when you've been away and come back and you're still no use!).

Fueled by a couple of muffins I had bought the night before, and the in-room coffee, I set out at 5:00 a.m., in the rain (I won't mention that word again), with the temperature barely one degree above freezing.

The sky was just beginning to pale, but the air was thick with moisture, often pooling in foggy banks in the valleys. Once again, the park's 45 mph limit was just about right, with due regard for the wet pavement, limited visibility, and the possibility of large animals suddenly appearing in front of me, especially in the hours around dawn.

Following the Madison River to the West Entrance (glad to be taking a different way out, and see at least a *little* more), the sky began to

clear, misty rays of sun cutting into the deep gorge. A pair of big bison ambled up the road toward me, and I decided it was wisest just to stop and wait, and try not to upset them.

A little farther on I slowed to read a sign that forbade parking along that stretch of road, to protect the nest of a bald eagle. Puttering slowly past, I saw the immense structure of the nest high in a tree just off the road.

Continuing west, I crossed into Idaho, out of the park and into more open ranch country and sagebrush rangeland. The morning grew clear and sunny, warming fast, and I could make good steady time along country two-lanes with infinite visibility. I passed long security fences with dire warning signs, road signs pointing to the Idaho National Laboratory, and a turnoff to a place called Atomic City. Then I rode through a typical-looking ranch town called Arco, Idaho, and its sign caught my attention: "The First City in the World Lighted by Atomic Power." Then I noticed a burger joint offering the "Atomic Burger."

Curious, I made a mental note to look into that town's story when I got home, and it proved to be an eye-opening piece of modern history. Arco began as a sagebrush cowtown fetchingly called Root Hog, until 1901, when the citizens moved the town to the banks of the Big Lost River, to put it at the junction of two stagecoach routes. They applied to the U.S. Post Office to name their new town "Junction," but instead they were advised to name it after a German count, Georg von Arco, who happened to be visiting Washington, D.C., at the time. Coincidentally, the count went on to be a pioneer in radio and the founder of Telefunken, and his namesake town would play its part in modern technology, too.

In 1949, the National Reactor Testing Station was established nearby, in a remote high desert location that was perfect for secret government operations—in this case, to develop peacetime uses for nuclear energy. In 1955, ten years after the atomic bombs had leveled Hiroshima and Nagasaki, nuclear power lighted the streets of Arco.

The Miracle of the Atom seemed to offer such a bright and shining future, with clean, cheap, limitless energy powering cities, ships, submarines, airplanes, and cars. Strange to think that such a utopian vision was born right near that little town in Idaho.

Like national parks and philanthropy, nuclear power was another world-changing American invention, but its effects were obviously more . . . complicated. In 1985, I wrote the lyrics for a song called "Manhattan Project," about the birth of the Atomic Age (*"The big bang, took and shook the world/ Shot down the rising sun"*). Unusually for the lyrics to a rock song, "Manhattan Project" required a great deal of research (in the days when research had to be done by reading a pile of books rather than pressing a few keys), and I learned a lot. Then I had to distill all of that knowledge into what would add up to only 167 words—and they had to be words that could be *sung*.

Once I had chiseled out a draft of what I wanted to convey, it wasn't easy to "sell" the notion of a historical rock song, even to my bandmates. But it was Geddy, thinking as a singer, who suggested that I construct it so the listener was *invited* to imagine the scene. (Moments of collaboration like that are galvanizing in two ways—first that someone else likes your idea enough to take it seriously, then suggests a way to make it better.)

> Imagine a time, when it all began
> In the dying days of a war
> Searching for a weapon
> That would settle the score
> Whoever found it first—would be sure to do their worst
> They always had before

As early as 1939, Albert Einstein wrote a letter to President Roosevelt urging him to pursue atomic weapons, because Einstein and other scientists believed the Germans were already working on such a program. (They were, but—in a prescient scenario—the scientists overestimated the enemy's progress with such weapons of mass destruction.)

> Imagine a man
> Where it all began
> A scientist pacing the floor
> In each nation—always eager to explore
> To build the best big stick
> To turn the winning trick
> But this was something more

Modern revisionists seem to diminish the historical reality of that time—for example, the appalling brutality and racial genocide the Japanese had been inflicting in China, Korea, the Philippines, and elsewhere. Mass killings of civilians (tens of thousands at a time, and totaling at least twice the Holocaust's grim toll), biological and chemical warfare, inhuman treatment of prisoners of war, slavery, forced prostitution, medical experiments without anesthetic, vivisection, cannibalism—it's a horrific list. To absorb that history, adding Japan's alliance with the Axis Powers and the devastating sneak attack on Pearl Harbor that began the War in the Pacific, is to share an outrage that would have deserved any level of vengeance, to make it stop, and to punish the perpetrators. Anyone who believes in the alternative—

that the "humane" way to end World War II would have been an invasion of Japan—would only shift that death sentence to the American lives that such a suicide mission would have cost.

> The big bang—took and shook the world
> Shot down the rising sun
> The end was begun—it would hit everyone
> When the chain reaction was done

In the early '90s, on a day off on a concert tour, I visited Los Alamos, "where it all began," and later that decade, on the *Ghost Rider* journey, I stopped at the Trinity Site in New Mexico, where the first tests were conducted. In the '80s, on a concert tour of Japan, I had looked out from the bullet train passing through Hiroshima, and thought about what had happened there, and why. Now I was riding through what had been the next chapter in that story.

It happened that one of my camera's settings got jostled in the tankbag, and I ended up with a series of unexpectedly artful Action Self Portraits taken in that region—red filtered out, while other colors were saturated. The effect does suggest the austerity, and serenity, of the high desert, a surreal emptiness that can seem otherworldly—especially when you learn its hidden secrets, like the story behind those streetlights in little Arco, where atomic energy was harnessed for the first time.

Alas, it would not be without human cost—in 1961, the reactor that had produced Arco's electricity suffered a steam explosion and meltdown (human error), causing the world's first peacetime nuclear fatalities—three of its workers. Comparable to the space program, perhaps, the progress of nuclear technology was slowed by human losses, but not halted, and reactors began to sprout around the world, powering electrical generators, ships, and submarines.

Then in 1979, a partial meltdown occurred at Three Mile Island in Pennsylvania (human error again). This time there were no fatalities, but unfortunately the accident occurred within two weeks of the release of a fictional movie called *The China Syndrome*, dramatizing just such an accident, using melodrama and pseudoscience to play on people's fear of what they didn't understand (a timeless strategy, in religion, politics, and entertainment).

Widespread hysteria ensued, fanned by self-appointed "experts" like the star of *The China Syndrome*, Jane Fonda, and the careerist fearmonger, Ralph Nader. The shrill reflex of the "no nukes" protests effectively ended the growth of nuclear energy in the Western world (though France quietly continues to produce three-quarters of its energy from reactors).

In 1979, the chief voice of reason against that howling mob was another dubious character—the scientist Edward Teller. Teller was a veteran of the Manhattan Project, the "father of the H-bomb," director of the Lawrence Livermore National Laboratory, and one inspiration for the character Dr. Strangelove in the movie of the same name (subtitled "How I Learned to Stop Worrying and Love the Bomb"). He was also the betrayer of Robert Oppenheimer, the leader of the Manhattan Project, and high on my personal list of "People of Interest." (Oppenheimer took the name of the Trinity Site, in the desert near Alamagordo, New Mexico, from a sonnet by John Donne, and after the first test of the atomic bomb was successful, he contemplated a verse in Sanskrit, "Now I am become Death, the destroyer of worlds.")

At a 1954 hearing to review Robert Oppenheimer's security clearance (apparently threatened because of an unstable girlfriend with Communist associations), Edward Teller was asked whether he considered Oppenheimer a security risk. He replied that he had repeatedly seen Oppenheimer act "in a way which for me was exceedingly hard to understand," then clinched it with a damning indictment: "To this extent I feel that I would like to see the vital interests of this country in hands which I understand better, and therefore trust more."

In 1979, the public may have felt the same way about Edward Teller, as he stood up in counter-campaigns and tirelessly tried to correct misconceptions and widespread panic. But as ever, science and reason had little sway over fear and ignorance—or misguided movie stars and professional muckraking malcontents in bad suits. Teller suffered a heart attack that year, which he half-jokingly blamed on Jane Fonda: "You might say that I was the only one whose health was affected by that reactor near Harrisburg. No, that would be wrong. It was not the reactor. It was Jane Fonda. Reactors are not dangerous."

Clearly, history has shown that Dr. Teller was a little over-optimistic there, but perhaps it was true that reactors were not as dangerous as some other threats to human life and well-being. Like, say, misguided movie stars and professional muckraking malcontents in bad suits—or the stripping away of entire mountaintops to dig up coal and foul the atmosphere by burning it.

A few years later, when I was writing "Manhattan Project" in 1985, the Cold War was still an international menace, and I was thinking of both nuclear weapons and nuclear energy in the second half of the chorus:

Big shots try to hold it back
Fools try to wish it away
The hopeful depend
On a world without end
Whatever the hopeless may say

I'm not sure if I intended that twist on "the hopeless," but I like it.

In any case, the verdict was handed down in the supreme court of public opinion, and the "fallout" was that the pursuit of nuclear power, for purposes both peaceful and warlike, was abandoned to less developed, or less conscientious nations—soon leading to the true disaster of Chernobyl, in 1986 (the year after "Manhattan Project" appeared on our *Power Windows* album).

In the last years of a corrupt and crumbling Soviet empire, a clusterbomb of human and mechanical failures caused a terrible explosion, killing two workers instantly, several dozen fire and rescue workers immediately after, and releasing four hundred times the radioactive fallout of Hiroshima. An international committee estimated that the eventual toll from the radiation and associated cancers might reach a couple of thousand—terrible enough, of course, but even that number could never match the deaths from, oh, mining and burning coal, for example.

Not to mention the religiously inspired terrorist attacks of September 11, 2001 . . .

But the "first world" had already reverted to a nineteenth-century dystopia of burning coal (as I have noted before, in another context, coal still produces more than half of America's electricity). Shunning the perceived dangers of nuclear energy, people seemed less troubled by the "simple" idea of burning coal, despite its very real and insidious dangers (here—now—real), while governments remain suspiciously quiet about its contributions to climate change. At the same time, we turn a blind eye to the medieval institutions of superstition, feudal rule, and misogyny in tyrannical kingdoms like Saudi Arabia, because we "need" their oil.

And to think that those troubles had a large part of their history written more than fifty years ago, right around little Arco, Idaho . . .

Today, the National Reactor Testing Station is the Idaho National Laboratory, the immense fenced-in compound I had been passing for miles (it covers an incredible 890 square miles!). No wonder such enormous secret government installations give rise to paranoia—and later that same day I would be passing the mother of all those paranoid obsessions, Area 51 and the Extraterrestrial Highway.

But there were a lot of high-desert miles between the two—over 500, in fact. And a wall of strong wind, an invisible barrier that drove against me on the endless open stretches of the Great Basin. The wind's power worked against my motorcycle's, and I noticed that it was burning through fossil fuel unusually quickly. Where I can usually average 180 miles or more on a full tank, my reserve light came on at barely 100 miles. Even with my spare gallon can on the back, that

could spell trouble in a region where gas stations were so far apart—where *people* were so far apart.

Riding through Arco, with its time-capsule feeling, both as a rural ranching town and as a purveyor of "Atomic Burgers," put me in mind of another Great Basin town, Ritzville, up in Washington state. A few miles later I found myself riding along and trying to put together the words of an old song, "Puttin' on the Ritz." That chorus, and the lines, *"Dressed up like a million dollar trouper/Trying hard to look like Gary Cooper*

(super duper)" were about all I could remember, except that the rest was complicated wordplay—but most of all I wondered why *that song* was in my head. The word for those songs or musical phrases that play over and over in your head derives from a German term that means "earworm," and they can be a torment on a long motorcycle ride, like a mental mosquito.

For once, I was able to put it together—"Puttin' on the Ritz" (Irving Berlin, 1929) was playing in my head because of Ritzville, and the Top Hat motel I had stayed at there in 2007 (see "Every Road Has Its Toll"). It was nice to be able to trace the source of that earworm—like another one, earlier on this trip: Riding up through southern Utah on the first day, I had wondered why I was hearing a reggae lilt, and singing, *"Don't gain the world and lose your soul/ Wisdom is better than silver and gold."* It was Bob Marley's "Zion Train," and I had just passed the exit for Zion National Park. The long-distance brain sometimes chooses its soundtrack in mysterious ways.

My only urban-traffic-and-construction obstacle that day was Twin Falls, Idaho, otherwise it was smooth sailing (on an upwind tack) all day. Down into Nevada on Highway 93 to Wells, gas up and buy a sandwich and a drink for later, strip off my inner layer (fifty degrees of temperature change by then, from the 30s to the 80s), then aim for Ely ("Elee"), battling that fierce wind and stopping for occasional road-construction zones (a good opportunity to eat lunch). It didn't look like my fuel would last until Ely, so I had to stop at McGill, though they only had regular gas. After Ely, with its Jailhouse Motel where Michael and I had stayed in 2007 on the way to a show in Salt Lake City, a sign on Highway 6 announced "No Gas For 167 Miles." Again, that wouldn't be a problem normally, but with that day's wind, I was worried that even my spare gallon wouldn't be enough to get me all that way to Tonopah.

At a crossroads called Warm Springs, where the Extraterrestrial Highway met Highway 6, I stopped in the shade of an abandoned building to pour in that extra gallon. This was the exact spot, recounted in *Ghost Rider*, where Brutus and I had also found ourselves running out of gas, after a fast run from the Little A'le'Inn in Rachel, just to the east (next to the legendary Area 51, hence the café's cringe-inducing name). That was in 1997, on the *Test for Echo* tour, and it was an early experience with the American West that taught many lessons—like the little red gas can that was saving me now.

Rachel had gas in those days (though not anymore, I noticed by a warning sign in that direction), but Brutus and I had looked at the map, saw Warm Springs at the next junction, and decided to carry on. At least the map I have now offers the printed word "(site)" after Warm

Springs, to let you know it's only a name, because there was nothing there—nothing but the boarded-up building I stopped beside this time. Back then, an old rancher hauling a horse trailer had pointed one way and said, "It's about a hundred miles that way to Ely," then turned and said, "And about fifty miles that way to Tonopah—nothing in between."

Even twelve years later, someone was still maintaining that old cinder-block building, for some reason, and I saw where graffiti had been whitewashed over, leaving the red-painted letters spelling Warm Springs Bar & Cafe. A metal post remained where the pay phone used to be—the one Brutus had used to try to call a gas station in Tonopah to come to our rescue. There had been no reply, and no choice but to keep going as long as we could, and maybe hitchhike the rest of the way.

A little farther west on Highway 6 we had come upon the Five Mile Ranch, and Brutus and I stopped and looked for someone who might sell us some gas. The place was deserted, but they had gas, and—at Brutus's insistence, as I would never have had the nerve—we ended up leaving twenty dollars and a "sorry" note, then pumping a couple of gallons each (when gas was a buck-something, mind you) from their big metal tank.

This time I paused at the ranch's gate and took a few photos to send to Brutus, then carried on to Tonopah. I had thought of stopping there, after covering 740 miles, but Tonopah was not a prepossessing town. A moribund desert mining settlement, it was now largely supported by a military installation, the Tonopah Test Range, part of the incredibly immense Nellis Air Force Range Complex, which also included the Nevada Test Site and the legendary Area 51 (altogether an unbelievable 4,700 square miles—half the size of Yellowstone National Park). Nothing especially against the town of Tonopah—not so different from, say, Ely, where I always liked staying, but Tonopah lacked any attractive motels, however humble, or restaurants. I always thought of Tonopah, Nevada, as a town that was good for filling up with gas and riding away from—and sure enough, after stopping at the gas station and cruising Tonopah's two highways, looking over the uninviting motels and restaurants, I said, "Phooey" (or words to that effect), and kept riding west. Even after all those hard, windy miles, somehow I was still feeling surprisingly fresh—tired and saddle-sore, yes, but not drowsy or crabby. All along I had been thinking about carrying on to somewhere more inviting, maybe Bishop, California— "only" another 130 miles, and I would gain an hour, crossing back into Pacific Time. Somehow that boost helped me talk myself into it (those can be contentious conversations).

Another mountain town, at 4,137 feet, Bishop sits in the pretty Owens Valley, nestled between the high peaks of the Sierra Nevada on one side and the White Mountains on the other. As well as bringing me that much closer to home for the following day, Bishop offered a few decent motels and a fair choice of restaurants. After 877 miles that day, in fourteen hours, I was ready for one of those restaurants, and a Best Western bed.

From Bishop on, the roads home were familiar and well loved. I was able to keep to the two-lanes-only route, save where the highway occasionally widened to four lanes, and where I had to use a mile or two of interstate to connect to the excellent Lockwood Valley Road and Highway 33 to Ojai, then a short stretch of 101 through Ventura to the Pacific Coast Highway. Otherwise, all the way from Yellowstone to Los Angeles I stayed on back roads, covering 1,252 miles on the southward run—only about 150 miles farther than the interstate route, not more than an hour or two longer, and a whole lot more interesting and enjoyable.

Altogether, in those five days I rode 2,500 miles, and was glad to pull into my own garage, and get off that bike. As I have quoted myself before, "When I'm riding my motorcycle, I'm glad to be alive—and when I stop riding my motorcycle, I'm glad to be alive."

That, I hope, will never change.

And I felt pretty good about the trip—despite all the rain, cold, and violent winds (and partly because of them), it had been an action-packed few days. My careful planning had paid off in all the important little ways, like the bike preparation, route planning, and wardrobe changes. (I laughed when I was pleased to note that I'd had "all the right gloves," always a critical detail in riding comfort. These days I carry three pairs: for hot, dry weather; wet or dry cool weather; and cold, wet weather.)

Most of all, as I laid out my tools to change the bike's oil, I had a feeling of Mission Accomplished—at last I had made it to Yellowstone National Park. I didn't feel I had seen much of it, of course, but that green area on the map in the corner of Wyoming meant *something* to me now—it was on my "mental map," at least, where it had not existed just one week before.

I can only hope that one day I will return to Yellowstone, maybe even to that little yellow cabin. And that wish gives rise to another line in iambic tetrameter—"If the fates are kinder, than they sometimes seem to be."

That line, too, just cries out to be sung, perhaps in a triumphant chorus, with harmonized backing vocals:

> If the fates are kinder, than they sometimes seem to be
> (A little yellow cabin on Yellowstone Lake)
> There will still be many journeys and adventures for me
> (A little yellow cabin on Yellowstone Lake)
> A million miles, a hundred songs in my head
> (A little yellow cabin on Yellowstone Lake)
> Till the stupid fates decide it's time to make me dead
> (A little yellow cabin on Yellowstone Lake)
> Yeah!

Now everybody . . .

THE BALLAD OF LARRY AND SUZY

SEPTEMBER 2009

In a previous story, "Under the Marine Layer," I wrote about watching a hummingbird build her nest in the bougainvillea vines on the wall of our house. She gathered dried grasses and flower petals and wove them into a tiny bowl bound with spider silk. The lining of softest plant down was shaped with her body, which was about the size of my thumb. The nest was an exquisite egg cup, crafted by a meticulous Fabergé. She belonged to a species called Anna's hummingbird, after a nineteenth-century Italian duchess, so I named her Anna. Once I had spotted that nest, I kept a vigilant, protective eye on it, day after day.

I felt an irresistible connection with Anna, and a strong guardian instinct for her nest, because as Anna was preparing to lay her eggs in late May, my wife Carrie was seven months pregnant. My anxiety about that enterprise was projected and distilled into Anna's little nest, filling it with my fears and dark forebodings. Some of those fears were garishly clear in harsh, unyielding memory, while others bred in the shadowy unconscious, in tormented dreams. *Tormenta* is Spanish for "storm," and my interior weather was ominous and unsettled, temperature high and barometer low. The gathering storm generated a kind of pathetic fallacy in reverse, manifesting itself in my anxious concern for the well-being of Anna and her nest.

That nervous watchfulness soon blossomed into an aching, near-obsessive fretting, and several times a day I would find myself detouring into the backyard, sometimes just for a peek, but other times staying for a while, taking along some reading and writing, or my Macallan on ice at the end of the day. I would sit at the outdoor table across the lawn from the nest—close enough to keep watch, but far enough not to be intrusive. From time to time I raised my binoculars and focused on Anna's perfect stillness as she sat there, hour after hour, and I wondered what she was thinking. Essentially, and profoundly, she was just doing what she had to do.

Anna settled into her nest and rarely left it, except briefly in late afternoon, when the sun was on the nest—to keep it warm, I guessed. She buzzed around the garden, darting from flower to flower for a quick feed, then perched on a branch above me, in sight of the nest, and groomed herself for a few minutes. While most birds preen themselves with their bills, Anna had to use her *feet*—she perched on one foot and used the other to comb her feathers, then switched over, because the long needle bill that was so perfectly adapted to sipping floral cocktails was not so adaptable as a grooming accessory. I watched her little string of a tongue flick out a few times, and from the other end, she ejected an impressive jet of liquid.

Then all at once, in a blur, she would be gone again, arrowing back to the nest, almost too fast to see. It was wonderful to study Anna's flight, to watch her hovering in place while she fed, even flying backward among the flowered vines. If any other hummingbirds approached within about thirty feet of Anna's patch of bougainvillea, she would zip out like a fierce bullet and drive them off. No wonder hummingbirds' hearts can pump at over 1,000 beats per minute, and that they have to eat the equivalent of their own body weight every day to sustain that outpouring of energy.

One afternoon in early June, Anna was away from the nest, perched in a tree above my table and taking a little "me time" in the lowering sun. I fetched my ladder from the garage, leaned it against the wall, and climbed as high as I dared. With one hand holding onto the wall, my other hand reached my camera as high as I could above the nest, then aimed it downward between the leaves (my remote-framing ability practiced by the Action Self-Portrait photos I took on my motorcycle, as seen in many previous stories). When I viewed the resulting image, I was delighted to see two tiny white eggs, each smaller than the tip of my baby finger.

I also saw that I wanted to improve my nest-photographing techniques, and worked on that in the coming days. I found myself growing ever more attentive, visiting the backyard many times throughout the day, just to check on her. One morning I heard a commotion outside, and the squawking of crows—notorious nest robbers. With a start of fear, I raced out to chase them away, hoping I wasn't too late, but the bird community had the situation well in hand. Four different species, a robin, a mockingbird, a sparrow, and a hummingbird—Anna—were working together, mobbing a pair of crows, driving them away from all of their nests. I had never witnessed that kind of inter-species cooperation before, and it made me smile—and not only from relief. It is common to see a pair of sparrows or starlings harassing crows that way, and crows routinely nag at patrolling hawks, but that alliance of so many different birds was like a scene from a Disney movie.

I did some research into the nesting habits of hummingbirds, and learned that Anna's eggs should hatch in a little over two weeks. During that time, there were many dangers and disturbances I had to guard them against. One morning a team of workers came to spray around our house—a necessary retaliation against a recent invasion of ants (a transplanted Canadian like me appreciates the lack of mosquitoes and black flies in Southern California, but I can still be appalled to walk into the kitchen in the morning and see *thousands* of ants swarming over any dishes left in the sink, and over the dog's food bowl). The pest-control company claimed they sprayed with "green" insecticides, but I warned the workers not to spray near Anna's nest, and to try to stay clear of the area as much as they could. I was afraid too much human activity would drive Anna from her nest permanently, for if birds are kept away from their eggs too long, they will abandon them. I couldn't stand for that to happen.

Later in the day, when the workers had gone, I sat outside and watched to make sure that Anna was back on her nest—surprised at the intensity of my relief when I saw her return and settle herself above the eggs. A few days later, another team of workers came to work on our air conditioning system, replacing the air pumps behind the garage, right near the nest. Once again, I warned them sternly against disturbing it, and when they were gone, I was back at my table, watching to make sure Anna had returned.

Late in June, I started to see Anna making brief forays away from the nest all through the day, and I wondered if the eggs had hatched. When the afternoon sun was on the nest, I saw Anna perched above me, attending to her own grooming for a few minutes. I got out the ladder again and climbed up to aim my camera down into the nest.

When I looked at the screen to see what I had captured, I was thrilled to see two tiny little babies, still almost featherless, their bright orange bills half open. (Many young birds of different species have that fluorescent kind of beakage, and it is thought to help attract their mothers to *feed* them.) You can see there was nothing recognizably "hummingbird" about them yet.

Carrie was almost eight months pregnant now, so it was a matter of only a few weeks, even, possibly, days. (A phrase from the Summer of Love I somehow remember, "Love comes like birth, knowing its own time.") As that time grew steadily more imminent, yet remained uncertain, unknowable, the prospect assumed greater size in my imagination. My worries swelled and multiplied, and I began to feel a constant state of tension, even dread, added to what I came to realize was an attempt at inner *resolve*. As if trying to warn myself, prepare myself, *convince* myself, I was thinking, "Whatever happens, you're going to have to be ready to *handle* it."

I began to think of those two baby birds and their mother as My Little Metaphors.

Soon, though, they had real names. I sent this photograph to my friend and fellow bird-lover, Craiggie, and when he showed it to his eleven-year-old daughter, Selena, she said, "Ooh! They're so *cute*! Tell Neil to call them . . . Larry and . . ."

She paused. "Hmm. Rose? Sally?"

She fidgeted and thought, swaying from side to side, then said, "Oh, I know—Suzy! That's a good name."

So Larry and Suzy they were. There was no way to tell them apart, of course, or even their genders—like most young birds, baby Anna's hummingbirds are indistinguishable gender-wise. However, I was under no scientific responsibility to avoid anthropomorphism, and as they grew and developed I invented characters that fit the behavior I witnessed. Typically, a hummingbird's second egg is laid a day later than the first, and thus hatches like that, so the second chick remains smaller and less developed. With some bird species, the firstborn chick, larger and stronger, will heave the smaller one right out of the nest—either accidentally or on purpose, jockeying for more food. (The common loon of our northern lakes is one species I

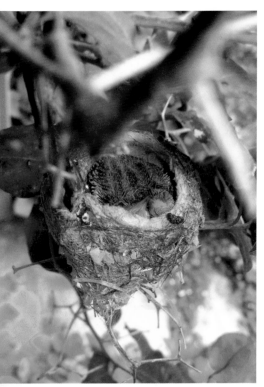

know where the parents will even begin to *ignore* the smaller chick at feeding time, letting it starve—perhaps at a time when fish are scarce, and thus maximizing the odds for one survivor.)

Nature's only two commandments for living things: Survive and Reproduce.

So I started to worry about Larry or Suzy falling out of the nest and tumbling to the ground. Even a metaphorical parent has so much to worry about—and, as I knew too well, the worries are, literally, endless.

One day I noticed that an overflow pipe up by the eaves was dripping a little water down above the nest. Though it was pretty well sheltered by the bougainvillea vines and leaves, I worried that even a drop or two of water would be enough to soak Larry and Suzy, or the tiny nest around them. I had dark imaginings of hypothermia, picturing them shivering and helpless in their cold, wet bedding. While I fretted thus, I saw Anna fly to the nest and perch on its edge, but she was obscured by leaves, and I couldn't see if she was feeding them. It looked to me like she wasn't moving at all, and I pictured her just sitting there, looking down mournfully at her dead babies. As soon as she left again, I reached up with my camera and took a photo—to reassure myself that Larry and Suzy were still alive.

There they were, dry and cozy, looking like a pair of fuzzy brown caterpillars, or tiny down sleeping bags—each of them still smaller than the end of my little finger.

Every day—many times a day—I kept watch from my outdoor table, seeing Anna fly off to feed and bring back a gullet full of nectar, and (I learned) the occasional small insect, caught on the wing or scavenged from a spider's web. I certainly had never thought of hummingbirds as carnivores, but years ago I was surprised to learn that many other birds I used to think of as vegetarians, like finches and sparrows, actually flew north to breed in the Arctic regions because that intensely buggy zone provided a high-protein diet of insects to better nourish their young. When birds have babies to feed, they want more than seeds and berries.

I tried to take at least one photograph of Larry and Suzy every day, and I was astonished to see how fast they grew—just on regurgitated flower nectar and occasional little bugs. Within a few days I was catching glimpses of tiny orange bills poking up out of the nest, gaping wide as they waited for food. Larry and Suzy were still incredibly small, but their bills lengthened noticeably every day, and their feathers grew into a comically spiky plumage. (Larry and Suzy's inevitable punk stage. I'll write a verse like that for their Ballad.)

I loved to watch Anna feed them, too—flickering in behind the leaves to perch on the edge of the nest, while Larry and Suzy's orange bills pointed up and gaped even wider. She would stick her long bill way down their throats, then shake with a kind of rhythmic convulsion, head pumping like a sewing-machine needle as her tongue transferred the nourishment. Each chick got two quick feedings, then Anna was gone again, to gather their next meal.

Witnessing these scenes, I swelled with a sense of feeling *privileged*—somehow *honored* to be able to share this intimate view of a wild family, miraculous, adorable, and somehow more than just "natural"—maybe "supernatural." I had never seen anything like that, in fifty years as a casual birdwatcher ("casual," because I have never kept a life-list of all the birds I've seen, and unlike serious birders, I've never traveled anywhere just to see birds—but wherever I do travel, I always love to look at the birds and learn their names).

As Larry and Suzy grew larger, they seemed to be crowding each other right out of the nest. Like two overgrown adolescents on a school bus, they jostled for space, occasionally flexing their little wings and giving them an experimental flutter, always in each other's way. One

time I laughed as Larry was waving his wings around, and with every stroke one of them banged into Suzy's head. She just sat there, looking indignant, but patient. I never saw them act aggressively toward each other, but I did notice they often faced in opposite directions, either for more space, or to avoid the very sight of their annoying sibling (anthropomorphizing again). But I still worried that one of them was going to shove the other out, and I pictured it tumbling helplessly to the ground. I wondered what I would do if that happened. Would I "play God" and rescue the fallen one, return it to the nest?

The answer seemed clear, "*Hell yeah!*"

Even as Larry and Suzy continued growing, so too did Carrie's belly, and the baby inside. Ultrasound examinations had revealed that she was a girl, and that—alas—she seemed to have Daddy's nose. I hoped she would grow into it . . .

Carrie and I attended a couple of lengthy birthing classes, which included graphic, gory DVDs of the labor and birth process, and there were painful-sounding descriptions of the complicated (and risky) series of steps, each one demonstrated with a life-size doll and model pelvis bones. So many things had to happen *just right* that you wondered how anyone managed to be born successfully.

Most significant to me, so many things could go *wrong*.

We toured the birthing unit at the local hospital, shared another in-depth class on newborn care, and I signed up for a one-and-a-half-hour course on infant car-seat installation and adjustment (seriously—and it was *necessary*). The last time I became a father was thirty years ago, when my daughter Selena was born in 1978, and it can hardly be overstated how much things have changed in three decades—not least my own blithe self-confidence that, in those days, allowed to me trust that everything was going to be all right. Since Selena's death in 1997, at age nineteen, I no longer had that faith.

What I did have was a bottomless well of fears for all those I cared about, and in this case, not just for all that could go wrong with the developing baby, and with a mother in childbirth, but recognizing that even given the best-case scenario—a healthy baby—my fears would only be beginning.

August 10 would be the twelfth anniversary of Selena's death, and Carrie's due date was August 12, so I was also sending out supplications to any available deity that the new baby not be born two days early—it would be awful to have her birthday fall on what would always be the worst day in my calendar.

By mid-July, Larry and Suzy had been growing for three weeks, and they looked pretty grown-up. The nest seemed impossibly crowded now, and I knew they would be leaving soon, but I was still surprised when I came out one morning and saw only one baby in the nest. Larry was gone—though he hadn't gone far. I spotted him perched on a nearby vine, as still as a flower, and it was a wonderful opportunity for me to get up close and marvel at his delicate plumage, its gemlike spots of metallic green, the combination of chestnut and buffy white, and the dark tracery edging his wings. I stared long into the shining bead of his eye, but as with all wild creatures, it revealed nothing of its depths.

From the table across the yard, I continued watching through my binoculars, and several times that day I saw Anna perch beside Larry and feed him, then continue on to the nest to feed Suzy. Larry didn't move all that day and night, for I found him in the same spot the next morning, but later that day, he was gone. It bothered me to think that I would never be able to be sure of seeing Larry again, among all the hummingbirds that visit our flowers (the avian franchise of Bubba's Bar 'n' Grill).

Suzy, meanwhile, was obviously nervous about taking that first flight. On one visit I would see her perched on the outside of the nest, as if ready to try her wings, but the next time I looked I would see her back inside its safe haven, having failed to summon enough courage to go.

That occasional dance to the outside edge of the nest, then back inside, continued for two whole days, until finally, on the morning of the third day, the nest was empty. My first and dominant emotion was *relief*—that they had both survived long enough, under my vigilance, to gain their independence—but of course I felt a little regret, too. I joked to Carrie, "Now what am I going to do?"

I had been watching over Anna's nest, her eggs, and then Larry and Suzy, since late May. In those six weeks I only missed five days, while I was away on my motorcycle journey to Yellowstone National Park. From then on, all through the writing of that story, and the other activities of a busy life, I had been slipping outside to check on the nest, or settling at the table to read over my work with my binoculars at hand—infatuated with the growing family, inspired and delighted, somehow even comforted by them, while at the same time feeling tense and fearful for their survival.

Those feelings had ramped up as Carrie's due date approached. For the first time in many years, my fingernails were nibbled raw, and in those final weeks I had been trying to keep myself usefully occupied—working out at the Y, spending several days up at the Drum Channel studio exploring some rhythmic ideas (plus enjoying the wonderful drive up and back on the Pacific Coast Highway in my old DB5), and planning, shopping for, and preparing nutritious meals for Carrie.

Our five-year-old golden retriever, Winston, needed extra attention, having been a "mama's boy" all his life, and—with his sensitive heart and genius brain—sensing change in the household atmosphere. With Carrie suffering from insomnia and growing discomfort, I spent more time caring for Winston, feeding him and taking him outside, occasionally for father-son walks in a nearby canyon, and trying to give him at least some of the infinite amounts of love he required (since puppyhood we had called him the "genius love-sponge").

All the while, wherever I roamed, my cell phone was always near at hand—ready for that call, and trying to remain prepared, remain *resolved*.

"Whatever happens, you're going to have to be ready to *handle* it."

When I was a boy of six or seven, I remember fervently believing that I could prevent bad things from happening if I *worried* about them enough. Now I recognize that atavistic urge as a primitive kind of *prayer*, and I was still superstitious enough then to believe in magical thinking. Hoping to escape being found out in a lie, or punished for something I had accidentally broken, I would worry about it long and hard. If, despite all that prayer, my crime were discovered, I would decide that I had simply not worried enough. All unknowing, I had invented my own little religion, the Church of Worry, and it worked the same as all the others: If something bad happens, it's your fault for not having prayed enough.

This time, I guess I must have prayed enough—so far, at least. On August 12, 2009, Olivia Louise Peart hatched into the world.

In early discussions of a possibly long and painful labor, I had said I might not want to remain in the delivery room. People seemed to think I was squeamish about blood, but it was actually about the *pain*, I wasn't sure how much of Carrie's suffering I could bear to witness. Blood I can take, in small doses, and my own pain I can stand, to some extent, but not a loved one's agony.

But it worked out all right, and I was able to be in the operating room, masked and shrouded in sterile green, for the entire procedure—holding myself *resolved*, ready for whatever I might have to *handle*. Later, I said to Carrie's mother that such a situation seemed to require holding a stance that was truly *cool*—unselfish, detached, neutral. You quite literally have to set your own feelings aside. As has often been observed about behaving well in a crisis, it's not that you don't have feelings—usually quite the contrary—but at critical moments, when cool and efficient action is required, your own feelings are a temporary liability, an *indulgence* you cannot afford. That way lies surrender and failure. As I mentioned in a letter to my mother a day or two later, what I needed was that old Hemingway quality, grace under pressure.

". . . as I've learned before, you don't know what you can take until you've been *tested* (and ain't *that* the truth!)."

Lately I had been thinking of an early Hemingway masterpiece, a story called "Indian Camp," where the boy, Nick Adams, accompanies his doctor father to attend to a young Indian woman who had been in labor for two days, a breech-birth, and was screaming in agony. In the bunk above the suffering woman, her husband lay immobilized by a logging injury, and while Nick's father performed a Caesarean section with a jackknife and fishing line, and no anesthetic, it was the husband who succumbed to the unbearable pain.

The story also has one of those peerless Hemingway ending lines, "In the early morning on the lake sitting in the stern of the boat with his father rowing, he felt quite sure that he would never die."

A couple of times lately in Bubba's Book Club I have touched on the notion that "being good" often simply means "behaving better than we are." Now it occurs to me that being good can also be about behaving better than we *feel*.

Very important, that notion.

Years ago, on a grueling concert tour, the guys in our road crew came up with an ironic expression of that existential reality. Their slogan began with an upbeat, confident boast, "We have the technology!", then descended to a whiny, abject lament, "But we don't feel so good."

Sometimes in life you simply can't afford not to "feel so good"— when it's showtime.

Within a minute after Olivia's birth, I was touching and holding her while the medicos cleared her breathing passages, dried her skin, and swaddled her. Then I carried the tiny bundle over to introduce her to her mother. A few minutes later, I accompanied Olivia on her first journey, down a long hallway to the nursery, where she was weighed (seven pounds twelve ounces) and checked over by the pediatrician.

While she lay there in the clear plastic bassinet, I tried to soothe her (the naked weighing had especially outraged her delicate sensibilities, yet I had smiled to hear her strong cry of protest). I reached my finger into her fist, and felt her tiny fingers close tightly around it.

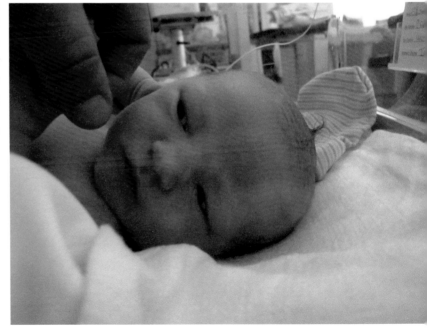

I whispered, "Hold on, baby, hold on."

I was talking to her, and to myself.

AUTUMN SERENADE

NOVEMBER 2009

It has been some years since I have been able to play the drums just for the pure enjoyment of it. Not performing or recording, not rehearsing or filming instructional material—just playing. The lack of a drumset at home is one reason, and that is partly because in seismically active Southern California, basements are rare. Given my rootless nature, I am always ready for the next move, the next home (in just the past nine years, five different homes in California, and three in Quebec), and it always seemed too troublesome and expensive to build the kind of sound-proofed drum rooms my friends Gregg Bissonette and Doane Perry have in their houses, or the cozy and well-equipped teaching studio Peter Erskine has in his back garden.

Another factor in recent years has been that I have spent so much time away from home playing the drums that when I did get back, it was kind of nice to step away completely from the "tools" for a while. If you have drumming in your very pulse, the flow of rhythm in your life is ceaseless, a constant kind of conceptual practicing. (Sitting at a red light, turn indicators set the tempo for an improvised cadenza on the steering wheel.) On the physical side, after forty-four years of playing the instrument, the language of drumming is wired deep in my brain and muscle fibers. So, as one does, I simply adapted to the way things were, and made a virtue of a necessity—"that's how it is, so okay" (a very grown-up philosophy, indeed). When I needed to rehearse for something, I found other ways—sometimes heading for Toronto a week or two early, or in recent years to the Drum Channel studio, a beautiful hour's drive north along the Pacific Coast Highway, if they had some downtime.

When I studied with Peter Erskine in 2008 (see "The Drums of October"), he restricted me to high-hat and metronome only, so I was able to practice every day without being as anti-social as a full set of drums requires, even at my house on the lake in Quebec, where sound *really* travels over the water and through the woods.

Inevitably, though, at some point I will be overwhelmed by a strong desire to play the drums for real, and that fever came upon me in late summer of this year. As often happens, the urge was sparked by listening to a couple of great drummers: Jack DeJohnette and Ian Wallace. Some musicians react to another player's greatness with envy, or even *despair*—like Eric Clapton's claim that he wanted to burn his guitar after hearing Jimi Hendrix, or Miles Davis allegedly making Wynton Marsalis want to smash his horn. But for me, hearing another drummer who impresses me (a long list) makes me want to go home and *play*. That's how it was when I was a kid, and it's still true today—not just an urge to practice and get better, but a response to *inspiration*.

Quite a few days this summer and fall I have been able to use Drum Channel's studio when it wasn't busy, playing a beautiful practice kit (its finish an autumnal harmony, too) provided by neighbor and benefactor, Drum Workshop. That was how I had that rare luxury of just playing, rambling aimlessly for hours.

These fine photographs by Rob Shanahan capture one of my "Autumn Serenades," a lyrical expression with mallets improvised over a relaxed tempo in my beloved 3/4 ostinato (a repeating rhythmic foundation—from the Italian for "stubborn," funnily enough, like "obstinate"). It is my personal adaptation of Max Roach's "The Drum Also Waltzes," and that rhythmic frame remains a comfortable and creative warm-up every day, as it has for many years. Slowly, gradually, I moved on to some more recent experiments in rhythm, first with wire brushes (I've had a long secret love affair with brushes, unexpressed professionally as yet—note to self), then with sticks.

I once picked up a quote (though I've never learned its source) that I applied to Buddy Rich: "Genius is the fire that lights itself." It is also true that it is often in the nature of genius to light a fire in others. This year I have been listening to a variety of Jack DeJohnette's incredible span of work over his long and artfully productive career, including a stellar recording called *Parallel Realities*, with Pat Metheny and Herbie Hancock, and an entrancing duet called *Music from the Hearts of the Masters*, with Foday Musa Suso, a West African playing the kora (a stringed instrument resembling guitar and harp). Jack DeJohnette bridges the traditional and modern styles of drumming more than perhaps any living player, and his boundless virtuosity and improvisational eloquence lit that fire for me. (I wrote to Jack about the *Parallel Realities* album: "If I could play like one drummer in the world, it would be like you on that record.")

The late Ian Wallace spent a long and fairly successful career as a journeyman rock drummer, backing a wide range of artists from an early stint with King Crimson in his native England, to touring and recording with the likes of Bob Dylan, Jackson Browne, Don Henley, the Traveling Wilburys, and "the French Elvis," Johnny Hallyday. However, Ian had always wanted to be a jazz drummer, and later in life, he studied with my long-time teacher, Freddie Gruber. Typical of Freddie's other prominent students, like Steve Smith and Dave Weckl, and my own experience with him, one of Freddie's great gifts as a master teacher is that he is a different guide for each of us, according to what we need and want. Thus Freddie guided Ian in becoming the jazz drummer he wanted to be, and Ian's mastery of the style, plus his own confident and original voice, were beautifully evidenced on a CD called *King Crimson Songbook*, from a project close to Ian's heart, the Crimson Jazz Trio, which interpreted King Crimson songs in a traditional piano, bass, drums format. (Speaking of brushes, check out Ian's dazzling brushwork on "21st Century Schizoid Man.")

Ian was only sixty when he was struck down by cancer (I always have to think of it as *stupid* cancer, but sometimes only other bereaved survivors understand) in 2007—just at the moment when he had achieved a lifetime goal of supreme expression on his instrument. He had recently recorded a second CD with the Crimson Jazz Trio, and was planning a tour of jazz festivals for the following year, when all at once, *ba-da-boom*, it was all over for Ian Wallace. (And people believe in benevolent deities . . .)

Ian's widow, Marjorie, and his bandmates Tim Landers and Jody Nardone saw that second CD into production (*King Crimson Songbook Volume 2*), and my delight in Ian's playing on it is only partly because he was a lovely man with a tragic fate. His command of time and subtleties of dynamics, facility as a soloist, and faultless accompaniment to the other musicians all stood as a shining inspiration to me.

A highlight on that recording was the daring Latin feel Ian applied so successfully to "In the Court of the Crimson King," which inspired me to investigate a rhythmic area that in the past I had only "admired from afar," as it were.

One Big Concept I was determined to work on was a rhythmic approach I have wanted to explore for years, but have always set aside because I knew it would require a lot of time to develop. In the best layman's terms I can muster, it is a hybrid of two rhythmic paradigms: the emphasis on the upbeat or the downbeat. The upbeat tends to drive certain styles of music, like jazz and reggae, while the downbeat is the fundamental language—or at least the *accent* of the language—in blues and rock. I wondered if they couldn't be combined in a way that didn't shift between one and the other, but actually blended the two, playing both at the same time— what is called a polyrhythm.

F. Scott Fitzgerald once wrote, "The true test of a first-rate mind is the ability to hold two contradictory ideas at the same time." Well, I can't necessarily do that, but with a dedicated sufficiency of time and effort, I have found that my *body* can express one idea, and my mind the other—for example, after years of practice with the waltz, my feet can sustain a steady 3/4 pattern all day, while my brain directs my hands at improvising with complete freedom, playing absolutely anything, any time signature, any tempo. It took years, but I got there—conquered the ostinato by being obstinate.

The concept this time was to have my left foot keep a constant upbeat, as it would in fast swing music, say, while my right foot and hands would syncopate freely around the downbeat feel of rock and funk music. Sounds simple, and perhaps for some drummers it would be, but for me it was like the waltz had been at first—it was all I could do to keep that high-hat going, and play the simplest figures against it. The critical essence is that both rhythmic accents have to be *felt*, not just played, so in effect, you have to play two different songs at the same time.

Breakthroughs came slowly, one figure at a time, and along the way I discovered amazing relationships to well-known rhythms in that tension between upbeats and downbeats: samba, various jazz feels, West African patterns, ska and reggae, and the so-called second line style of drumming from New Orleans.

And it was so *musical*, I could play it for hours, because, like the waltz again, to improvise in that pattern was to play a *song*. An "Autumn Serenade."

The title comes from a big-band hit by Harry James, reflecting the kind of music I've been listening to a lot lately—a satellite music channel called '40s on 4. Artie Shaw, Benny Goodman, Gene Krupa, Buddy Rich, the Dorseys, Duke Ellington, Count Basie, Frank Sinatra, Billie Holiday, and so many great female "band singers," like Jo Stafford, Helen Forrest, Ella Fitzgerald, Eydie Gormé, and Anita O'Day—what a treasurehouse of classic, timeless music. (And a fine soundtrack for cooking at Bubba's Bar 'n' Grill!)

Also, when I started thinking about what I wanted to put into this story, I decided I wanted to make it a *song*—a serenade for the late summer and autumn of 2009.

"Autumn Rhythm" was another title I considered for my percussion *études*, and for this story, after a masterpiece by Jackson Pollock, exhibited at the Museum of Modern Art in New York City. Pollock's wife, Lee Krasner, was an important modernist painter in her own right, and she once offered a fundamental distinction that lesser artists often overlooked: "An abstract painting is still *of* something." I learned to understand that profound quality by experiences like standing before Jackson Pollock's monumental *Autumn Rhythm* in New York, and finally *getting* it. No reproduction can possibly hint at the effect of works like that, or his *Lavender Mist* at the National Gallery in Washington, D.C. Like Picasso's *Guernica*, van Gogh's feverish paint-handling, or major works by the Hudson River school, you have to witness their majestic scale, see the paint, its texture, the lyrical, even *sensual* power of its application and arrangement on the canvas.

In *Autumn Rhythm*, Pollock's gestural arabesques of dripped house-paint and carefully chosen tones and cadences *expressed* (that's where "Abstract Expressionism" comes from) the feeling of autumn by transcending the observed reality—the mood a representational painter would render in brightly colored trees and floating leaves on a mill pond (like those great lines from "Moonlight in Vermont": "Pennies in a stream/ Fallen leaves of sycamore"—more from '40s on 4).

My own favorite "Autumn Rhythm" is found in the Laurentian Mountains of Quebec. The blazing colors of fall foliage are the result of a certain combination of climate, elevation, and varieties of deciduous trees, and their majesty is only fully expressed in the boreal forests—in Canada, the Northeast U.S., Scandinavia, and Siberia. The Laurentians get that formula exactly right on all counts.

It has been quite a few years since I visited Quebec in autumn, and I was very excited about getting up there. I arrived on October 6, just at the "tail of the peak" for the fall colors, before wind and rain brought them down to carpet the forest floor, leaving the stark gray trunks and branches naked against the icy winds to come. The woods all around, and stretching away over the rounded hills behind the lake, were painted in brilliant reds, yellows, and oranges, all flaming among the dark green conifers. As I stood outside and looked around at the radiant beauty, the crisp air fragrant with wood smoke from my own fireplace, in a silence complete but for the hushed murmur of the stream, I uttered an involuntary, "Oh my."

Though my days there were gray and often rainy, the trees still seemed to gather and radiate color and light. Even indoors, the radiance was warm and luminous. Individual leaves of yellow or orange drifted down, turning and wafting like butterflies. An occasional leaf storm whirled about the house, a harbinger of blizzards to come.

Autumn is said to be a season of nostalgia, "pain for a lost home," and in the following rainy days, lazing and reading by the fire, I was reminded of other autumns, especially in that same area. Back in the early '80s, my bandmates and I were recording at nearby Le Studio. (Working there had introduced me to the Laurentian region, where I have had a home for almost thirty years.) The studio's guest house overlooked a small lake, with a steep wooded mountainside rising behind it, and that was the view from our breakfast table. On those brilliant October mornings, we noticed how the colors on that vast canvas of forest changed visibly from one day to the next—a new blaze of red, a flash of orange, a wash of yellow. One afternoon when the studio crew were busy with some technical job, Alex and Geddy and I rowed across the lake and climbed that mountainside, up to where I knew a ski trail crossed its high ridge.

It was a steep climb, but the October air was cool and delicious, and as we struggled upward, clinging to granite boulders and maple trunks, we laughed a lot at our lifetime's worth of shared jokes. Catching our breath at the top, we looked down over the kidney-shaped lake, with the guest house at one end and the studio at the other, then far away south over the low, rolling mountains in their polychrome paint.

I took out my Swiss Army knife and started carving our new band name into the smooth gray bark of a beech tree. It has long been our habit to invent sub-groups that encourage us to write and play in a different character than "us," and the early '80s version was a new-wave outfit called The Fabulous Men (responsible for such songs as "Vital Signs" and "Digital Man").

Another favorite sub-group was Rockin' F, which was more of a roots-rock combo, and often applied as an adjective: "That's Rockin' F!" Masquerading as Rockin' F gave us things like the second verse of "The Spirit of Radio" and the verses of "Force Ten," "Dog Years," and "Spindrift." (Riding through the Texas Hill Country on a hot July day last summer, I laughed to see a ranch called the Rockin' F—and later regretted not stopping to take a photo. I think it was just too hot.)

Somewhere up on that mountain in Quebec, along the Portageur ski trail, there's a beech tree with "The Fabulous Men" carved into it (if it hasn't grown over or fallen down in over twenty-five years).

In this autumn of 2009, the three of us are poised on another kind of "reinvention." We have agreed to meet in Los Angeles in November, and discuss our future. We learned many years ago that when we finish one long project—like a two-year tour following a year or so of writing and recording for *Snakes and Arrows*—we don't make any further plans for a while. It's good to feel truly *free* for a time, and to clear your mind to focus on what you'd really like to do next.

Of course, these are parlous times in the music business, so our time-honored pattern of touring, recording, and touring is no longer the obvious way to do things. The music world—or at least the *business* of it—is very different now, even since 2006, when we began work on *Snakes and Arrows*. The importance of "the album" is not what it was, and there is currently a reversion to a musical climate rather like the 1950s, when only "the song" matters. Radio, downloads, and "shuffle"

settings are inimical to collected works. Because of that reality, record company advances that used to pay for album projects are a thing of the past, so if that was what we wanted to do, we'd be on our own.

"Crisis is both danger and opportunity," goes the Chinese saying, and rather than lamenting the passing of the old way, we will figure out how to work with how things are now. In Nelson Algren's *The Man With the Golden Arm*, Frankie Machine explains to Sparrow why their neighborhood, and their lives, are going to hell: "That's just the new way of doin' things we got these days."

A resigned irony is conveyed there, and it applies to my feelings about some of the changes going on around us. It may not be the way we would choose, but I defer to a favorite expression of Professor Gruber's, drawn from a worldview dating from his childhood in the Bronx in the 1930s: "It is what it is."

I have been surprised to see that phrase mentioned as the "most hated" by some people, when I think it expresses a simple practicality of making the most of the current reality, not getting all exercised by what can't be altered. As stated earlier, "That's how it is, so okay."

The German philosopher Ludwig Wittgenstein gave this definition of reality: "The world is all that is the case." Typical of philosophical aphorisms, it is a deep little statement, but it certainly includes the idea that "It is what it is." I guess idealists ("It's not what it ought to be"), paranoids ("It's not what it seems"), cynics ("It is, but not very"), reactionaries ("It's not what *I* want it to be"), self-deluders ("It's not *my* is"), and rationalizers ("It's not my fault") would have trouble with that concept.

To this point, the three of us haven't even discussed what we might discuss, so to speak—so our ideas and shared enthusiasm for the entity of Rush will be fresh, spontaneous, and quite likely exciting. For myself, I'm open to anything we can all agree on. (I've pointed out before that in a three-piece band, we need *consensus*, not democracy—it's no good having one outvoted and unhappy member.) My favorite group activity is always songwriting and recording, and I've got some lyrical ideas and those new drumming frontiers to explore. However, those rhythmic concepts would also be inspiring for a new drum solo, if we decided to do a tour of some kind, maybe with an orchestra. We could write and record just a few songs, and release them some way. Or there were a couple of film-and-music projects we had discussed in the past. In any case, there are enough possibilities for future collaboration, and I am curious to see what we'll come up with.

Meanwhile, I'm watching the October rain fall, warmed by a blazing fire, and as always, delighted by the steady flight of visitors to my bird-feeder, Bubba's Seeds 'n' Suet. There's the inevitable cheerful throng of chickadees, occasional crack-head mobs of blue jays, a red-breasted nuthatch, downy woodpecker, hairy woodpecker, a few charcoal-gray juncos feeding on the ground, and some birds that are uncommon in winter, like white-crowned sparrows and goldfinches, probably stocking up before they move farther south. The finches are already fading from their brilliant yellow and black summer plumage to the dull buffy outfits they wear in winter. The first time I saw a goldfinch in its winter colors, I drove myself mental trying to identify it, until I found that season's wardrobe illustrated in the big *Birds of Canada* book.

My gallery of picture windows frames a series of watercolors of the autumn woods, vibrant hues subdued and softened by a wet gray haze. The rain on the metal roof is a delicate pattering of wire brushes on a snare drum, the fire a hiss and murmur of mallets on a cymbal, syncopated by sparks and snaps in a polyrhythmic Latin flourish.

Johnny Hartman sings the Harry James standard on '40s on 4:

Let the years come and go
I'll still feel the glow
That time cannot fade
When I hear that lovely autumn serenade.

FIRE ON ICE

FEBRUARY 2010

For once, this complicated and far-ranging story involves quite a lot of sports, and only a little news and weather. But let's start with the music.

"The Hockey Theme" was composed in 1968 by Vancouver native Dolores Claman (who would also be recognized by Ontarians of a certain age as having written "A Place to Stand" for the Ontario pavilion at the World's Fair in Montreal, Expo 67). Over the next forty years, Dolores Claman's theme became synonymous with the CBC's *Hockey Night in Canada* broadcasts. It is considered by many to be "Canada's second national anthem," as nearly every Canadian can hum that melody on demand, and serious hockey fans have the ringtone.

In 2008, some complicated publishing maneuvers resulted in the CBC, Canada's government-sponsored network, losing the rights to that music to Canada's largest independent network, CTV.

"Foul!," cried the congregation of devotees to *Hockey Night in Canada*—the time-honored and widest-received Canadian broadcast.

Hockey's place in the Canadian sensibility is hard to explain to citizens of other nations, and the effect of merely moving a TV theme song to another network is a fine example. The event caused an angry public outcry, with celebrity hockey fans like Mike Myers chiming in to criticize the CBC for letting that iconic music get away.

Meanwhile, CBC executives huffed and puffed, sternly insisting, "It's not about the song; it's about the *game*." Eventually the CBC's *Hockey Night in Canada* replaced Dolores Claman's dignified theme and its stately French horns with a Celtic-rock composition chosen by popular vote.

For their part, CTV planned to use the traditional theme for hockey broadcasts on their satellite sports network, TSN. A director at TSN, Eric Neuschwander, attended the Toronto performance of Rush's *Snakes and Arrows* tour, and at the climax of my drum solo, with the horn shots and big-band action, Eric thought, "Wouldn't it be cool if Neil played like that on 'The Hockey Theme'?" He brought the idea to Andy Curran at our office (who has since been promoted to Vice President of Hockey Affairs); Andy mentioned it to our manager, Ray, who then conveyed the offer to me.

My first reaction was to laugh out loud—at the incredible *irony* of it all. As a kid, I was skinny, weak, non-athletic, and spectacularly bad at every sport. On skates, my little twiggy ankles folded right over, and I more-or-less shuffled along the ice, until I fell down. At least the hockey stick was a helpful crutch to lean on, because among the stronger, faster boys, I never got near the puck—unless I wanted to play goalie—a cold, lonely, and often painful fate, without helmets, masks, or pads.

For a Canadian boy in those times, it was a humiliating struggle growing up that way, and—here's the thing—it would eventually be *drumming* that would make my redemption against those feelings of inadequacy, and against the bullies—the jocks and frat boys—who tormented my childhood and teenage years. And now, here I was being asked to play a drum solo that would open every NHL broadcast on TSN.

On the day of the recording and filming sessions for my version of "The Hockey Theme," I emailed this photograph to Mom and Dad— me standing behind my drums that were custom-painted with all the NHL logos, holding THE Stanley Cup, and about to record "Canada's second national anthem."

My caption was "Take *that*, bullies from fifty years ago!"

Clearly, many unanswered questions already leap up, waving their hands frantically. What about those fancy drums? Why was the Stanley Cup there? What's with the hat?

All will be revealed, patient reader, in the fullness of time.

Growing up in Southern Ontario in the 1950s and early '60s, hockey pretty much dominated our lives for half the year. Backyard rinks and frozen ponds, schoolyard debates about favorite teams and players, street hockey (as portrayed wonderfully, by Mike Myers again, in *Wayne's World*—"Car!," move the nets off the street, then back out, "Game on!"), little tabletop games with rods and levers, collecting hockey cards and clothespinning them against our bicycle spokes for that "motoring" sound, watching games on black-and-white television (old Uncle John always called it "the hockey match"), my father listening to games on the radio, or the sports report after dinner every weeknight at 6:45, Rex Stimers on CKTB (that broadcast is extra clear in memory, because 7:00 was my bedtime). Rex was a classic old-time sportscaster, and his game coverage was punctuated with colorful phrases rising to an intense shout: "He winds up and shoots—a *bullet-like* drive!" "Ohhh—a *ten-bell* save!"

Dad sometimes took me to the Garden City Arena (later the Rex Stimers Arena) on Sunday nights, to watch our Junior A team, the St. Catharines Teepees (for their sponsor then, Thompson Products, the automotive parts factory across St. Paul Street West from my dad's International Harvester dealership). The team's name was later changed to the St. Catharines Blackhawks, when they became a farm team for the Chicago Blackhawks in the NHL, back when there were only six in the Big Leagues: Toronto, Montreal, Chicago, Detroit, Boston, and New York. (As the league expanded to today's thirty teams, those became known as "The Original Six"—the inspiration for the hats I had made for this project, with their logos circa 1950.) With players moving up and down between St. Catharines and Chicago, and similarly with the other Junior A teams who came through, we saw many of the era's greats, and despite being nearer to Toronto and the Maple Leafs, surrounded by fans of that team or the arch-rival Montreal Canadiens, we became Chicago fans. They were the players we "knew."

At age eight or nine, I saw a notice in the *St. Catharines Standard* announcing tryouts for kids' hockey teams. I wince with sympathy now for my deluded little self, and for my mother—who must have known better, when she drove me to the arena that Saturday morning. I shuffled out on the ice among an army of ragtag boys, and followed the coaches' directions. (I'm pretty sure the backward skating was my real downfall, metaphorically and literally.)

I must have known I was hopeless; yet somehow I was not without *hope*—the teams would be announced the following week, and I actually ran for the paper and checked to see if I was on the list. I guess I imagined that my "secret talent" might have been recognized by a discerning coach. But no.

Another psychological awakening occasioned by hockey occurred one bitter winter day at around the same age, when my parents drove my friend Rick Caton and me to Martindale Pond, a broad expanse of ice big enough to be called a lake in many parts of the world. Rick and I had our sticks and a puck, but it was a one-sided game—Rick would just steal the puck from me and skate away effortlessly, every time. I became more and more frustrated, and was finally overwhelmed by a wave of murderous rage, the red mist. Some animal combination of envy and humiliation made me want to take my stick and swing it at Rick's head—anything to stop him.

Lucky for both of us I had no chance of catching him, but still— the power of that violent urge, and my own revulsion at it, was an early life lesson. It was the first time I remember feeling an inner moral reflex that would return many times in my life, when I would tell myself, as I did that day, "I don't want to be like *that*."

After another thirty years of observing myself and others, and many times thinking, "I don't want to be like *that*," I addressed the subject on a Rush album called *Hold Your Fire*. The lyrics of the individual songs shared the theme of "instinct," good and bad, and this one was called "Lock and Key."

> We carry a sensitive cargo
> Below the waterline
> Ticking like a time bomb
> With a primitive design
> Behind the finer feelings
> This civilized veneer
> The heart of a lonely hunter
> Guards a dangerous frontier
>
> The balance can sometimes fail
> Strong emotions can tip the scale . . .
>
> I don't want to face the killer instinct
> Face it in you or me
> So we keep it under lock and key

A few years after the Martindale Pond Incident, Rick Caton would be part of my young life's redemption—drumming—as he was the lead singer in my first band, mumblin' sumpthin'.

(The name—I know. Forty years later, I'm still having to explain it: a) It was 1967. b) We were fifteen years old. c) It came from a *Li'l Abner* comic strip.)

In adult life, music took precedence over sports, but my bandmates liked to watch hockey games on motel and studio lounge televisions, for example, so I did not escape observing and even getting *involved*—feeling the pain of becoming emotionally invested in something you were powerless to affect—like watching "your" team struggle and fail (that would be Toronto's Maple Leafs). Alex and Geddy had grown up in Toronto with longtime Montreal Canadiens forward Steve Shutt, and we would sometimes meet up with "Shuttie" in cities where we were both playing. (Further irony: Throughout our career, the band played in all of the NHL arenas, sharing the same "office space" as the hockey players.)

In the early '80s, touring with another Canadian band, Max Webster, we rented small hockey arenas after shows, suited up in skates and pads, and—in the middle of the night—played outrageously inept hockey for a couple of hours. (My ankles were stronger by then, and skates were better—but I still basically shuffled around the ice. Fun, though.)

Having lived mostly in the United States for the past ten years, whenever I get to my Quebec house in winter, I like to sit in front of the fire on a snowy evening and watch a hockey game. The whole experience—the game, the players, the fans, the announcers, the commercials, the weather—is like an intravenous shot of Canadiana.

And I guess that is how my lifetime relation to hockey could be described: basically "intravenous."

The timing for "The Hockey Theme" proposal was perfect. The band had been off that year, after three years of writing, recording, and touring, so I was eager for a new musical challenge. This one would be especially demanding, but I would have the time and energy to devote to it. And with the Blessèd Event of Olivia Louise's arrival that summer, it was great to be able to work close to home.

As recounted in "Autumn Serenade," I was deeply engrossed in drumming at that time, exploring styles and exercises that would feed straight into my approach to this performance. For example, I establish the Latin feel under the beginning, and the rolling tom sections echo my experiments in polyrhythms—staying firmly rooted to the downbeat, while my high-hat foot is playing alternating upbeats. Couldn't have done that a year ago.

So I had the time, and I had the place—Drum Channel boss Don Lombardi had been letting me use their studio when it wasn't busy, for practicing and working on ideas, and Garrison from the neighboring Drum Workshop factory had been setting up the "practice kit" for me. (I have referred to Terry Bozzio before as Drum Channel's "Artist in Residence"—now I was their "Student in Residence.") Right away Don and I were excited about documenting this project, and decided to film each step as it developed and grew—bigger than we ever imagined.

The time and the place—now for the people. The foremost collaborator I needed was an arranger, and once again, earlier musical adventures came into play unexpectedly, and combined to grow into an even *greater* one. For the previous year's Buddy Rich tribute concert, the bandleader had been Matt Harris (Buddy's last keyboard player, before his passing in 1987). Matt had done a terrific job of leading the band through a long night, with seven different drummers, and had also written some arrangements for Chad Smith and Terry Bozzio that I admired. I thought he was probably the perfect man for this job—and it turned out he had been a hockey player in his youth, and had gone to a hockey camp in Southern Ontario. An experienced musician and arranger, respected music educator at Cal State Northridge with a master's degree in music and a smelly hockey bag in his closet. I had found my man.

Don's crew filmed the first meeting between Matt and me, as we sat at the piano and discussed ideas for the arrangement, then played piano and drums (brushes) to explore different feels and tempos. The parameters were simple: I wanted to pay due respect to Dolores Claman's original composition, and the equally classic orchestration, to some degree, while making it more of a "solo drums" performance.

That performance had to be one minute long, no more, so that was a limitation of its own. I was determined to get "everything I know" into that one minute, so it would be as action-packed as I could make it. Matt and I discussed having a quiet passage, for example, a Latin feel vamping away softly as a contrast to the full-out drums-and-horns sections, but soon decided, "We don't have time for that."

Matt would contract the musicians for the actual recording, from the cream of L.A. session players, and also offered to set up a rehearsal with his students—as he had done before the Buddy Rich concert in 2008. It would be a great experience for them, and a chance for Matt and me to iron out any problems in the final week before the Big Day—now finalized as December 7, six weeks away.

As I started working on my drum part, Andy (Vice President of Hockey Affairs) brought me a request from Eric, the director at TSN—he wanted me to record the performance first in a recording studio, then move to a soundstage (on the same day) and reproduce it for the cameras—without microphones all over the place, and with more control of lighting and camera angles. At first I was reluctant. You can't "lip-sync" drums, of course, as drumming is so physi-

Matt's students appeared as background musicians in the film shoot

cal that it's not "fakeable." When you watch somebody try, and hear something completely different from what you're seeing, it's painfully, humorously obvious.

Ideally (freighted word), I would have preferred to record and film it live, as a matter of "purist" authenticity. But I understood the director's wish, from a visual professional's point of view, to make it look as good as possible. The alternative—recording in a giant soundstage where they could also film, would be a compromise acoustically. At least doing it their way would result in the best possible sound, and that was the main thing. And in any case, I always hate to seem "difficult." Half-jokingly, I told Andy, "I can do it—because I am a *professional.*" In the filming of past band videos, I had simply played along to a part I knew well, so the experience was the same for me, and hopefully similar for the viewer. But the gist here was that I would have to work out "a part I knew well," with no unrepeatable improvising, and deliver it exactly the same, again and again. It's one thing to do that for a song, becoming familiar with it through the process of writing, rehearsing, and recording—over a period of many months, usually—but for this action-packed minute, with only a few weeks to prepare, I would have to refine every beat into a seamless, repeatable sequence of drum events.

Meanwhile, Andy was looking into studios and soundstages, and had talked with Rush's recent coproducer on *Snakes and Arrows*, Nick Raskulinecz (Booujzhe). He was excited about the project, too, and having Booujzhe onboard to supervise the recording and mixing was a major boost to my confidence in the outcome.

I had the time, the place, and the people—now I needed the drums.

For those, I simply went across the road from Drum Channel to the offices of Drum Workshop, builders of the world's finest drums. (Handy, that.) The last two Rush tours, *R30* and *Snakes and Arrows*, featured lavishly customized drumsets, while for the Buddy Rich tribute DW built me a beautiful set in classic white marine pearl with gold hardware.

A tribute to Drum Workshop's artistry is that for over a year the R30 kit has been on display at the American Motorcycle Association's museum in Columbus, Ohio—along with the *Ghost Rider* bike—and was a centerpiece at the instrument maker's trade show, NAMM, then did a tour of drum clinics across the U.S. and Canada—just the drums, not me! Plus DW built thirty replicas (each costing an equal number of thousands of dollars), which found enthusiastic buyers. The *Snakes and Arrows* set was recently exhibited at the Percussive Arts Society's trade event in Indianapolis, and the Buddy Rich tribute kit was bought off the stage after that concert and is on permanent display at a drum store in Pennsylvania. We only jump ahead in the story a little to reveal that the "hockey drums" would be exhibited at NAMM in January 2010 and were later a major display at the Hockey Hall of Fame in Toronto.

(To jump ahead just a little farther, my bandmates and I will be inducted into the Canadian Songwriters Hall of Fame in March of this year—along with Dolores Claman! A total, wonderful coincidence.)

(And isn't it funny that by then the band will have been represented in the Motorcycling Hall of Fame, the Hockey Hall of Fame, the Canadian Music Hall of Fame, the Songwriting Hall of Fame, and the Modern Drummer Hall of Fame—but not yet in the "official" rock pantheon? Passing strange . . .)

Between the *R30* and *Snakes and Arrows* tours, 2005–06, I had been using a less-decorative "recording kit" from DW, in a beautiful natural wood finish. Those drums had sounded fantastic through some recording I did for Vertical Horizon's *Burning the Days* album, and all of the recording for *Snakes and Arrows*. They had since been outdone in both sound and looks by the *Snakes and Arrows* touring kit, with further developments in shell design as well as the flashy Aztec Red, gold leaf, and black nickel hardware, but I suggested to DW's drum guru John Good that we take the recording kit out of the warehouse and refinish the shells in some hockey theme.

It just seemed resourceful to me (I'm all about Reduce, Reuse, Recycle), but John would have none of that. He shook his head firmly, "We have to start from scratch." He knew he could make something better.

The date of that meeting was October 21, 2009, and the shoot was scheduled for early December, so there wasn't an abundance of time. John and I met in the DW boardroom with shell-construction foreman Shon, hardware specialist Rich, artists' rep (and invaluable member of my West Coast Pit Crew when my drum tech Lorne Wheaton isn't available) Garrison, and the company's great artist in drum finishes, Louie. Don and cameraman/editor Jose captured the scene for our "Making Of" documentary.

Back in September, in the "Autumn Serenade" period, my mom and dad were visiting, and I took Dad for his second tour around Drum Workshop. He said later, "It's just wonderful to see people so *enthusiastic* about their work." That describes the atmosphere at a meeting to discuss a new drumset.

John offered his thoughts on the selection of wood plies and reinforcing hoops he would apply to each of the different shells, and consulted with Shon on the materials and methods. Louie had already looked into the different team logos, and had some ideas for the basic finish I wanted—"ice-blue pearlescent," we called it, like the color of artificial ice. Louie had looked up the geometry of the NHL hockey rinks, red lines, blue lines, and faceoff circles, and we agreed to try to bring that into the design.

I quizzed Louie on whether the center lines were solid or dotted, and he reported, "Five of the six Canadian NHL rinks have dotted lines." He had done his research. And he had his work cut out for him, too. Each color, on each logo—thirty different ones, on nine different-sized shells—had to be masked and sprayed separately, one tiny patch of color at a time. Every few days I would drop by the factory, with the Drum Channel cameras, to watch that work in progress. (One small preference I expressed to Louie was to give "pride of place" to the logos for teams for which I felt a "hometown" affinity: so those for Toronto, Montreal, and Los Angeles are featured in front panels.)

I had a vision of blue chrome hardware ("like icicles," I described it to the DW guys), and wondered if that might be possible. Rich showed us some colored finishes that were powder-coated or anodized, but what I wanted had to be shinier. Since this drumset wouldn't have to go on tour and suffer the ravages of the road, it was decided that *painting* was the solution—Louie would ghost a translucent blue over the chrome, and although it would be fragile, it would look like blue chrome.

Matt prepared a demo of an arrangement for me, and I started working with it—playing on the "practice kit" described in "Autumn Serenade." Again and again I played along with that "one hot minute," as I had come to think of it. (On Day One, I learned to start the iPod and drop it into my breast pocket facing *outward*, or while I played along, the heat building inside me had the same thermo-sensitive effect as a rotating finger, and pinned the volume.)

Imagine, if you will, air-drumming as hard and fast as you can for the next minute. (Try it if no one's watching.) That will give some idea of what it means to say, "I played that one-minute piece of music fifteen or twenty times a day, three or four times a week, for six weeks."

Every few days, I would record an updated version with Drum Channel's audio engineer, Kevin, and go away and listen to it. Then I would think, "Another drum figure would fit there—and there."

"Gotta smooth out that transition from straight time to triplet feel."

"Maybe I could get that hockey stomp, '*Boom—Boom—Boom-boom-boom, Boom-boom-boom—Boom—Boom*,' under that snare roll."

(During the previous couple of tours, whenever we played in hockey arenas, I had been adding that "stomp" to the improvised part of my solo—a subtle joke you hope the keen-witted might catch. Or at least you might amuse your bandmates and crew.)

I'd go back and practice some more, then record yet another version to check out in the car and at home. About two weeks into it, Matt sent me a new arrangement, which put more of the drum action at the end instead of the beginning. Being already so "deep" into the previous version, I was a little daunted at first. But I saw what he intended, and reconfigured my part to suit.

The "Drummers Only" version of this story will appear in a more detailed beat-by-beat breakdown (drummer porn), via Drum Channel's "Making Of" documentary. However, among the lively photos taken by my friend Craiggie (*Dunkelkammer*), one tells a very expressive story of things I have learned about playing the drums, and tried to express in educational material.

My hands and arms are flailing away, far over to my right, pounding those floor toms with all my might, while my body and face (and blazing eyes!) are focused on where I'm going next—that sixteen-inch crash cymbal in front of me. Such an alignment, an advance setup, as it were, will allow me to make the transition smoothly, under control, and be centered and balanced to keep playing at full force.

In a recent edition of Bubba's Book Club, I wrote about a novel called *The Art of Racing in the Rain*, which contained thoughts about driving a racecar that I had found to be true. One of those—"The car goes where your eyes go"—has a nice relation here, as does something I learned while trying to master telemark skiing (pathetically, but earnestly, as usual). While wobbling my way down the hill, picking myself up from yet another fall, I overheard an instructor tell another beginner, "Always keep your upper body pointed down the hill." So he'd be able to pivot his legs and arms around a stable base, I realized. "Well, yeah," I thought, "why didn't I think of that?" (Because I *never* think of things like that—it's why I always need good teachers.)

I think I have remarked before about riding a motorcycle on a racetrack, "If you're in one corner, and not already thinking about the *next* corner, you're in trouble." It's true with a car, too. And, per the above, on the drums. The heat of inspiration and adrenaline must be cooled by reason—restraint. In an interview for a motorcycling magazine, I described it as "poise in motion." It could also be defined as "Fire on Ice"—heat tempered by conscious control. (Like that violent temper—another intentional twist on the album title *Hold Your Fire*.)

Somewhere along the way, "Fire on Ice" was a title I proposed for the theme music—indeed for the whole hockey project, the whole *concept*. A description of the game itself, a title for TSN's broadcasts, the visuals they could use in a montage to go with the opening theme (flashing skate blades leaving a trail of fire; a "hockey stop" in a shower of sparks; a puck blazing like a meteor and scorching into the goalie's glove in a sizzle of smoke). The title had been used for a book about one team's Stanley Cup win, for a figure skater's autobiography, and—I was told—for an Ice Capades show, but not for anything like this.

However, no one else up the ladder at TSN seemed to take up the vision, and it wasn't my place to do anything more than share the idea. So I decided to use the title for my own story, at least, and maybe Drum Channel's documentary.

Another vision I had was for Booujzhe to produce an "extended mix" of that one-minute performance, in the spirit of the over-the-top dance mixes of the 1980s. We could deconstruct the orchestration and experiment with rhythmic loops and such—have fun with it, and easily make it several minutes long. With that in mind, I decided to work up a "quiet version" of the theme, in which I would minimize the drum part and play it softly, with a view toward adding percussion overdubs for texture and atmosphere. Perhaps TSN could use that as an "outro" theme, under their credits, or at least, the elements would be useful in that extended mix.

Working on that "Quiet Version" gave me a nice physical break from the "Loud Version," and—perhaps surprisingly—took just as much painstaking labor to refine. It is less "pyrotechnical," drumming wise, but required a delicate touch, superhuman restraint (merely keeping time through the "solo" sections), and perfect control and feel—the kind of approach I had worked on in my studies with Peter Erskine in 2008, so it was great to have a chance to *express* it.

December 7, 2009, the Big Day, was uncharacteristically rainy for Los Angeles, but as I drove east to Hollywood, hissing along Sunset Boulevard toward Ocean Way Studios (where Booujzhe and my bandmates and I had mixed *Snakes and Arrows*), my excitement was certainly not dampened.

One of Frank Sinatra's best television specials, "A Man and His Music" (1965), opened like that—a shot from a distant rooftop of his sleek, elegant Dual-Ghia driving through a dark, rain-wet studio lot and up to the door of a soundstage. Nothing and no one else around, Big Frank walked from the car and opened a door into a large, bright studio full of musicians. That's how I felt pulling up to Ocean Way in my sleek, elegant Aston Martin—though unlike Frank's suave entrance, I had to run through the rain. (No one can ever be as cool as Frank Sinatra. As his friend Dean Martin put it, "It's Frank's world— we just live in it.")

The above photo shows me giving my "speech" to the musicians before we began—about what this piece of music signified to Canadians. "Just remember that every man, woman, child, granny, moose, and beaver in Canada will hear this performance."

And . . . while we recorded, we were inspired by the presence of a sacred hockey icon, the real, actual Stanley Cup, sitting in the middle of the room.

It happened that a representative from the Hockey Hall of Fame was in town to display the Cup at a Los Angeles Kings game the previous night, and he was able to bring it by the studio for a few hours.

The Cup's traveling companion and attendant, Craig, allowed me to lift that treasured Canadian symbol (more than a hundred years old) out of its road case and hold it up high (it weighs thirty-five pounds), like I was a hockey player whose team had just won the Stanley Cup. The earliest inscription was inside the bowl, for a game in 1904, in which "The Kenora Wanderers Beat Ottawa." Every winning team since was engraved on silver bands around the sides (they add another level to the base when it gets too full). I stood behind my drums for the cameras, holding up that Cup, and thinking, "Take *that*, bullies from fifty years ago."

Thanks to that inspirational presence, the ace musicians, Matt's charts, my preparation, those state-of-the-art drums, and Booujzhe—who produced a magnificent drum sound, and worked well with Matt to get the best out of the orchestra—we were able to get the music recorded pretty quickly that morning. First we did the "Quiet Version," then the "Loud Version."

Then the drums had to be moved to the soundstage, and were broken down by Garrison, his partner in my West Coast Pit Crew, Chris from cymbal-makers Sabian, and some of the Drum Channel crew. (I told Don later that it was wonderful to see him, the president, with his rain-wet hood over his head as he helped with the loadout.)

My one regret is that I was called over to the soundstage for the filming just as percussionist Brian Kilgore was preparing to do his overdubs. When I heard the "Loud Version" later, the tympani notes he added were just *perfectly* placed, either reinforcing my parts or finding gaps I hadn't imagined (like after my little splash-cymbal slapstick), and the orchestra chimes gave it a proper, classical grandeur. But in those parts, Brian was just playing (however perfectly) what Matt had written. For the "Quiet Version," the percussion parts would be entirely improvised, and that's where Brian really shone. On my way out, I had suggested perhaps he could try bongos and congas, and that I was looking for a certain "Lalo Schifrin" vibe (like the original *Mission Impossible* theme). When I got back, and Booujzhe played me what they had done, Brian's contributions on shaker, rainstick, and bongos were creative, tasteful, and atmospheric. What a pleasure it was for me to work with musicians of that caliber.

I had mentioned to Andy early on that the film people couldn't expect me to do limitless takes of this performance. As I said, there was no "faking it," and I knew from my rehearsals that my One Hot Minute was a killer to keep repeating.

But they too were professional and well organized, and managed to keep it down to eight separate performances, for different lighting and camera angles. Again, I just played my carefully orchestrated and rehearsed part as well as I could, while they did their work.

Having completed the film shoot, and an interview in front of TSN's cameras, by late afternoon I was back at Ocean Way, sipping a Macallan in the control room while Booujzhe started mixing. The hard stuff was over now, and I was happy just to sit back and listen to the results, over and over, and later that night, have a CD to take home with me.

The rain had tapered off, but the neon and streetlights reflected on the wet pavement of Sunset Boulevard. Now I could finally start to get some perspective on the day's events, and I realized it had gone, well, *perfectly*. Thanks to all that preparation, and to a great team of people, I had delivered the performance I wanted as accurately as I could have hoped (and quickly too). I smiled to think that, all told, it had been one of the great experiences of my life. How rare and wonderful to be able to "think that out loud"—to make such a plain statement of superlative fact, without exaggerating or "playing to the crowd" one little bit. All of that work had been worth it.

One of Craiggie's photographs that really spoke to him and me is an image only a friend could have captured. Between takes at the film shoot, I was looking over at Craiggie on the sidelines, smiling as if to say, one Canuck to another, "Pretty neat, eh?"

Or that smile might be saying, "Take *that*, bullies from fifty years ago!"

19

TIME MACHINES

MAY 2010

It was a summer Saturday in 1970, and I was playing with the band J. R. Flood in St. Catharines, Ontario. We were set up on the back of a flatbed trailer on James Street, closed to traffic for a Saturday "whoopee." The idea was for us to entertain the youngsters, confound the adults, and share a $250 fee. Pictured are the late organist Bob Morrison and guitarist Paul Dickinson, and we had bass guitarist Wally Tomczuk and singer Gary Luciani. I was seventeen.

All of those guys were pivotal in my musical development—each in his own way. Bob as a consummate, consumed artist; Paul as an exacting, disciplined, yet passionate musician; Wally as a solidly grounded person whose equally grounded bass playing kept my flights of fancy rooted in "real time"; and Gary as a lead singer, lyricist, and front man who somehow managed to leave ego out of that job description (and who was the first singer to sing my lyrics).

An old photograph is a powerful time machine. Personally, I haven't kept any scrapbooks or albums for a long time, but lately a lot of my "pre-modern"—even *ancient*—history has been emerging from heaven-knows-where, sent to me in emails and envelopes from various sources.

Now I wonder with some trepidation, "What will they find a photograph of *next*?" It seems every possible file of ancient yearbook photos has been finely combed, and many dusty boxes of black-and-white prints by amateur photographers have been found in basements and attics.

Back in the late '60s and early '70s, hardly anyone I knew had a decent camera, and considering the cost of film and developing, the few that existed were more sparingly used. Nowadays every handheld device can take a picture.

(That was one of my suggestions for the title of our tour this summer: "RUSH: Handheld Devices." But eventually, for all good reasons, "Time Machine" won out.)

In any case, it is remarkable that such images as these were taken, saved, put away and lost for several decades, and found again. Then that they made their way to me—forty years later and 3,000 miles away.

Looking at this particular image can send me off in so many directions. My eyes go straight to those drums, the first good set I ever owned: gray ripple Rogers. Not long after that photo was taken, I stripped them down to the bare shells in my bedroom, painstakingly disassembling all of the hardware, and covered the gray ripple wrap with "chrome" wallpaper, to emulate Keith Moon's *Tommy* kit. Only two years or so previously, I had added the second eighteen-inch bass drum (little cannons like that represented a certain "style" then—a hangover from mod, I guess), and another twelve-inch tom. In addition, I had a fourteen-inch floor tom, a chrome "Powertone" snare (a model below the Dynasonic I coveted), thirteen-inch high-hats on a stand with a homemade height-extender, and two Zildjian cymbals, a twenty-inch and an eighteen.

That day, I remember my twenty-incher was cracked, and I couldn't afford a new one. A friend of the band's, Greg, was a local drummer who had a somewhat less *violent* playing style than my own, but he lent me his twenty-inch Zildjian for that show. I still consider that a brave and generous act. (I didn't break it.)

My pantlegs are rolled up like a clown to prevent the bass-drum-pedal beaters from fouling in my flares (I use a bicycle clip these days), and the drumsticks are played backward, "butt-end," because I couldn't afford to replace broken ones, so turned them around and used the other end. I'm sitting on a little square pillow ("liberated" from my mom) atop an upturned metal barrel (in which my dad's farm equipment dealership sold calcium carbide for bird-scarers—*sigh*, so much needs to be explained when you're telling about a time machine: Those bird-scaring devices looked like a long megaphone atop a box, and they made a loud explosive noise from time to time, to scare birds out of orchards and vineyards). That steel barrel also served as a hardware case, because after the gig I could fill it with the stands and pedals.

A drumset is a time machine, literally speaking—a machine for keeping time—though a drummer has to be the clockwork device to subdivide rhythm—to *bring the time*.

In those days, I was not that drummer.

In the opening photo, guitarist Paul is giving me what I can only describe as an "incredulous" look (he was both disciplined and disciplinarian, and I learned a lot from Paul in those days, like how to watch his tapping foot—a time machine if ever there was one—to keep the tempo). At that moment, I was probably racing away. When I hear the demos we made in those days, I find myself thinking, "For heaven's sake—give that drummer a *Valium!*" (Or a metronome.)

The spectacles on the optician's sign remind me of the eyes on the billboard in *The Great Gatsby*, which Fitzgerald used as a symbol for an impassive onlooker, a remote, uncaring deity, seeing all, changing nothing. "The stars look down."

To any drummer who has sweated over a particular set of drums, they represent another kind of time machine—like a classic violin or guitar, a part of one's life. Still, I don't get emotional about my old drumsets, and have given most of them away.

Happily, the Rogers are still in the possession of my friend Brad, who has restored them beautifully, stripping off the cheesy chrome wallpaper to reveal the classic gray ripple finish. A couple of years back I had the opportunity to play them again, in Brad's basement, with him playing guitar, and we had a fine time.

No, I didn't feel transported into the past, but it was fun to *share* a piece of it. And I wished I could have communicated a few observations to that kid who used to play those drums, so many long years ago. Even just to tell him, "Your 'time' will come."

Going back even farther in the Wayback Machine—early 1968 is my best guess—the previous shot is a kind of miracle. Amazing that it was taken at all, and that it survived, got passed around, and made its way to my mailbox (thanks Joe) more than forty years later. "Garnet's Head Shop" is the scene, in a former barber shop near the intersection of St. Paul and Geneva Streets in St. Catharines (and right near Ostanek's Music Centre, my other favored hangout in those days).

Garnet, second from the right, later went even farther into outlaw territory, becoming a biker gang leader, while the future me is in the middle, fifteen-going-on-sixteen, girlfriend Debbie behind me, beside her best friend Linda, whose fringed jacket I was wearing—with flood pants and penny loafers, retina-bruising T-shirt, and unruly bangs. I am captured midway between geek and freak, I guess. Behind the girls is Norbert, our token U.S. draft dodger, and popular guide for people taking their first acid trips. This single image could be a photo-essay from the pages of *Life*.

All kinds of time travel in this shot, too—past, present, and future. The car is the actual time *machine*, a 1964 Aston Martin DB5. It evokes an era, the early '60s, I didn't really live through, as an adult (I was twelve when it was made), but even today it represents a purity of driving involvement and mechanical art to which I certainly *aspired*. In its day, the DB5 was the ultimate Grand Tourer, hand-crafted, powerful, luxurious, and elegant (Italian styling allied to the British "feel" for engineering). After being featured in several James Bond movies, beginning with *Goldfinger* (1964) and continuing to *Casino Royale* (2006), the DB5 became known as "The Most Famous Car in the World" (though the first Aston Martin I remember seeing a photograph of as a boy was an earlier model, the DB Mark III, which was actually Bond's car in the *Goldfinger* novel).

As a general thing, I try to avoid talking about the material things I have been fortunate enough to acquire, not wanting to seem to brag—and definitely not wanting to arouse in others the evil worm of *envy*. One psychologist theorized that the possession of material things was a prop to make you feel good about yourself—but I thought that theory went two words too far. For me, owning a fine car, a fine watch, or a fine set of drums just makes me feel *good*, period. Some owners of old cars like to brag about how much *attention* their pride and joy receives—but I consider that a downside. Sometimes I wish I could press a button and make my DB5 look like, oh, a Prius—not to arouse envy, or even *notice*, in passersby.

For some, the fantasy might be that if you can afford to buy a beautiful old car, then you could just drive around in it, looking surpassingly cool.

Oh no. Nothing is that easy. An old car—especially an old *English* car—will *test* you.

You have to man up to that challenge, and become *engaged* with the machine. I suffered through many "adventures" with that DB5 (recalling the rally driver's comment, after her car skidded off a snowy road and rolled onto its roof: "Adventures suck when you're having them"). Breakdowns, overheating, having to refuel without turning off the engine (it wouldn't start when hot), flatbed recoveries, and roadside repairs with Swiss Army knife and emery board were part of that adventure.

After three years, including a couple of concert tours and lengthy service visits that kept me from driving the car, the "testing" has stretched over 12,000 miles, and we've been through all that now—me, the car, and master mechanic Ken Lovejoy, who loves the car nearly as much as I do. His shop is "conveniently" located 350 miles from my home, up in the Bay Area, but that has allowed for many memorable road trips, often with my friend Matt Scannell, who also loves cars and journeys (and gosh, we make each other laugh), and occasioned some "adventures," too. An overnight in Big Sur, one of my favorite parts of California, is a bonus—breaking down there, not so much.

Having invested in mechanical rebuilds and upgrades, and survived the adventures, now I have a reliable more-or-less daily driver (proved by the cloth grocery bags in the trunk—or, "boot"). More old cars perish from neglect than from overuse, and the more I drive it, the better it runs.

As for the reward for all of that effort and expense, it can still best be expressed by the time machine of a song—"Red Barchetta." Written thirty years ago, set in a future dystopia that still looms in the fears of paranoid petrolheads—a time when motorcars, and motorcycles, are outlawed—its description of driving pleasure remains as evocative as I could hope to express now.

> Wind in my hair
> Shifting and drifting
> Mechanical music
> Adrenaline surge
>
> Well-weathered leather
> Hot metal and oil
> The scented country air
> Sunlight on chrome
> The blur of the landscape
> Every nerve aware

The idea of rewriting those lines, vis-à-vis the DB5, came to mind:

> Wind in my hair

[Windows always open, 'cause there's no AC]

> Shifting and drifting

[Slipping and sliding on those skinny bias-ply tires]

> Mechanical music

[Vroom-vroom—ka-ching!]

> Adrenaline surge

[The clutch pedal just went to the floor and stayed there]

> Well-weathered leather

[Need to repair passenger seat-back]

> Hot metal and oil

[Is that temperature gauge creeping up too high?]

> The scented country air

[Windows always open, 'cause there's no AC]

> Sunlight on chrome

[Note to have the door handles redone]

> The blur of the landscape

[With due regard to the California Highway Patrol—and at night, the failed speedometer light—requiring an occasional check with Maglite]

> Every nerve aware

[Is that temperature gauge creeping up too high?]

A modern car—like perhaps the DB5's present-day descendant, the DB9—is another kind of time machine: a glimpse of the future. So far superior in power, handling, and sheer *competence*, the DB9 is a space ship—yet one that would be recognizable to Jules Verne or H.G. Wells, its streamlined aluminum hull comfortably upholstered in wine-colored leather and polished walnut.

In the previous photograph, I was driving the old DB5 home from Drum Channel, south on the Pacific Coast Highway near Zuma Beach—with California fan palms tossed in the onshore breeze—after a hard day's drumming. Next to Zuma Beach is Point Dume, pronounced "Doom" (both Chumash Indian names, like Malibu and Topanga), and that always reads to me like a cryptic kind of cautionary tale—Zooma to Doom.

The first three weeks at Drum Channel were just me and Lorne "Gump" Wheaton, my drum tech for almost ten years. Playing through the songs, learning them in some cases, revisiting them in others, I was also building up my calluses, and my stamina, to "performance grade."

And what a clockwork complication of thoughts revolved in my brain during that one-hour drive up to work and back—"Remember that fill in 'Camera Eye,'" "Have a listen to that part of 'MalNar' and get it right," "Try that Latin bass-drum ostinato under the African samples for the solo."

During the first three days, Gump and I were joined by the band's longtime keyboard and sampling consultant, Jim Burgess, and he and

I auditioned about 200 sampled sounds—industrial, ethnic, manufactured, and electronic—looking for new material for my drum solo. I selected three different arrays of sounds, tonal soundscapes, that I improvised on every day, looking for shapes and patterns that pleased me, and working out a new "architecture" for this tour's solo.

One interesting insight: Among those 200 sounds were arrays of drums from West Africa, India, Asia, and the Middle East. I was curious about that last category, because I never think of Middle Eastern music as particularly rhythmic. And sure enough, all of those drum sounds were flat, toneless, and uninspiring, as compared with some of the West African ones, or the Indian tablas, which expressed such a *complexity* of tone and timbre. Musical history states that only European composers ever developed harmony, but I remember mentioning to Jim about a drum from Benin—its sound did contain harmony, as does the West African djembe, now that I think of it, a range of pitches that give voice to far more power of communication than the dull "thud" of the Middle Eastern drums.

Over lunch one day with some of the Drum Channel guys, and visiting percussion master Alex Acuña, I suggested that perhaps Islamic extremism had arisen from just that unfortunate deprivation—a lack of decent drums.

"Why do infidels have all the good drums? They must die! Derka, derka, muhammed jihad!"

The previous photo was taken at Blackbird Studios in Nashville, on Tuesday, April 13, 2010, while I was being the "time machine"—recording drum parts for two new Rush songs. Alex, Geddy, and I had put them together over the winter and spring, mostly by long distance (Geddy emailing me from Toronto to report on his and Alex's progress in his home studio, and to request lyrical alterations), even as we were planning our *Time Machine* tour. We had never done anything like that before—write, arrange, record, and release just two songs, instead of a whole album—then go out on tour and play them, along with what we thought was an inventive selection of our older songs. But the real-time time machine—*life*—has brought many changes to what used to be called the "music business," and we thought, "Why not?"

I was using the *Snakes and Arrows* kit for that session, and now, rehearsing for the tour at Drum Channel, I was playing a mish-mash of a setup, based on the "Hockey Kit," that Gump had successfully assembled for me to work with—because just around the corner, at Drum Workshop, a spectacular new drumset was under construction, down to the final details of finishing and assembly. Sometimes Gump and I took a "field trip" over to the factory, to check on its progress.

As I played through the old songs the three of us had agreed to resurrect for the *Time Machine* tour, some of which I hadn't played live in ten years, twenty years, or *ever*, it occurred to me that the ultimate time machine might be a *song*. What else can immediately take you to a particular moment in time—an indelible memory that overwhelms you with its completeness? Smells are famously powerful memory stimulators, and—as we have seen—images of the past can have an intense effect of revitalizing the olden days. But when it comes to really *taking* you somewhere, there is nothing like a song.

And it doesn't have to be only about memory. It happens that the two songs we recorded that day in Nashville are detached from the past, rooted in the present, and pointed toward the future. Because they are the first two parts of what we envision as an extended album-length story, they truly are a work in progress, and thus a glimpse of our own future. Some sneer at the notion of "progressive" music, but I am pleased to note that I'm still progressing—several elements of my drum parts in those songs contain discoveries in technique and knowledge that I have only acquired in the past couple of years—studying with Peter Erskine, playing the Buddy Rich tribute concert, recording "The Hockey Theme," and just generally moving through time, as a drummer.

(No one moves through time like a drummer!)

Books, I think, are a different kind of time machine. Instead of reminding you of a lost world, they create one for you. More personal, more intimate—unlike movies, say, the world you experience while reading a book has been lived and envisioned entirely from the *inside*, and its contours are yours alone.

This pile of volumes represents my reading list for ten days in late February, a solitary winter retreat that was somewhat marred by bad weather, and being under the weather, so I had nothing better to do than lie by the fire and turn the pages. (If there *really* is a heaven . . .)

Obviously these titles are all future material for Bubba's Book Club, but just looking at the *spines* now, the stories, images, scenes, characters, and moods conveyed to me, as the reader, are near infinite. A treasure chest, a time capsule, a time machine with access to so many worlds.

"Oh, the places you'll go," said Dr. Seuss, and for this traveler, there's no way I'd rather go than by motorcycle. And it too can be a time machine, taking me to places where the past seems alive, but carried forward into the present. And that present—the day's weather, scenery,

wildlife, and humanity—is experienced with raw nerve-endings.

As for the future, it's always right there—the road ahead of my front wheel.

But so far humans don't really have a way to send ourselves into the future—with the sole exception of transmitting our DNA through the delightful medium of *babies*. Some might say creating something beautiful that endures is a kind of immortality, but even if a story or

a song survives into the future, it can't take *you* with it.

Baby can do that.

Carrie and I had welcomed Olivia into the world the previous August, and I was surprised to find that even as our home was caught up in a tempest, a whirlwind, a tornado—which carried us not to Oz, but to Planet Olivia—I was still inspired to *work*. Stories, book reviews, recipes, days of drumming labor on "The Hockey Theme," and a whole album's worth of lyrics, all were created in moments stolen from the compelling priorities of helping to care for baby, and feeding the family (indirectly in Olivia's case, but still . . .).

No doubt part of that urge was a result of the hardwired male conditioning to be the "breadwinner," to bring home the bacon (as well as "fry it up in a pan"), but some of it was a response to the *muse*.

We all revolved around Planet Olivia, orbiting like weather and communications satellites, fixed by her gravity, and by her radiance. Psychologists tell us that nearly everything men do is in some way related to the primal desire to "impress chicks," and that reflex seemed to be working its mojo on me. This little bundle of bittersweet joy was telling me to quit messing around and get to work.

But first, let's play and read books.

And so we did.

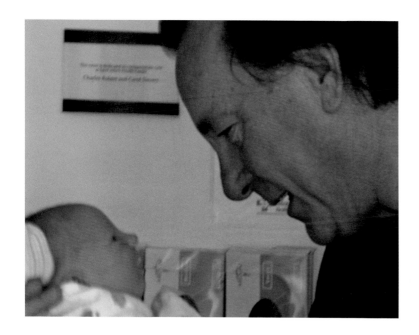

20

THEME AND VARIATIONS

AUGUST 2010

Since at least 2004, during the thirtieth anniversary tour I wrote about in *Roadshow*, I have been talking about a theme for a book, and even chipping away at it (mostly in my head, but partly in these stories). I referred to that imaginary book as *Roadcraft: How to Work the World*, and the aim was to assemble a set of rules for travelers that deliberately paralleled rules about living, working, making music—metaphors, like.

However, the more I continued to think about that goal, the more I realized it was not a book you could just sit down and *write*—it would have to *accumulate*, like experience, a journey, a life, and (indulge me here) a drum solo. In the flow of rhythm, dominant patterns arise and gather gravity over time, and suggest parallels that can be further developed and expressed—variations on a theme.

It has become obvious to me that my ambitions for *Roadcraft* represent the project of a lifetime, really, to be gathered and shared along the way. And in any case, those observations would certainly demand more than one book—more than one *lifetime*. But, what the hey—I figure I'll just start trying to nail down any principles I can, for as long as I can, then pass the project down to the next generation of travelers . . .

I: The Art of Improvisation

When I see a sign like the one here, I pause and think it over. Should I continue, trusting that I'll find my way through, or should I turn back and find another way?

In such moments of decision (or indecision), a number of factors are weighed and compared, using a combination of imagination and experience. Do the map and GPS agree that this is in fact a "road"? If so, is it really "closed," or just "unmaintained"? My riding partner Michael and I certainly don't mind a challenge, and sometimes enjoy a few obstacles difficult enough to raise our heart rates and pump some adrenaline. But . . . will there be an impassable point? A locked gate, a fallen tree, a rockfall, a swampy morass, a wall of snow, or a collapsed bridge? All of those barriers have turned us around in such situations, from California to West Virginia, Oregon to Vermont, because as shunpikers (see "Shunpikin' It Old Skool"), we deliberately seek out such roads.

When you're riding a heavy motorcycle on a narrow track, it's always better to *choose* where you're going to turn around, and not have it forced upon you. Your only "reverse gear" is *pushing*, so you don't want to be pointed downhill against a fence with boulders on both sides. (It happened to me—but only *once*.)

Facing a Road Closed sign like that, I will also be weighing how much time I should allow to explore it, if it turns out we have to backtrack and go another way. On days off I don't worry about time so much, but on show days, it is everything. Recently I had to explain my show-day mindset to a friend who wanted me to stop at his house for lunch on the way to work. I coined a new word (a "Neilogism") to describe my feelings on such a day: "I am 'anxty,' which combines 'antsy,' 'anxious,' and 'angst-ridden.' On work days, I really just want to keep moving—have as good a ride as possible, and arrive in plenty of time."

This particular Road Closed sign greeted us in the woods of Pennsylvania, on our way to a show in Camden, New Jersey (across the Delaware from Philadelphia). But although it was a work day, it was still early morning, and we had only a hundred miles or so to go. I felt we had a little time to mess around, so I waved Michael onward, and we rode away—into the unknown. The very *interesting* unknown.

In a sense, Michael and I had been down that road many times before, or ones like it—but they are all different. We couldn't know if that track would bring us out somewhere in the general direction we were headed—even though I had traced it on the Rand McNally map

of Pennsylvania, where it was marked as an unpaved road, and Michael had found it on his computer GPS program, Mother, making it part of the route that was then downloaded to our on-bike units, Doofus and Dingus (though those occasionally demented geniuses continued to insist that the muddy track we were on was "Highway 97"). Many different fates have awaited us at such signs before, but hope and optimism carried us forward.

And that day, a fairly common pattern was repeated. At first the road got worse, deteriorating to a muddy, puddled pair of ruts through deep forest, and I began to keep an eye out for turnaround places (a slight uphill is handy). In the photo above, showoff Michael is riding straight into one of those opaque brown puddles, which is photogenic, but generally best avoided—because it is impossible to read how deep they might be, or what rocks, roots, or ruts might be hidden in their depths. It's best if you can get through by riding between the risky puddles, or beside them. However, that choice puts you in the slippery, equally treacherous grass and ferns, and that terrain requires delicate, precise balance, steering, and throttle use.

After a worrisome couple of miles, there were gradual signs of fresh gravel, a glimpse of a boarded-up hunting cabin through the trees, then a little farther on, a mildewed old mobile home. These habitations indicated at least *seasonal* use, and finally, all worries were allayed by the sight of an actual house, a small farm, where the track once more became a road that people used, and which led us out to more well-traveled highways.

So . . . when I stand before a Road Closed sign, it's all a matter of reading the "signs," literally and metaphorically, and deciding whether I wish to proceed in that direction, while accepting that I may not be able to. That is "Roadcraft," and it occurs to me that I have been finding a *musical* parallel lately.

This tour I have deliberately designed my drum solo to be more improvisational than ever before, and that has led me into some "adventures" that have their analogues to the art of traveling.

Even as I consider that comparison, it makes me smile—because sometimes on the drums it absolutely *does* feel that I'm playing myself into a Road Closed situation, with dark forest all around, treacherous puddles ahead, and an unknown outcome to this rhythmic path I've set myself upon. I can only hope I'll come upon a mobile home and some fresh gravel to lead me back to the "paved road."

Certain wilder places I have ridden, like the African Sahel, or the Sahara, resemble the "map" of my solo. In the open stretches, there may be scores of separate tracks, where cars, trucks, and motorbikes have chosen their own routes. Then at some fixed point—a ridge in the rocks, or a graveled wash—all of those paths will come together into an established road.

My solo is built on three rhythmic foundations, which I think of as "The Steampunk Waltz" (freeform melodies and rhythms in 3/4 time), "The Steampunk Stomp" (polyrhythms in 4/4 with upbeats against downbeats), and "The Steampunk Mambo" (a Latin ostinato, or repeating rhythm—regular readers will recall its root in the Italian word for obstinate, or stubborn). Through a couple of different variations, including the electronic drums at the back, I continue to explore and stretch my limits in all of those frameworks, and all of them converge toward the end—the big-band climax of "Love For Sale."

So, in general, I know where I'm going, but not how I'm going to get there.

Other principles of roadcraft apply to both drumming and motor-cycling—like a phrase uttered by producer Peter Collins years ago, during the recording of *Test for Echo*. I was describing to Peter how I had constructed the drum part for "Resist" to be as improvised as possible, by playing along with the song many times and experimenting with all of the elements that *might* work, especially for the drum fills. Then when I performed that song, like for the recording, all of those ideas were expressed in a random order, different each time. Peter smiled and said, "Don't leave spontaneity to chance." A great observation, and it became a chapter title in my subsequent instructional DVD, *A Work in Progress*.

The same principle of preparedness as a *liberating* force is true on the motorcycle. Michael and I rode past that Road Closed sign on capable, well-maintained motorcycles, with good tires and plenty of gas. We wore all the protective clothing. (I have just read of an acronym

for my rule in regard to wearing full riding gear—helmet, armored suit, gloves, and boots—on every ride: ATGATT, for "all the gear, all the time." Sadly, us ATGATTs represent a tiny fringe element in the fashion spectrum of motorcycling, but all I can do is stick to what I think is right, and set a good example—roadcraft again.) Apart from the GPS units, I carried paper maps, plenty of tools, a tire-repair kit, some water, and even a first-aid kit, while Michael added a satellite phone to our "improvisation supplies." So we were properly *prepared* to make that spontaneous choice.

Don't leave spontaneity to chance.

Here is an example of a time when Michael and I were faced with a rapidly worsening track ahead of us—and took the opposite approach: turned around and got out of there. It was during the full production rehearsals in Albuquerque, when we had a few days to explore the beautiful state of New Mexico. One day off, we rode 500 miles around southeast New Mexico, touring Guadalupe Mountains and Carlsbad Caverns National Parks (two new passport stamps for my new journal!), with a nibble of Texas, and curved back north for a night in Artesia. (As a title, that sounds poetic—"A Night in Artesia"—but the reality was actually a prosaic Best Western with a Chinese buffet—though decent, and good value, at $11.50 each.) Early the following morning, Michael and I were headed north to Albuquerque for the final rehearsal, with over 300 miles to go. We followed the winding roads up through the Sacramento Mountains near Cloudcroft, at about 9,000 feet, when Doofus and Dingus led us onto this backwoods specimen.

Truth to tell, this photo shows me riding back out the way we had come, after only a few miles in that wilderness. Apart from the sharp rocks that made up the rough logging trail and menaced our tires, the track soon began to descend steeply into a pine forest that looked sodden, boggy, and forbidding. As mentioned, it's awfully hard to turn a heavy motorcycle when it's pointed downhill on a narrow, muddy track, so I waved Michael to a halt, parked my bike, and walked down for a look. It didn't look promising—the sharp stones had been bad enough, but the downhill slope was raw, rutted dirt, wet looking, with football-sized boulders and knotted roots, and the dark sheen of blackwater puddles in the shadows downslope.

I looked back to Michael and shook my head, giving him the "turn around" signal. (And some other signals, too—we're very profane.) We bounced our way back to the paved highway, and headed down from the cool mountains into the sweltering sagebrush plains, near Trinity Site, the location of the first atomic bomb explosion, in July 1945—just weeks before that terrible invention ended that terrible war, in Hiroshima and Nagasaki.

Near the site, we paused at a signboard that quoted Manhattan Project director Robert Oppenheimer's statement on that day, from the *Bhagavad Gita*, "Now I am become Death, the destroyer of worlds."

Thinking back to both of those little motorcycle adventures, and their different outcomes, the lesson is clear: in roadcraft, you have to know when to struggle on, and when to make a graceful, *planned* retreat. Both decisions were "improvised"—extemporized, invented on the spot, based on experience and imagination—and both could sometimes be right, and sometimes wrong.

Other times, your progress may be halted by causes in which *adaptation* to the journey is no longer an option—because the journey has suddenly halted, and become an entirely different enterprise. Like, for example, if your motorcycle's fuel pump fails in the middle of the busy, speeding traffic of I-40, surrounded by the endless sagelands of eastern Arizona, on an afternoon when the peak temperature of 107°, along the banks of the Colorado at the California-Arizona border, had settled to a steady 100°. (As I like to point out, it is indeed a "dry heat," but so is an oven.)

That happened on our first day out. After leaving Los Angeles early in the morning, Michael and I had already covered 600 miles, and according to my (always tentative) plan, we would have stopped in another fifty miles or so, in Gallup, New Mexico. (One of my favorite church signs in such cases: "Want to Make God Laugh? Tell Him Your Plans.")

But this setback was only a nuisance—not a disaster. The first rehearsal would be the following night, so we had allowed plenty of time—and this was why. (In something over 250,000 miles of riding BMW motorcycles, I have only been stranded that way three times, and two of those—note to BMW—were failed fuel pumps.)

As I was riding along in the left lane of I-40, at a decent velocity, passing the many semis and other slow traffic, my bike's power just *ceased*, suddenly and completely, leaving me coasting, and rapidly losing speed. With a quick glance over my right shoulder, I saw traffic coming up in both lanes behind me, so the safest thing was to signal left and coast into the median. Michael pulled off behind me, and we surveyed the situation. On both sides, steady traffic roared and wailed

by, punctuated by the mighty passage of many tractor-trailers on that busy trucking route, each one vibrating the ground and the air around us as they dopplered past.

While I had a look over the bike's various mechanical bits, hoping to spot something obvious, like a loose cable or wire, Michael got on the phone to BMW Roadside Assistance.

In these times, with countless satellites in geosynchronous orbit above us, distributing communications and pinpointing navigation for geniuses like Doofus and Dingus, you would think it would be a simple phone call—"We've broken down at such-and-such latitude and longitude, in the middle of I-40, please send a flatbed." But to my increasing disbelief, as I walked around and photographed our plight, dodging the steady, fast, and loud streams of traffic, I saw the phone stay at Michael's ear. When I looked a question, he said, "I'm on hold." That would continue for long minutes, then he would get another question from the dispatcher: "Have you passed Highway 77 yet?" Another long hold, then, "Have you passed Petrified Forest National Park?" It seemed they were gathering all this information before the flatbed had even started in our direction—from who knows where, given that we were as near to the middle-of-nowhere as it's possible to get on an interstate in the Continental United States.

Fortunately Michael is cooler tempered than I am, because that one call went on for an incredible forty-six minutes. Later, I said to him, "Man, I would have been screaming at them, '*We're in the middle of frickin' I-40—he'll SEE US!!*'"

To which Michael replied, "It's hard to scream when you're on hold."

I didn't think so—but good for him!

Once our situation had became starkly apparent—we were stranded in the baking desert and could only await rescue—I accepted that lousy fact, and soon could even think of all the ways it could have been worse.

Michael suggested I take his bike and carry on. He said he would wait for the flatbed and deal with my bike, saying, "It's part of my *job*, after all."

That was true, in his capacity as my riding partner (though Michael's job also embraces multiple levels of security work for me and the band, as well as being my longtime "Director of Homeland Security" in California). The idea was that if we had a problem on the way to a show, I would take his bike and continue. In fourteen years of doing concert tours by motorcycle, well over 100,000 miles and hundreds of shows, that had never happened—but it was the reason I always had a riding partner.

However, in this case, I didn't feel like it was an *emergency*—a show day—and in my "traveler's heart," I felt that it was my "situation," so I ought to see it through (the Roadcraft Code).

We changed out of our heavy riding suits, and settled down to wait, in the sage, prickly grasses, and talc-dry dust of that shadeless inferno. The "No U-Turn" sign was apt.

An hour went by, and then two. The science of meteorology must offer a formula to multiply two hours by 100°. Fortunately we had bought sandwiches and water at a truck stop earlier, intending to have a quick lunch at a rest area in Arizona—but that troubled state, like

California and a few others, has been closing its rest areas for "budgetary" reasons (so uncivilized and ungracious to travelers), and we ended up eating in the shadow of an undercrossing beneath I-40—loud and charmless, but the only shade we could find. But now at least we had some extra water, though it was soon gone.

At one point Michael and I were both huddled in the paltry shade of my motorcycle, and started getting delirious—on purpose, though, entertaining ourselves and each other. We had dodged a few showers that day, and had seen a few *virgas*, gray veils of rain that evaporated before they reached the parched ground. A rainbow appeared in the east, and I asked Michael if he'd like to hear one of the stories I had been reading to Olivia in our early morning times together, called *What Makes a Rainbow?* He said he would, and I recited the tale in which Little Bunny asks his mother how a rainbow is made, and she tells him to ask his friends. The ladybug tells him you can't have a rainbow without red, the color of her wings; the fox tells him he needs orange, like his fur; the grasshopper tells him he needs green; the chick yellow; and so on. Michael listened with his head cocked, then asked, "Is this some kind of *inclusionary* story?"

I said I guessed it was, and camped it up. "Yeah—you know, it takes all your friends, of all different colors, to make a rainbow world."

He shook his head and smiled, "That's so *gay*."

I tossed my head and turned away, "You say that like it's a *bad* thing."

We received a call from the flatbed driver around that two-hour point, saying he was a half hour away. I started to contemplate the next stage—my bike would be transported to the BMW dealer in Albuquerque, which was still around 240 miles east. The thought of sitting in the cab of that flatbed with "my new best friend" made me decide what I had to do—I would "commandeer" Michael's bike after all.

I felt a little bad about it—but only a little. And not for long.

However . . . it was getting toward dark by then, and all day we had noticed the chunks and coils of thick black rubber that littered that interstate, from failed retreaded truck tires (ought to be banned). "Retread gators," I called them, as they could be as big as alligators, and as deadly. We could dodge those gators in daylight, but at night they would be much less visible. In any case, on general principles I don't like to ride at night—no scenery, and lots more dangers.

But . . . it was time to improvise again.

After this visibly intense portrait in the failing light, I didn't take any more photographs that night—keeping my concentration riveted on the pavement ahead of me. Even with Michael's good auxiliary lights, I had about two seconds between seeing something and hitting it—one-Mississippi, two-Mississippi—so my eyes were fixed on the farthest edge of that ellipse of light. Tense and vigilant, I had the clear thought, "This is an adventure—and I can't *wait* till it's over."

It ended up being the longest travel day I think I've ever endured—by the time Michael and I were in my Albuquerque hotel room clicking our plastic cups of Macallan on ice (toasting our arrival with very *expressive* faces), it was nearly midnight. Including that two-and-a-half-hour "rest" in the middle, it had taken seventeen hours to cover 850 miles.

That is a record I devoutly hope never to break.

Just as this is a sight I devoutly hope never to see again (though without faith that it will be so).

It happened two days later, in the Jemez Mountains west of Santa Fe (my motorcycle had been quickly repaired and returned by Sandia BMW), and every time I look at this image it sends the same chilling flash of fear through my insides. However, the real outrage this time was that we were pulled over for speeding—*on a gravel road!*

That had never happened before. And, if you note the radar detector perched beside my mirror, we seldom get taken by surprise that way, except in purposely radar-blind speed traps. We heard and saw this guy coming at us—Michael even waved at him—then we saw and heard him coming up *behind* us, lights and siren on. Still, we thought he just wanted to *pass* us, on his way to some *real* emergency or crime. But no, he was pulling us over.

He spent the usual long time in his truck, checking our documents, and when he finally got out and went back to speak with Michael, I snuck this photograph. He let us off with what can only be described as a "stern warning," and as Michael and I rode away again, we shook our helmets at each other—"What the . . . ?"

Later that day, we talked about our adventures in those first two rides of the tour, and decided that perhaps we had gotten rid of our potential mechanical and legal demons in that first thousand miles. And so it proved, at least for the next 7,500 miles (making the highest total we've ever logged on a single leg of a tour). Thirteen shows, 8,500 miles, three oil changes, two sets of tires—and a month away from home.

That is the greatest cost of all.

Just before setting off on a concert tour, I am often perplexed when friends at home ask, "Are you excited to be going on tour?"

Of course a deeply ingrained fantasy is at work there, and to answer in the negative seems jaded, cynical, *wrong*. However, to put their question another way—*should* I be excited to be leaving my wife, my ten-month-old daughter, my home, my kitchen, my desk, my books, my pleasures and treasures, my toys and joys?

Another client that Michael works with, Elliot Mintz, is a veteran public relations man, going back to the time of the Beatles, and these days he represents the surviving members of John Lennon's family, Bob Dylan, and other celebrities. A diminutive, nattily dressed man, he attended one of our shows at the Hollywood Bowl a few years back, and I spoke with him after.

I was telling him that I didn't really like touring, but somehow felt it was something I had to do—if you call yourself a musician, it is kind of your *duty* to play live.

He nodded, looked up at me with a serious expression, and said, "You have to do it—because you can."

That simple phrase stayed with me for a long time after, as I wrestled with its implications. Recently I shared Elliot's insight with Geddy, at dinner in the dressing room before a show, and he nodded and said that statement expressed the reality about as well as he'd ever heard.

A friend of Geddy's was visiting that night, a friend who lived in "the normal world," and he remarked that it seemed like we had a pretty good life.

Geddy said, "Yes, it is a good life—but it has a *price*."

Any phrase that includes the words "goes without saying" is suspect, but I would be clear—I wouldn't trade jobs, or lives, with anyone. In our song "Bravado," there's a fitting line I adapted from John Barth, "We will pay the price, but we will not count the cost."

That cost has many facets—physical pain; exhaustion; psychological alienation from home, family, and friends; homesickness; performing even when you feel bad; and all the while, missing out on days and nights and countless little events in the lives of your loved ones. A whole part of your life goes on without you. Why the "fantasy" other people imagine doesn't include these elements is because they don't know what it's like to *miss* those moments of everyday life, so they don't value them highly enough.

But this time the price was made especially sharp for me. Before starting this tour, I had spent nearly every early morning with baby Olivia, all through her ten months of life, quietly watching sunrises together, playing on the floor with her toys and books, sitting side by side on the sofa, my arm around her little form, while I read aloud from *What Makes a Rainbow?*, *Wake Up Little Ones*, or *Big Red Barn*.

Then, after a month away, I returned home to an eleven-month-old baby who didn't know me, shied away from me, and clung to her mother.

I know I just have to hang back until she gets comfortable with me again—but it still aches.

II: Ride for Peace

One reason I like to arrive early on a show day is that there's always so much to do—bike maintenance, personal maintenance, catching up on emails, and, always, getting out the maps and improvising our motorcycle route for the next couple of days—exploring my way from one show to another, seeking the smallest roads with my pink high-lighter ("Yes, Michael, it's pink—you say that like it's a *bad* thing"), and stitching them together. In the larger view, I'll try to include a medium-sized town every couple hundred miles, for fuel and possible lunch stops, and consider potential overnight destinations—towns big enough to have motels and restaurants.

Some of those towns prove to be delightful discoveries in their own right: Recently we have had unexpectedly enjoyable nights off in Iowa City, Iowa; Jim Thorpe, Pennsylvania (what a story surrounds *that* pic-turesque little town—I must tell it one day); and several delightful resorts across Ontario and Quebec.

Michael showing off; Brutus laughing—the old story

Those last destinations were courtesy of my earliest riding partner, Brutus, who joined Michael and me for the rides to the Canadian shows. With the added tension and social demands of those "hometown" events, it was a pleasure for me to turn the navigation over to Brutus—a past master at the high art of riffing on a map: improvising. Being conversant with not only paper maps, but with the computer variety, he could also take over Michael's role of tracing the routes on Mother, then downloading them to the boys—now reunited as Doofus, Dingus, and Dork.

The average riding temperature on all of those 8,500 miles must have been above 90°, the average only cooled that much by a couple of rainy days. From New Mexico through Kansas to Wisconsin and Ontario, the most common reading on my bike's thermometer seemed to be 95°. Riding into Chicago, and on the way to the last show at Jones Beach on Long Island, I saw and felt 102°—and it was *not* a dry heat.

On one such hot afternoon in Ontario, we followed a series of little roads, some paved, some not, framed in green fields and woods. There was almost no traffic, and as I've described such roads before, they were the kind that nobody travels unless they live on them.

A word to describe the mood of that ride came to me—it felt so *peaceful*. I would reflect on that word again a few times, on those certain kind of perfect roads that lead from nowhere to nowhere. There is no peace to be found in traffic, on freeways, in towns, and certainly not when I'm playing in front of an audience or bouncing through the night on a roaring bus—but once in a while, for a few miles every few days, I could feel it.

The same word suggested itself to me in regard to my pre-show warm-ups, on the small drumset in the Bubba Gump room. A half-hour before each show, I go in there and just start *playing*, working out on the same three rhythmic foundations I use in my solo, but without *consequences*. There is no such thing as a "mistake," never mind a Road Closed, and for fifteen or twenty minutes, I just wander in rhythmic space.

It occurs to me that opposites do not always include a negative, and if "excitement" is one polarity of "peace," it too is a wonderful and necessary component in life. Motorcycling is certainly exciting, but so too is working on a story, or playing the drums—especially in front of an audience (we had some wonderful audiences at those first thirteen shows, and so *many* of them, too—I'll have more to say about that part of the journey in a later story). But even excitement is a tenuous condition—it can easily tip into anxiety, just as peace can devolve into tedium.

Excitement is found along the road, not at the end, and likewise, peace is not a fixed point—except perhaps in the unwanted "rest in peace" sense. Peace is the breathing space between destinations, between excitements, an occasional part of the journey, if you're lucky. Peace is a space you move through very rarely, and very briefly—but you're not allowed to stay there.

You have to keep moving, and go do what you do.

Because you can . . .

21

CRUEL SUMMER

SEPTEMBER 2010

Always preferring to start a story (or a day) with the "good news first," this photograph illustrates the pleasant ride that began this second leg of the *Time Machine* tour. It was August 5, 2010, in western Wyoming, on the way to a show in Salt Lake City. The gravel road lay like a brown ribbon over the rumpled blue-green sagelands, tracing away toward the upper right of the photo. Ahead of us, the mountains of Utah began to rise in the distant west.

The night before, Michael and I had flown into Denver to meet Dave and the bus, and slept aboard while Dave drove us to a truck stop in Rock Springs, Wyoming. In the morning, we unloaded the bikes and set out on our "commute" to work. (Sure, we could have just flown into SLC, but if you have to ask . . .)

We followed that peaceful road for a good forty miles, through that wide-open rangeland and occasional isolated ranches. Then we turned south and west, riding high up into the Uinta Mountains, on a highway only open in the summer months, over Bald Mountain Pass, at just over 10,000 feet. Descending to Park City, we had to "sniff" our way to an old favorite bicycle route of mine called the Guardsman Pass—also almost 10,000 feet up, unpaved, closed in winter, and all but unsigned and unmapped. (I learned of it from an old cycling map, and it doesn't appear on the Rand McNally or GPS computer maps—I think on purpose, for the same reason a couple of miles at the summit are left rough and unpaved these days: to discourage its use as a summer shortcut between Park City and Salt Lake.)

We paused at the top of Guardsman Pass to enjoy the view, and I told Michael that I had crossed that pass before, and the Bald Mountain Pass, by bicycle, after riding Highway 150 down from Evanston, Wyoming, back in the late '80s. It was about 150 miles, with those two 10,000-foot passes, but I must not have hated it—I did the same bicycle ride again a couple of years later. (A photo appears in the original *Counterparts* CD foldout, of me setting out from the bus at an Evanston truck stop.) Hearing that story, Michael was impressed, held up a gloved fist for a "bump," and said, "Dude!"

Winding down through Big Cottonwood Canyon to Salt Lake City, we crossed that ever-expanding conurbation from east to west, arriving in plenty of time for a good show at the amphitheater that night. (After a break of even eight or nine days, my bandmates and I often feel as though we have probably forgotten all the songs, but of course they come right out again—plus we're all rested and refreshed, and don't hurt anywhere yet, so that first show back is always a pleasure for us.)

All that was nice, but the next day things started to edge into the more "dramatic" theme that would dominate this cruel August. (T.S. Eliot famously described April as the "cruelest month," but I've got news for him.) On the bus after the Salt Lake show, Michael was up most of the night with an attack of food poisoning. In the morning, at a truck stop near Boise, Idaho, I saw the state all that "evacuating" had left Michael in, and insisted he stay on the bus and rest. (I pretend not to care, but I can't help it.) I told him I would ride that day's route alone, and he could stay on the bus and have Dave drop him and his bike later, to meet me at Connell, Washington, at the good old M & M Motel—my planned destination for the night, where I had stayed a few times before, right back to the *Ghost Rider* journey.

Setting out on my own, riding north from Boise on a warm, sunny morning, I decided I was going to be *extra* careful. I knew that if anything happened, Michael would never forgive himself. (Oh, he pretends not to care, but he can't help it.) Despite my own good intentions, however, within the first twenty miles I had a very close call—a deer went bounding across the road in front of me so close that I'm sure my front wheel shaved the back of her legs.

She was pretty big, too, and I realized that if she had jumped out just a few milliseconds earlier, she and I would have made an awful mess of each other. After having hit a deer before ("Every Road Has Its Toll"), and having another near miss in the Santa Monica Mountains near home not long ago, I was starting to feel increasingly nervous about those all-too-common hazards. Deer are pretty and everything, but their ever-growing numbers in many areas, and their carelessness about looking both ways before crossing a road, are literally *deadly* for motorcyclists.

Shortly after that little existential reckoning (and you can bet I was "reckoning" on that near-death experience for some time after—still am), I followed my GPS unit, Dingus, onto an unpaved road near the frontier outpost of Idaho City. I had mapped a road like that into my route, but that plan was for *two* riders, and once again, I felt nervous being alone in such a remote and risk-filled environment. Then the road began to deteriorate and dwindle to a pair of rutted tracks, bumping up and down and forking off here and there into little logging trails. Dingus couldn't decide whether we were actually on the right road or not—the purple line that represented my route kept separating itself suspiciously from the little motorcycle icon that was supposed to be me.

With superhuman resignation, I actually turned around and went back. (See previous story, "Theme and Variations," for thoughts on turning around when you want to, not when you *have* to.) Just outside Idaho City, I pulled up by a pair of fishermen on a bridge over a stream. When I asked if I could get to Placerville that way, one of them said, "You *might* get through that way," then he pointed at my bike, "but not on *that*." He said a lot of people made that mistake, and directed me to the real Placerville Road—still unpaved, but graded and navigable.

Michael and I met up that night in Conner, and next day had an enjoyable ride across Eastern Washington's irrigated hayfields and hops farms (apparently a prestigious and tightly regulated crop, we had once been told by a local policeman who had stopped us for a speed infraction, but was friendly and "forgiving"), and over the Cascades (and into rain, predictably). After the Seattle show, we rode the bus down to Roseburg, Oregon, where we were met in the morning by Greg Russell on his Halloween-colored KTM. He would join us for the ride to the next show in the Bay Area—by way of Crater Lake National Park, Lassen Volcanic National Park, and some remote and adventurous back roads in Central California. Then it was south to L.A., where the real trouble began . . .

After two shows there—an indoor one at the Gibson Amphitheatre and outdoors at Irvine Meadows—Michael and I were planning to motorcycle to Vegas on the day of that show, so Dave drove the bus and trailer out of the Irvine show early. The bus developed engine trouble in the middle of the night, leaving Dave crawling up a long, long grade on Interstate 15, near the California-Nevada border, at twelve miles an hour. By the time Dave made it to the summit, the bus was engulfed in smoke, and his drive was over. The diesel's turbocharger had disintegrated—after Dave had just spent a day in the shop in L.A. having it repaired. Our longtime lead truck driver, Mac, carrying the band's stage gear, caught up to Dave and stopped to keep him company, and our band-crew bus driver, Lashawn, came up and hooked our motorcycle trailer behind her bus. (We're running seven trucks and five buses this tour, and they all leave at different times after the show, according to which gear and crew they're carrying: stage gear, PA, lights, rear screen, and so on.)

One can imagine that there are not many flatbed trucks that can carry a 45-foot bus, and dawn was breaking in the eastern sky over the cluster of casinos on the Nevada state line, before the rescue was complete.

(Don't you have to wonder about all those headlights driving away from Vegas that early on a Saturday morning?)

Dave's drive was over, but his day was not. Not only did he have to make sure the bus arrived at the shop, and that somebody was actually working on it (they weren't), but at the previous show I had asked Dave to set me up for an oil change in Vegas. (For that routine, before my arrival Dave lays out the tools, oil, filter, drain pan, and a rug for me to lie on while I work, and I just roll up and get the job done, while the oil is still hot and holding any contaminants in suspension.) Under the circumstances of that day, I certainly would have understood if that "sideline" operation got overlooked. But no—when Michael and I rode up beside the MGM Grand Arena (in 112° heat), Dave had the oil-change setup all ready. Champion's points for that.

However, our little world was still in "crisis mode." Dave, Michael, and I lived on that bus, sleeping on it every show night in the truck stops of America. Everything we had, everything we needed, was in the drawers, hanging lockers, shelves, and nonslip surfaces of that bus. When Michael and I set off for an overnight ride to the next show, we just carried a day's worth of supplies on our bikes.

Now it was Saturday, and no work was going to be done on that bus at least until Monday, and there would be parts to order—it seemed likely that we could be busless, homeless, for days. The dead bus had been carried to a shop forty-five minutes away from the MGM, and Michael and I prepared a list of all the stuff we'd need to live and travel for . . . who knew how long. Clean clothes, for a start, maps for the upcoming days, cell-phone chargers, Michael's professional security apparatus, computers, Canadian cigarettes, Scotch whiskey—a daunting list. It was like suddenly being forced to evacuate your house, from a distance, and trying to remember everything you might possibly need from it.

Also, it happened that Michael was flying ahead to Denver to deal with some security issues, and I was scheduled to meet up with my friend Chris Stankee from the Sabian cymbal company, on his Ducati Multistrada, for that show-day ride to Red Rocks. However, our ren-

dezvous in Arizona had been based upon me riding the bus overnight after the Vegas show toward Colorado—now I was going to have to ride each of the 745 miles (even taking the interstate route) to Red Rocks.

Chris received my news by text while he was heading for our previous rendezvous in Arizona, and altered his route to meet me in Vegas. Since he and I would have to ride out after the show by motorcycle anyway, we decided to get a bit of a head start that night, and ride east a hundred miles or so, to Mesquite, Nevada.

Riding my own motorcycle out of the MGM Grand Arena that night after the show was certainly a novel experience (unique, even, as I have never actually left a show by motorcycle), and I confess that I was mildly thrilled at having our two motorcycles led by two police bikes, with flashing lights and everything. (Nice to have them in front of me, for once, instead of behind.)

After the motor officers had smoothed our way out of town, Chris and I set out across the dark Nevada desert on Interstate 15. I was tired enough after two shows in a row, and that day's 340-mile ride across the Mojave Desert in 112° heat (and an outdoor oil-change ditto), but felt no drowsiness—I was both exhilarated and powerfully alert.

The Ducati's headlight behind me was pale and yellow, and easily lost in other following traffic, but I tried to keep Chris in my mirrors all the time. Occasionally I slowed a little to make sure there was still a single headlight behind me, and there it was—though suspiciously slow and far back. Finally I got worried and pulled over to the shoulder, four-ways flashing in that inky darkness, with speeding traffic roaring up from behind.

I looked back and watched that single headlight come up on me, then cursed as I saw that it was a one-eyed SUV. Pulling the handheld device out of my tankbag, I saw a text from Chris. "Rear tire shredded. Calling AAA."

It was after 1:00 in the morning by then, and I called Chris to discuss our options. I suggested he get the flatbed to carry him back to Vegas—if there was anywhere in the world where he had a chance of getting a new rear tire on a Sunday morning, it was Vegas.

I rode another fifty miles into Mesquite, checked into the Best Western, and considered my own options. Even given the sudden change of plans with the bus out of the picture, I had mapped a scenic ride for Chris and me, down through Utah and the Four Corners region into Southwestern Colorado, then on to Red Rocks on the show day. Now even that indulgence seemed irresponsible (first priority always, I needed to get to *work*), and I was thinking I really ought to take the most direct route. Pacing around my little room, ruminating over a long-awaited Macallan at nearly 3:00 in the morning, I caught my reflection in a mirror, and a little voice addressed it: "Just get up in the morning when you can, eat breakfast, and start riding."

And that is what I did.

It must be said that if you need to devour some miles on an interstate, I-70 across eastern Utah and into Colorado is about the prettiest freeway in the land. From the redrock ramparts of the Book Cliffs you are funneled into the green valley of the Colorado River, climbing in serpentine, narrowing curves toward the Vail Pass, at over 10,000 feet.

Chris was able to get his tire replaced early Sunday morning, and met me that night in Moab, after an epic ride of his own. From there we started early and took a brief tour of Canyonlands and Arches National Parks, then got back on I-70 and rode together to Red Rocks. (That was the longest show-day ride in my career: 420 miles.)

As always, the show at Red Rocks was unforgettable—such a stunning setting, and as I wrote in *Roadshow*, the audience is arrayed in *front* of the band, rather than below, and it makes the whole event feel more intimate. Nowhere does the audience feel more part of the show to us.

Dave and the bus rejoined the tour that day (hurray), and Michael and I were glad to be aboard it after the show that night—"home again." From a truck stop in Limon, Colorado, Michael and I set off in the morning across the plains of Eastern Colorado into Kansas. With flat green rangelands to either side, we followed some enjoyable gravel roads. Our front wheels found the smooth wheel-tracks among the loose stones, and we could maintain a decent, safe speed. I was wondering if Greeley County, Kansas, was named after the New York journalist named Horace Greeley (turned out it was—the seat of Greeley County is named Horace), who famously wrote, in 1865, "Go West, young man." (In fact, the full quote was, "Go West, young man, go West and grow up with the country.")

So I was riding along through that big open country and feeling good. (Though our run of bad luck hadn't run out—in Denver, Michael had discovered a flat rear tire on his bike as well, and had it replaced.) The wide blue dome of the Great Plains sky above us was blotted by a few distant dark clouds and gray veils of rain, but right around us we endured the same hot, dry weather we had been suffering for many days—reaching 105° that day. So if anything, I was thinking a brief rain shower might cool us off a little, while Michael hoped it might lay the dust somewhat—because he was riding behind me (though I courteously moved to leeward on the road when I could, so the dust was blown away from him).

As we drifted along a desolate, empty dirt road, through that vast empty country, a strange phenomenon obscured the road ahead of me—the brown track seemed to disappear into a windblown lake, with lapping waves of rain driven across its surface by a fierce wind. Suddenly we were engulfed in a roiling tempest, the sky instantly dark, and the wind pelting us with rain and hail. It stung even through our armored suits, and rattled against our helmets like thrown gravel—but we had no time to attend to that sensation, because we were busy trying to stay *upright*. The previously firm road became a slick pool of goopy clay, and our front wheels went slewing around, while the rears spun helplessly.

Our boots were down like outriggers for balance, and they and our spinning tires were coated in thick mud, gaining no purchase on the greasy surface. I could crank my handlebars hard over, turning my front wheel all the way to either side, without affecting my direction at all.

And still the wind, rain, and hail lashed at us. At one point I was blown helplessly across the slippery track, into the shallow ditch, and right up onto the open field to the north—all the while sure I was about to fall down, and just trying to control when and how that fall was going to occur.

(Roadcraft lesson—the counterintuitive trick is to do *nothing*. No braking, no steering, no accelerating—just hold on. JUST HOLD ON. Very often that's the right thing to do in a difficult situation—nothing at all—but it can be awfully hard to tell yourself that, and make your body *do* it.)

Anyway, it seemed miraculous to me, but I stayed upright until I could coast to a trembling stop on that grassy plain. After a long breath, I carefully angled my way back to the muddy road—but, almost immediately, my motorcycle was skidding sideways, pirouetting under me, and I jumped clear as it went down on its side. The squall had passed away to the north by then, but we hardly noticed.

Michael came up to help, and it was all the two of us could do to raise the heavy bike, skating around in the slippery mud. We decided to try riding in the ditch, where at least the grass might give us some traction. That worked for a while, but soon the ditch was filling with water—as ditches will do in a rainstorm—and I looked back and saw Michael struggling to steer his bike up into the open field beside us, but he wasn't getting anywhere.

I parked my bike upright—easy enough in the middle of a narrow ditch—and walked back to give him a push. We managed to maneuver his bike up onto the open field, but not without his spinning rear tire painting me in mud, like a Jackson Pollock drip painting. I had my revenge when Michael had to push my bike up out of the ditch.

Once we were both up in the open prairie, we could ride all right, but had to dodge a lot of big gopher holes, with mounds of dirt around them. When we paused for a moment, Michael said, "Those could *so* put us down!" I told him that in the Old West, it was considered foolhardy to trot a horse across country like that, because the horse could easily break a leg in one of those holes. He said, "Only *you* would know that." I said, "Only you *wouldn't*." Then we called each other some bad names, and continued picking our way across the lone prairie.

A mile or so like that brought us to some dry gravel, and we headed for the nearest paved road—hoping to find a spray-wash, for both the bikes and ourselves. Around then I reflected that only two other riding conditions I had experienced compared to our predicament in that mud—places where forward progress simply seemed *impossible*, yet there was no going back either.

Several times in the Canadian Arctic, I had been mired in a similar swamp of slimy mud, wheels spinning, feet sliding, and motorcycle falling down. In Tunisia, on the edge of the Sahara, Brutus and I had lost track of what passed for a road around there, and found ourselves sinking into tire-spinning, clutch-burning sand.

So, the adventure traveler's bucket list ought to include the Arctic, the Sahara, and Greeley County Road F in Western Kansas during a thunderstorm.

For motorcyclists in general, another roadcraft lesson I have been considering is a metaphorical rule-of-the-road: "Lead Left."

Back in 2002, on the *Vapor Trails* tour, Michael and I first rode with Brian Catterson, a vastly experienced motorcyclist on everything from dirt ovals to Grand Prix roadracing tracks, and nowadays he is the Editor in Chief at *Motorcyclist* magazine. Before setting out from a truck stop in Gallup, New Mexico, that morning, we asked Brian if he had any particular preferences about riding with others.

"All I care is lead *left*. I hate following a rider who leads from the right."

Point taken—me too. Because nearly always the proper lane position on a two-lane road is in the left wheel-track: it's nearest the center, providing the most options in case of surprises, like cars pulling out from the right, scattered debris on the road, or—perhaps deadliest of all—a sudden deer.

It is also a matter of protecting your "territory" on the road, a very important principle in its own right. There are a few exceptions to the "lead left" rule, like when a vehicle is approaching you from the other direction, and you move to the right wheel-track of your lane, so that any driver behind that first vehicle who might want to pull out and pass will see you first. Or in the outer lane of a four-lane road, you lead right, to block that piece of road from any would-be intruders from the inside lane. (Given the chance, they will edge right over on you.)

"Lead Left" can also stand for a principle of leadership I have been thinking of, first phrased in a way that sounds a little schmaltzy on its own, but carries a worthy meaning: "Lead with your heart."

On a motorcycle, leading one or two riders (no more than two, for this leader—I couldn't imagine being part of one of those Sunday "processions" Michael and I always see, with a dozen or more bikes), I believe that a good leader makes exactly the same strategic decisions regarding lane position, speed, route, and overall *pace* as he would if riding on his own. The difference is in the leader's *consideration*: maybe just of an upcoming yellow traffic light, choosing to stop for the others rather than slip through alone. Or it could be more long-range calculations, taking note of a following rider's endurance, fuel range, and bladder capacity.

Ride with your mind, but lead with your heart. (It's on your left side, too, as it happens.)

Of course there's a political parallel to "Lead Left" as well, though I haven't hammered it out quite yet. Ideally, such a metaphor would have to include flying with both "wings." (The terms left and right wing date from the French Revolution, when royalists and revolutionaries sat on those sides of the National Assembly.) A good leader would have personal integrity, be the same person in every situation—like Atticus Finch in *To Kill a Mockingbird*, the same good, honest man in the courtroom that he was at home—and lead with basically conservative values, protecting the "state of the ride," but would also have a quality of *compassion*.

Such reflections have led me to define myself in recent years as a "bleeding-heart libertarian."

Do I believe in the sanctity of the individual and all freedoms and rights?

Certainly.

Do I believe that humans should generously help others in need, and voluntarily contribute to public works of mutual benefit?

Why, yes, of course.

Do I believe that the general run of humanity can ascend to those noble heights of . . . humanity?

Alas, I do not.

So . . . lead left.

Meanwhile, back in Kansas, we were cruising eastward on paved Highway 50, once again in fierce 105° heat and a strong wind. I noticed a small grassfire at the roadside, flame and smoke in the middle of nowhere. Some genius must have tossed a cigarette butt out of his or her window. In that heat and wind, the fire was already the size of a car, flames rising orange even on the windward side, so this was serious. I pulled over to call 911, and Michael said he would ride ahead and find a mile marker. As I watched, the fire doubled in size every thirty seconds, and there was a dry cornfield beyond the roadside that would soon be ablaze. I told the dispatcher our approximate location, east of Syracuse and about forty miles west of Garden City, but she said, "You're at mile marker twenty-two." Must have traced my cell phone. Having done our civic duty ("Lead Left"), we rode on and found a car wash, and used up many quarters spraying away the mud that encrusted our bikes and our riding suits.

All of these events occurred within one cruel week—between the Irvine show on August 13 and the one in Wichita on August 20. In that time, I motorcycled 2,650 miles, played five shows, and was beginning to feel like I was just hanging on by my fingernails. It was indeed becoming a cruel summer.

But wait—there's more!

The story's title was inspired before the tour even began, back in late June, on the first day Michael and I rode out of L.A., on our way to the full-production rehearsals in Albuquerque (recounted in the previous story, "Theme and Variations"). After a seventeen-hour day, in which I had ridden 850 miles, with a breakdown and a two-and-a-half-hour wait in 100° heat at the 600-mile point, I finally pulled up in front of the hotel in Albuquerque at about 11:00 at night. Under the marquee lights of the portico, I kicked down the sidestand and lifted a weary leg over the saddle, pulled off my helmet and removed my earplugs. Unusually, loud music blared from outdoor speakers, the 1983 pop classic by Bananarama, "Cruel Summer."

"It's a cruel, cruel summer—leaving me here on my own."

I was only hearing it with one ear, though, because a chronic problem with ear infections was already flaring up on this tour, and my left ear was entirely blocked. (Later on, as the condition grew worse, I would play at least six shows with that handicap—an unrewarding way to perform, of course, and it required me to *imagine* what I and the band were playing rather than *respond* to it. Plus there was pain, especially when inserting or removing the in-ear monitors.)

As I stood by the bike and gathered myself to go inside and check in, an apparently drunken beggar, middle-aged, unshaven, sheepishly smiling, possibly under more than one bad influence (alcohol, drugs, mental deficiency) swam into my orbit, jabbering at me with his hand out. When I waved him away, he started trying to sell me the beads around his neck. I just kept saying, "No, no, no."

Then—something that has almost *never* happened when I travel on my own or with Michael—another guy came up and said, "Are you Neil Purt?" (A widespread and enduring mispronunciation of "Peert.")

Oh, did my heart sink. Could the timing possibly be worse?

However, I do maintain that I have never been rude to anyone who wasn't rude to me first. And this guy had a nice, friendly face—no fanatical burning eyes, or hyperventilating with embarrassing excitement, as some strangers do in such situations. After taking a deep breath, I just said, "Not right now" (true enough, as I was about to check into the hotel as "Johnny Gilbert"), and continued rooting around in the tankbag for my wallet. The guy was still saying things, but between Bananarama (followed by Squeeze's "Tempted," I recall), and my one ear, I really couldn't understand him.

Looking into the guy's face with all sincerity, hoping a simple explanation might make him understand that now was not the time for a meet-and-greet, I said, "Look, I just rode 850 miles, all the way from Los Angeles."

He nodded eagerly and said, a touch wistfully, "That sounds cool!"

Oh dear. My reaction was like one of those cartoons, or a slapstick act, where the character's mouth opens to say something, then snaps shut again, in hopeless resignation. I just mumbled something neutral and headed inside.

However, as I wandered through the chlorine reek of the hallways around the inside pool in search of my room, the guy was suddenly there again—thrusting out a rumpled keycard envelope and a pen, saying, "Would it be too much to ask . . ."

With a sigh, I tried to comply, but his pen didn't work. I held up an open palm, meaning "wait," and dug in my bags to fetch my own pen. I scrawled an unsatisfying signature across the shabby bit of paper. (If I'm going to sign an autograph, I like them to be *nice*. That's why I don't like signing T-shirts or drumsticks: You can't make them nice.)

Six weeks later, in mid-August, as the trials of our second leg of the tour continued, the title "Cruel Summer" kept recurring to me. The opening verse, about hot summer streets, pavements burning, strange voices saying things I can't understand, *"this heat has got right out of hand"*—I knew about all that.

112° in Vegas, 105° the next day through Utah, an all-time record for Denver of 101°, 105° the next day during our playing-in-the-mud games in Kansas, and from then on, every day was at least in the 90s.

Worst of all was a day-off ride, about a week later, down through the Ozarks of southern Missouri and northern Arkansas, between shows in Wichita and St. Louis. It was "only" 100°, but in that part of the country, the humidity was that high, too, and in our heavy riding suits, we were wilting. By the time we reached our night-off destination, Mountain Home, Arkansas, we didn't even bother with our usual survey of the motel possibilities—just stopped at the first one we came to, and checked in.

And even in the air-conditioned room, I was still mopping sweat from my forehead for a half-hour—much as I am on the bus after a show—and it seemed we couldn't drink enough water (and other more "medicinal" liquids). At around 6:00 a.m., I was awake and thirsty for something besides water, and wandered out in search of a soda machine. It happened that from the room next door, Michael's dark shadow ghosted out, bent on the same mission. I said, "You know, since we're up this early anyway, why don't we ride out by 7:00, and get in some cool hours before breakfast?"

Even Michael couldn't argue with the good sense of that idea, and we rode off into the sunrise together . . .

That was one of many less-cruel moments in our days and nights of August, for truly, there was much to celebrate as well—the shows, for example, and the *audiences*. This summer of 2010, and the seasons leading up to it, have been a cruel time for many people, economically, and as we planned our tour, we couldn't fail to be aware that there had been other concert tours that had been suddenly "rescheduled" (canceled, in fact, due to low ticket sales).

So as always, we remain grateful and delighted that after so many years, people still come to see us in such numbers—and with such *enthusiasm*. While we are the ones supposed to be doing the entertaining, I have written before that we are always entertained by our audiences, too. And *inspired* by them—when other people care so much about what you do, you can hardly do less than care about it more.

Another theme I've touched on before is how different one tour is from another—not just in its itinerary, but in its musical dynamic among the three of us. In *Roadshow*, writing about the thirtieth anniversary tour in 2004, I described how a run of good shows would be punctuated by one "magic" show, in which we would transcend ourselves and feel the band, crew, and audience swept into an ineffable vortex of musical elevation.

However, in 2007 and 2008, during the two summers we spent on the *Snakes and Arrows* tour, I wrote that the dynamic seemed completely different—we established a benchmark "good show" early on, then continued improving on it incrementally, show by show, without any that seemed particularly set apart, or "magic."

This summer, on the *Time Machine* tour of 2010, it has been different again. At dinner before the fourth or fifth show, Geddy, Alex, and I were talking about how the shows were going, and Geddy said, "I don't think we've peaked yet."

And he was certainly right. Even well into the second leg of the tour, after almost twenty shows, I felt that we seemed to enter a new "zone." The basic structure of the show, the details of arrangements, tempos, and transitions, had been refined night after night as we went

along (noting that we rehearsed for two months for what was to have been a three-month tour), but once we had nailed down the foundation, each of us was reaching *higher*. More determination and care were being poured into our individual performances, and together those energies were fusing into a white-hot unit that surprised even us. Raw energy sparked in our improvisational sections, especially—Geddy in the bass rideout to "Leave That Thing Alone," Alex in his new acoustic piece (following from his previous such performance, "Hope," I believe he's calling this one "Hopeless") and in his frenetic leadwork in the middle instrumental section of "Working Man," in which he plays with what a long-ago reviewer called "seeming teenage abandon." During that part, at the end of the night, when I look out from the drums and see Alex skipping back as we begin the ensemble section out of that solo, I can't help but smile at the crazy guy I've been watching for thirty-six years.

So magic still happens.

(Though not always: I loved the line Geddy delivered one night when our opening movie malfunctioned. He apologized to the audience, then casually remarked, "Sometimes magic *doesn't* happen.")

This shot was taken at the Minnesota State Fair, on August 27—Alex's fifty-seventh birthday. (The special T-shirt was made up by the crew for everyone to wear that day, and just after dinner more than thirty of us gathered in front of the "dressing trailer" to sing "Happy Birthday." I decided to wear it onstage for the first set.)

John ("Boom-Boom"—our pyro technician and photographer of daily events) was able to capture this shot of me while walking across the stage in the hotdog costume (you have to have seen our show to get that reference, I guess), with his Nikon and fisheye lens around his neck.

Of course I had to smile at that.

More than one friend has already remarked that this photo captures the "real me" they know, and that's nice. My mother has always complained that I don't smile enough onstage. But it's a grim, arduous, sometimes painful job, and I never trust a drummer who smiles too much while he's playing. Back in the old days, when more drummers performed solos in their band's shows, some guys told me they "held back" before their solos. I would never do that—I prefer, like the hockey players say, to "leave it all on the ice."

I can tell that the photo was taken in the middle of "Leave That Thing Alone," the "jazzy" bit, because of my traditional grip on the sticks—which I only use in that part, the opening of "The Camera Eye," and in one part of my solo. (All those sections demand rudimental, parade-drum patterns, and I learned all that stuff with traditional grip.) That part of "Leave That Thing Alone" incorporates ever-changing variants of rudimental patterns on the snare between the accents.

The headphones I'm wearing also round off the ear-infection story, for now—or at least suggest the short version. After much experimentation with eardrops, creams, and hypotheses, two excellent doctors, Dr. Buzz Reifman and Dr. David Opperman, persuaded me to visit their clinic in Denver, specializing in "Care of the Professional Voice," but also a musician's ear, nose, and throat problems. Both ears were badly infected, aggravated by wearing the in-ear monitors onstage, and perhaps by wearing earplugs on the motorcycle, too—heat and moisture create a rainforest environment for bacteria, fungus, eczema, and psoriasis. The doctors prescribed a heavy regimen of three different antibiotics, and recommended that I switch to headphones (and no earplugs on the bike, but its Cee Bailey windscreen is pretty quiet). Within a few days, they had given me back two reasonably healthy ears. Never again will I take for granted simply hearing what I'm playing, what the other guys are playing, and—in everyday life—what people are saying to me. (Like when "Cruel Summer" is playing.)

Unknown to anyone else, I also suffered a little from a problem with my right foot. It didn't *hurt*, but I seemed to be gradually losing speed on the bass-drum pedal. At first I chalked it up to advancing years (just turning fifty-eight as I write), and it troubled me—the first time in my life I've felt my ability to play the drums receding instead of improving, and that particular apex is an awful prospect to contemplate.

However, I noticed that if I tucked my knee under the snare drum, it was better, and I started to wonder. The new *Time Machine* setup had the same layout as the previous *Snakes and Arrows* kit, but small differences were inevitable, with hardware changes and such, and I asked Gump to try moving the snare drum to the left about three-quarters of an inch. That's all it took—that small ergonomic change. Up to that point, during rehearsals and the first half of the tour, I had simply adapted to curving my knee slightly around that angle, causing the whole geometry of my leg, knee, ankle, and foot to be altered. The real story appeared when I happened to look at the sole of my right drumming shoe—it was only worn on the *outside*, in a perfect oval, while the big-toe side, which ought to have been doing the work, was unmarked.

I hadn't even noticed, but just adapted, until I felt the loss of foot speed. Over the next few shows, I had to consciously keep trying to rotate my foot inward, to align it properly with the pedal, and of course I was powerfully relieved not to be "losing it."

I felt that same sense of relief—reprieve—on the day off between the two Red Rocks shows, earlier in August. I was hiking to the summit of Mount Evans (14,264 feet) with my friend Kevin Anderson. Kevin has climbed all fifty-four of Colorado's "fourteeners" (peaks over 14,000 feet), often dictating chapters for his novel-in-progress to a recorder while he hikes. Kevin offered to guide me up my first "fourteener," and along the way we could discuss some ideas for a writing project on which we hoped to collaborate.

It had been some years since I had hiked at such a high elevation—since climbing Mount Kilimanjaro (19,334 feet) back in 1986 or so. As Kevin and I neared the summit, still able to walk and talk in the thinning oxygen, I told him I was glad to find that I could still *do* such a thing—also referring to my fear of the day when I might discover that I was losing my drumming fluency, or any number of other abilities, to the ravages of aging and Time (aptly described by John Barth as "The Destroyer of Delights").

I said to Kevin, "It's inevitable that one day there will be a last show—a last hike."

He grinned and said, "Not today!"

Other good memories stand out from that August, too. After our week of constant crisis, all that riding and all those shows, by the time of the show in St. Louis on August 22, I was *tired*. Plus, we were on our way back to Chicago the next night, to replay a show that had been canceled due to threatening weather on the first run. (I had already done my warm-up and was just about to get into my stage clothes when the decision came down—it was an awful feeling.) So including the first Chicago show two days prior to that, when it had been 102°, I had already ridden into downtown Chicago in withering heat twice this summer, and wasn't eager to repeat the experience.

So—a day off. Michael and I and friend Tom Marinelli rode the bus straight to the venue in Chicago, surprising the crew at breakfast catering (they had an *omelette station!*), then spent a pleasant couple of hours at the Art Institute of Chicago. I had visited there many times over the years, and offered to be "tour guide."

"Leading left," I didn't want to drag them through room after room of medieval religious paintings or too much inscrutable modernity—I just guided them to my personal "highlights"—the American and European artists of the late nineteenth and early twentieth century, like Sargent and Whistler, Edward Hopper's *Nighthawks*, Grant Wood's equally iconic *American Gothic*, and the van Goghs and Gauguins. (I knew Michael would appreciate those, because he likes what he calls "LBGs"—little brown girls.)

After that night's show (blessedly undampened by rain this time), Michael, Tom, and I spent the next couple of days looping around the back roads of Nebraska. We rode west to the lovely Sand Hills region, under the rarest of summer skies—a crystal dome of pale aquamarine, the "robin's egg blue" more often described than actually seen. Oh, it was hot again, of course, but pretty and peaceful.

We had another little drama on the show-day morning, leaving Ogallala, Nebraska, for Omaha, when Michael's bike failed to start. With a boost from a pickup, he got it running again, and we agreed that he would ride straight for the BMW dealer in Omaha, and get it sorted. (He needed a new battery.)

Later that same day, I had an awful computer incident. Just trying to copy some photos for Tom of our travels together, suddenly my whole desktop disappeared, and I was left with a blank, generic computer screen. Forensic experts Michael and Kevin worked on it, and got most of it operational again, but could not access my all-important photo files. During the previous break I had backed up everything at home, but there were almost two hundred new photos in there *somewhere* that I couldn't get at. It was distressing, to say the least (and is the reason there are so few photographs of some of our adventures in this story). All I had were unprintable "thumbnails"—which I started to feel I was hanging from.

All the while, Dave's troubles with the bus continued, with tire problems one day, and a failed water system the next. Our little team was facing an unending series of challenges getting through that second leg—but we did manage to make it to seventeen more shows, via another 7,366 miles of motorcycling (thirty shows altogether, and almost 16,000 motorcycle miles).

After one long day of battling heat and traffic in the East toward the end of the run, in late August, I remember thinking, "About one hour of that seven was actually *enjoyable*." But there were many good rides to remember, like up into Minnesota, to Voyageurs National Park (new passport stamp) and a wonderful family resort called Arrowhead, right near the park. It was owned by a friendly couple and their in-laws, and offered cozy cabins on Lake Kabetogama (I was determined to learn to spell and pronounce that name) and a casual dinner at the lodge.

The sign above the dining room door read "Dinner Choices: 1) Take it; 2) Leave it," because they only offered one choice—though that night it happened to be barbecued ribs and fresh, local corn that was unbelievably tender and succulent, so we didn't complain.

In farthest northern Minnesota, hard by the Canadian border, we had no cell service, so Michael brought out our satellite phone so I could call home. It was a beautiful scene, sitting on that dock, on a night off in the middle of a peaceful ride (500 miles around Minnesota with hardly any traffic, and without a single radar beep, or even seeing a cop) under that same robin's egg blue sky. But I was feeling pretty sad and lonely on that dock, 2,000 miles away from the ones I love. Not for the first time, I felt worse after calling home than I had before. After thirty-six years of touring life, I'm pretty good at blocking out thoughts that will only make me feel bad—but it is especially hard to maintain that "distance" with the video calls we've also been trying: looking right at your home, your family, your dog, and *not being there*.

But if I couldn't be there, at least I got to be here, sitting by a lake on an August evening that was both beautiful and cruel.

THE POWER OF
MAGICAL THINKING

22

NOVEMBER 2010

We all have our own brands of magical thinking, and mine brought me to this "pass," as it were. While my supernatural beliefs do not include skygods or "visualization techniques," they do embrace the equally irrational pursuits of dreaming, daring, and hoping. Those are the very qualities that made me believe I could do a concert tour of Brazil, Argentina, and Chile by motorcycle.

When the South American tour was being planned, for October 2010, I started to dream about riding it; then I dared to think it out loud, and from then on, it was a matter of hope. I knew it wouldn't be easy. My longtime riding partner, Brutus, would handle the route planning and logistics (even traveling to Brazil ten days early to do "advance reconnaissance"), and ride with me. For myself, I would provide the opportunity, by performing on the drums with Rush in São Paulo, Rio de Janeiro, Buenos Aires, and Santiago (to earn our "gas money"), and I would provide and prepare my two BMW R1200GS motorcycles, with fresh oil and tires, heavy-duty luggage cases, spare gas cans, and kits for tools, tires, and first aid.

In the past Brutus and I had both done a considerable amount of adventure traveling by motorcycle, often together. We knew how to prepare for a trip like that, and how to improvise around various obstacles along the way. But still—we would also need to be *lucky*. That's where the magical thinking came in.

It would be my first time motorcycling in South America, and the first time I had tried to combine "adventure travel" and "business travel." A bicycle tour in China in 1985 introduced me to adventure travel, and led to further journeys on pedaled two-wheelers, in Europe, North America, and many countries in West Africa. On concert tours, I had used bicycles and motorcycles as a kind of "getaway vehicle" for many years, but until now I had always kept the adventure travel separate from the business travel.

As the dates in South America drew nearer, I admit I was increasingly nervous about it, defining my feelings as "anticipation and apprehension—in about equal measure." Hope and fear, in other words. In the van from the airport to the first hotel, in Campinas, near São Paulo, being driven (and armed-guarded) along the dark highway, I even felt a little *dread*. After the first show, in São Paulo, when Brutus and I started riding, it felt like I had a knot in my stomach, and I carried that anxiety with me the whole way. There were many times when I thought, "This was a bad idea."

Many others would have agreed with me, and had *always* thought it was a bad idea—my wife, Carrie, for example. When she got wind of my plans to ride to the South American shows, she was appalled and incredulous. My mother didn't like the idea either. My American riding partner, Michael, who I have also described as my "Director of Homeland Security" (which surely includes *me*) tried to discourage me. Manager Ray and bandmates Alex and Geddy must have had their reservations, but wisely left them unspoken. (They know I can be impossibly stubborn, perhaps *especially* when I am in the grip of a bad idea.) Agents and promoters and crew members would have felt concern for their livelihoods.

But what could I do?

Seriously, as soon as I saw the itinerary, with four days off between the Brazil shows and Buenos Aires, and once Brutus had done some preliminary mapwork and determined that it *could* be done, it seemed like I didn't have a choice. It was a perfect example of the kind of decision that just seems *obvious* to me: I have four days off between those South American shows; what's the most *excellent* thing I can do in those four days?

Why, ride my motorcycle there, of course.

As if it would be that easy.

I conceded to my well-wishers (and my own selfish preference for survival) that we wouldn't ride in any of the big cities, or to the giant soccer stadiums where we would be performing. Apparently Brutus and I had more than *traffic* to fear there—like robbers, muggers, and kidnappers (oh my!)—so we would stage ourselves somewhere within an hour of those jobsites, then shuttle in and out of the cities by van, accompanied by Michael.

Brutus and me in Argentina's wine country

It all ought to work, as long as nothing went wrong. That was the act of faith—and magical thinking: dream, dare, hope . . .

As mentioned, Brutus and I had shared many adventure travels on motorcycles—to Arctic Canada, around Mexico, and even from Europe to North Africa and the edge of the Sahara. And on each of those journeys, something unexpected had occurred—a mechanical problem, bad weather, a crash—that had delayed us for a day or two and changed our plans. When an adventure trip is interrupted like that, you just stop and deal with whatever you have to, and make new plans to suit.

But we had no flexibility for anything like that this time.

On the "business travel" side, I have been motorcycling to concerts for fourteen years—hundreds of shows and tens of thousands of miles—and have yet to be late even for a soundcheck, let alone a show. However, this time I would not have the "support crew" of a bus and trailer in the general vicinity (following the interstates while I explored the back roads). No spare bike, no BMW Roadside Assistance and well-placed dealers, none of the "easy" rescues available in North America and Western Europe. We would be pretty much on our own.

As I wrote to Brutus early on, when he was painstakingly researching and planning the journey (for about six months), "You know that a lot is 'riding' on this little venture of ours, and NOTHING can go wrong."

He needed no reminding, but perhaps it was another kind of magical thinking to state it so plainly—a talisman to ward off the Evil Eye.

We did have a *real* "guardian angel" watching over us. Michael installed satellite tracking devices on our bikes, and while he traveled by air, with the band and crew, he could check his computer screen and follow our "breadcrumbs" (that's what they call the electronic tracks we left, in that curious, playful imagery that sometimes emerges from high-tech language—a contradiction that has fascinated me at least since writing the lyrics for our song "Vital Signs" in that style, in 1980).

It was kind of eerie to feel that you were being watched like that (once a day at least, I would look up at the sky, raise a fist, and say bad words at Michael), but it was reassuring, too. If any trouble *did* come our way, we would want as much help as we could get, as soon as we could get it.

The first day, navigating through the teeming traffic of Campinas, I felt like we were riding two ponies through a vast buffalo herd of cars, with trucks like elephants towering above, and swarms of gnat-like little motorbikes swarming all around.

From Campinas to the Rio de Janeiro area, then back through São Paulo and south, we traveled mainly four-lane motorways for long stretches, because we had so much distance to cover. As Brutus had warned me, trucks outnumbered cars by about ten to one, but the drivers seemed good, and we were able to pass easily on those roads. However, there were a *lot* of tollbooths (fifteen in just one day's travel), and in negotiating those, Brutus and I followed the same ritual that Michael and I always did in the U.S. Brutus pulled up by the toll window, and I stopped on his right. (Roadcraft tip: Avoid the greasy strip in the middle, where cars and trucks have dripped, especially on wet days.) While Brutus paid both tolls, the attendant raised the barrier once and waved me through, then a second time for Brutus—while he was collecting change and receipt, pulling on his gloves, and getting the bike in gear.

Away from the freeways (well, *toll*ways), things were much more lively and picturesque, of course. Here is Brutus on the road up to Petrópolis, a beautiful colonial city nestled in the mountainous rainforest north of Rio de Janeiro.

Typically, perhaps, things really started getting interesting when we became horribly *lost*—in southern Brazil, on the second day of our four-day odyssey to Buenos Aires. Back in Campinas, before we set out, Michael and Brutus had spent many, many hours (and many *caipirinhas*—Brazil's national cocktail) working on our GPS units.

After all that online work, and several long telephone calls to the manufacturer, the units worked fine for the 322 miles from São Paulo to Petrópolis, then 550 miles (a long day) south to another good-sized city, Curitiba. But shortly after leaving there, they began to "wander." Something similar had happened to Brutus and me a few years previously, in Poland and the former East Germany, and then as now, the purple line of our route remained on the screen—if not exactly on the road we were on, then near enough that we could navigate by it. This time we just figured we were riding through another poorly mapped area, and the GPS units would eventually steer us right. (Magical thinking again.)

We knew that generally we had to work our way west-southwest, toward the Uruguay River. There was only one bridge in that part of the country, where we would cross and carry on west-southwest to the Argentina border. As we rode along, we glanced occasionally at the purple line on the little screen, or switched it to the "compass" function, to see that we were still tending in the right compass direction. We figured we couldn't go too far wrong.

Until about the point where I took the previous photo. Riding out of one small town, the paved road petered out into a dirt track running along the wide brownish-green river to our left. It was late in the day, with nearly 400 miles behind us, and the shadows were growing long as the sun headed for bed. Still there was no bridge in sight—and no *bed* in sight, for us. Of course we had paper maps with us, but they were no use just then—because there were no towns, no signs, nothing to go by, and no people to ask. The best idea we could agree on was to make our way north toward where the paved road *ought* to be, and take it from there. The knot in my stomach was growing, and I said to myself, in roughly these words, "We are fornicated."

Even once we found our way to that paved road, we were confused, thinking we still had to go farther west along the river. So we headed that way, following a delightful winding two-lane along a ridge overlooking green valleys of woods and farmland, with only occasional trucks to pass. We didn't realize yet that we were *still* very lost, so we were enjoying a lovely late-afternoon ride. The Uruguay occasionally appeared in the distance—to the south, just where it ought to be. And yes, the purple lines on Dingus and Dork continued to assure us we were headed in the right general direction. (Idiots—them and us. They also often showed us riding in the middle of the river—a motorcycle icon in a field of blue—which should perhaps have alerted us to the machine's utter *lostness*. Michael would tell us later that as he watched our wandering breadcrumbs, he wished he could shout "down" at us, "You're really lost!")

As we rode through a small town called Itapiranga, the road suddenly dwindled to rough dirt once more, the trees shadowing darkly overhead, and we stopped and opened up the map again. Now that we knew where we were, exactly, we could see how badly we were *lost*, exactly. We had missed the turn for the bridge some hours before, and now were in the farthest corner of Brazil, with the river to our south, and, immediately west of us, the Argentina border running north and south. No roads crossed that frontier, or that river—and I knew right away what we should do.

"We'll stop here," I said, pointing back up the road to Itapiranga, "It was a nice-looking town—it might have a hotel."

"Yeah," Brutus said. "Then tomorrow—"

I cut him off, "*Fornicate* tomorrow—let's look after today first." (Roadcraft.)

As I led us back along the main street, I pointed up at a sign, in Gothic script, "Hotel Mauá." For a town of only 13,000 people, laying "at the end of the road" in more ways than one, the hotel was absolutely fine—small, austere, and scrupulously clean, much like you might come across in rural Austria, say, and with safe covered parking for the motorcycles.

My room, with its little balcony, upstairs at the Hotel Mauá, Itapiranga, Brazil. In the foreground, the idiot Dingus displays the motorcycle icon, representing me, in the middle of the river.

I had noticed a couple of restaurants in town, too, and we walked to a casual outdoor place, much like you might come across in small-town Italy. Speakers played music in a fetching hybrid of Brazilian and West African styles, and I had to ask our waiter to write down the names of the artists—handing him my notebook and making him understand about "*música*." Subtropical night, good hotel, outdoor dining, intriguing music—everything was working out all right now.

As I stood on the sidewalk in front of the restaurant talking to Carrie on my cell phone (which miraculously worked perfectly in that remote corner of Brazil), Brutus was talking in pidgin Portuguese with some locals. He learned there was a *balsa*—a ferry—right in Itapiranga, and in the morning we could take it to the other side of that major barrier without having to backtrack several hours. From there we could try to navigate (the old-fashioned paper way) to our border crossing, San Borja.

On the hotel's balcony, Brutus and I had arranged a still-life array of all of our "handheld devices" (still would have made a great tour name, as I have remarked before): cell phone, satellite phone, Nextel radio-phone, satellite tracking device (Michael's "eye on the breadcrumbs"), GPS idiot, paper map, and camera. (For "verisimilitude," we also added a whisky glass and a pack of Red Apples, as other important handheld devices.)

In contrast to that display of high technology, Brutus stayed up late with the paper maps, copying down village names, distances, and (where possible) road numbers onto sheets of paper, for the tankbag map-holders. (That's the kind of GPS I call "Get a Pen, Stupid.")

Up at sunrise, as we were on so many of those long traveling days, we had some bread and coffee at the hotel, loaded up the bikes, and headed down to the ferry landing. The *balsa* was just a small barge driven by an outboard-powered launch, but within a few minutes it had carried us across the expanse of river, shining blue over greenish-brown on that sunny morning, and we were immediately—lost again.

There was no there there, just a few small houses and a two-block grid of narrow lanes, brown dirt and rocks (not gravel—rocks). We immediately resorted to the most primitive form of GPS—finding a person and saying the name of the next village we were trying to find ("Gaucha Vista?" in this case) repeatedly, and pointing up the road interrogatively. Basically, looking like idiots.

The only downside to that method is that *you need people to ask*, and they were scarce along the little dirt road indistinguishable from driveways and farm tracks leading off in different directions. We often paused to consider choices—and look at our GPS compasses ("the idiots," as I routinely called those units now, and Brutus sneeringly referred to his as "the thousand-dollar compass"). There were no road signs—not one—and as I have remarked before about such unmarked tracks in Africa or Mexico, even when you're on the right road, you have no way of knowing it.

There was a certain extra anxiety about that day, too, as we really needed to get to the border crossing, in San Borja, as early as we could. The promoter had arranged to have an agent meet us there and help with our "formalities," and we were supposed to be there by noon. And there was still such a long way to go to Buenos Aires in the next two days.

But soon we encountered an important truth about Brazil—several truths, in fact. Sure, we were lost on a rough road in an isolated rural area, but Michael and I had found ourselves in that exact situation many times right in the United States. And similar to what happened then, once Brutus and I flailed our way out from the "beaten tracks" of that isolated rural pocket, we were on a nicely paved two-lane, with little traffic, passing through pretty countryside.

One telling detail: Along that dirt road, near the river, I saw a man driving a single-furrow plow with a pair of oxen, yet less than an hour later, along the paved road, we passed huge farms, and I saw many big, modern John Deere tractors and shiny green combine harvesters with sixty-foot blades. Subsistence farming might be the economic reality in such isolated, backwater areas, but even in the same region, those Iron-Age corners coexisted with large-scale mechanization and urbanization along the main roads and towns, all very much of the present day. Brutus and I saw undeveloped *pockets* in Brazil, and later, in Argentina too, but you certainly wouldn't say the countries were undeveloped—quite the contrary.

Most stories of motorcycle adventures in South America I have read have been concerned with getting *through* it—marathon riders traveling the Pan-American Highway from Alaska to Tierra del Fuego, for example. But I soon realized that you could certainly make a nice tour *around* South America. Those thin red roads, as they were shown on the *Guia Quatro Rodas* maps, were the key, and unlike São Paulo and Rio, the smaller cities and towns were entirely civilized and welcoming.

My own capsule definition for what some term "the Third World" is "any place where the air is redolent of human waste." (The reader may translate that freely.) Such a definition necessarily includes much of China, sub-Saharan Africa, and even parts of southern Europe—rural towns in Italy and Greece, for example. (It doesn't mean I don't *love* some of those places—I do—it just means they *smell*.)

In Latin America, only the biggest cities seem to fall under that rancid rubric—São Paulo, Rio, Mexico City—and then only because they are such magnets for hopeful young people. Magical thinkers. They dreamed; they dared; they hoped.

Brazilian cruise

In the late '90s, I visited Mexico City fairly often, and I learned that every single day, 1,000 new people arrived there—leaving their villages and towns and seeking a better future, carrying nothing but strong arms and hope. One thousand people a day—how could *any* city handle that sort of influx? To their compassionate credit, Mexico City tried—bringing electricity and piped water to the ever-growing shantytowns (as opposed to burning them out, as the U.S. government did in the 1930s)—but it could never be enough.

In such a confused megalopolis, expanding daily beyond any possibility of equal infrastructure, there will be bad smells—and bad behavior: crime. On the one hand, the cities are helpless to provide the necessary "facilities" for their new citizens, while the very rootlessness and helplessness of the newcomers alienates them from the sense of community—of home—that would otherwise govern, or at least moderate, their behavior.

All in all, it's pretty much a perfect recipe for disaster—stewed in its own smelly juices.

A tiny town like Itapiranga does not appear in the tourist guidebooks. Even in the vast and seemingly all-inclusive online resources, the most information to be found is that Itapiranga is "the westernmost municipality in the Brazilian province of Santa Catarina." Yet it was a clean, pretty, friendly place, with entirely adequate accommodations and nourishment for visitors, and Itapiranga lay at the end of some pretty nice motorcycling roads, too.

More than anything, it seemed like a *miracle* that we found Itapiranga just when that long, wearying day was growing dark. We had nowhere else to go—and there it was.

Magical.

As stated at the outset, I believe that everybody has their own version of magical thinking. My own "dream, dare, hope" approach to life is not based upon *reason*; it's a kind of *faith*—that I will be able to accomplish something about which I dare to dream. I once called it "Tryism," believing that if I tried hard enough at something, it would eventually yield and come to pass. The fact that such an approach sometimes works is no empirical proof of its *truth*, per se. I am reminded of a conversation I had after I hit a deer on my motorcycle ("Every Road Has Its Toll"). After that scare, I did some *serious* research about defensive measures such as deer whistles, which emit a high-pitched sound that's supposed to repel deer. I soon learned that those devices had been proven ineffective at best, and an actual *lure* at

worst. When I reported that to one friend, he said, "Well, I've got them on my van, and I've never hit a deer."

Well, that settles it, then. (Like a doctor who was dismissing suspected links between vaccinations and autism: "The plural of 'anecdote' is not 'data.'")

But that kind of subjective warp is just one variation of a human theme that ranges from four-leaf clovers and curative bracelets to sky-god temples like this one, in Petrópolis, Brazil.

In the incredible scope of impossibilities embraced by human faith (by definition, whichever one is correct, the others are thus "impossible"), it seems that the more outlandish those beliefs become, the greater are the cries of "intolerance" and pleas for "respect."

During the North American part of the *Time Machine* tour, over our post-ride cocktails and dinners, Michael and I had discussed that topic at length—the scale and power of magical thinking. (Our conversations aren't *all* gay banter and profanity—or at least they also contain the names of German philosophers and English metaphysical poets.) The subject of faith often came up when we had been riding in southern Tennessee, say, or even Pennsylvania (something of a southern state itself, I've come to think, outside of the cities). We would feel overwhelmed by the sheer numbers of churches and church signs, and the in-your-face billboards and bumper stickers, plus the prevalence of "boutique churches." Sometimes it seemed like every rural crossroads had three or four cinder-block churches, mostly different splinters of the Baptist cross.

"Tax them all," Michael says, and I would agree—churches are *products*, after all, like alcohol and tobacco, that provide a service that some find comforting and others find reprehensible. Call it a "sin tax."

As for tolerance and respect, we agree that tolerance is necessary—people can believe the crazy fecal matter of their choice—but we're not sure about respect.

Those who attribute spiritual power to geological formations, a humorless deity, or articles of clothing (think Catholic, Hasidic, Mormon, or Buddhist) are difficult to respect—not so much for their "magic," but for their *vanity*.

Fundamentalists of every stripe, and likewise conspiracy theorists, are pretty much impossible to respect, especially if they preach violence—pain to others, the *real* first deadly sin.

In terms of my simple moral compass (though like Dingus, it too was expensive to acquire!), if the greatest evils to an individual are pain, fear, and worry, then it stands to reason that the worst things you can inflict on another human being are pain, fear, and worry.

(One admirable part of the "gentleman's code" I ran across somewhere years ago was "A gentleman never inflicts pain intentionally." Likewise with fear and worry, I would think.)

Non-believers are always admonished to "respect" the beliefs of others, but are not respected in turn. Likewise, I don't believe for a second that Mormons "respect" the beliefs of Scientologists, say, or that Jehovah's Witnesses give equal weight to the teachings of the prophet Muhammad. Put ten believers from the major religions of the world in a circle, and their "thought balloons" are going to read the same as mine: "You believe *that*?"

I'm afraid tolerance is the best we can be expected to offer. People like that will just have to respect themselves . . .

But let's return to the flying carpet ride of magical thinking in action, and the bridge across the Uruguay River between Brazil and Argentina at San Borja. It would be our first South American border crossing, and we were a little nervous. (Well, a little *extra* nervous.) We were met at the border gates by the tour promoter's agent, Sergio, an amiable, bearish man, who spoke the necessary English, Portuguese, and Spanish. He had an assistant on the Brazilian side, and one on the Argentinian side, and they seemed to do the office-shuffling and line-waiting, which made the process much easier for Brutus and me—we just had to wait.

For a while we watched the computer monitor through the window of the Argentinian customs office, which was showing live footage of the rescue of the miners in Chile. For anyone not included in the estimated one billion people around the world who watched the events live, the short version is that in early August 2010, a notoriously unsafe copper mine in northern Chile collapsed, trapping thirty-three miners half a mile underground, three miles from the mine's entrance. A technological collaboration between NASA and the Chilean navy drilled boreholes down to the miners' shelter, at first delivering food, then winching out the stranded miners, one at a time, in cylindrical pods, up a perilous fifteen-minute ascent.

Over the previous few days, Brutus and I had come to feel we were *deep* in South America. (Nothing like getting really lost to heighten that sensation.) At that point, we were also close to Chile, both geographically and with its appearance on our itinerary in a few days. For those reasons, the story felt even more poignant—more part of *our* world.

In the ongoing bureaucratic process that presently defined our world, even with three people on our side, it still took two hours for the officials to decide that all of our papers were in order and properly stamped and signed in triplicate. (Sergio told us the Argentina border controls were the slowest and strictest in South America.) By the time we were free to ride into Argentina, it was 4:00, so we decided to run south for a couple of hours, then find a hotel before dark. The sky was gray, the air cool, and a few scattered showers were starting to spatter our windscreens.

(Of course, mid-October was *springtime* in the southern hemisphere, which took some getting used to mentally—and both Brutus and I had taken for granted that as we rode south, the weather would become warmer, when of course the opposite was true. *Everything was all upside-down!*)

Many things were immediately different in Argentina. We rode across the grassy plains called the Pampas, and the landscape resembled West Texas after a bit of rain—flat green grasslands patterned with occasional stunted, mesquite-like trees. A four-lane highway had been surveyed and partly constructed, but no recent work appeared to have been done. Traffic was almost exclusively trucks on the existing two lanes, and they often had to be passed in clumps of three or four at a time, as they bunched up in crawling, smoky convoys. But at least in flat, open country like that, visibility for passing was perfect.

Early in our Brazilian travels, tollbooths had been a constant interruption, but on the toll roads in Argentina, motorcycles were given free passage. However, we traded that for frequent barricades with soldiers and policemen slowing or stopping traffic. We were never questioned or searched, but a lot of truck and car drivers ahead of us were, some of them pulled aside for further scrutiny. As another indicator of the "undeveloped" (read "uncivilized," I think) world, any country that interferes with the movements of its citizens, and gives its armed officers the right to stop and search any vehicle they choose, is corrupting freedom. The worst examples of such countries I have encountered were in West Africa, China, northern Mexico, and . . . the Southwestern United States. (Derek Lundy's book *Borderlands* goes deeply into something I have experienced myself—the abuses the U.S. and border-state governments are perpetrating in the name of their citizens, and "homeland security.")

Even though we were not personally bothered by the armed roadblocks, of course traffic was slowed every time, and we had to wait behind it. The other obstacles for us were many construction detours, leading us through muddy off-road loops, a slippery mess, often pot-holed and puddled from recent rains. We slithered around the trucks, which loomed over us like hippos in a mud-bath. Soon our bikes and lower extremities were painted in brown slop, and the situation was even worse in places like this—a gas station's driveway.

We found refuge for the night in a somewhat run-down border town along the Uruguay River, Paso de los Libres. Across the river was Brazil's Uruguaiana, a major city with tall modern buildings and many more lights reflecting in the water. It was not quite a Ciudad Juárez–El Paso contrast, but the difference was striking.

Our hotel was a slightly shabby high-rise called Alejandro I (after Alexander the Great, apparently, judging by a huge bas-relief sculpture in the dining room). The ancient elevator was tiny, and had the old metal scissors-style gate, so I only rode it once—up with the luggage. From then on I used the stairs. I wasn't afraid of *riding* it, but did fear it might *seize* for some reason—they had earthquakes around there. And when I woke briefly around 5:00 a.m., with my curtains open, I noticed that the entire town was lightless—a power cut—while Uruguaiana glittered across the water. I definitely never used the lift after that.

The Alejandro I was a quaint old hotel, the kind where the front-desk guy handed us the TV remotes with our keys. The bellman came to our rooms to ensure they worked, and left us both with a different Spanish-language station on, each reporting on the successful rescue of the miners—all thirty-three of them above ground by then. After more than two months of darkness, they all wore dark eyewear, but smiled very brightly—all shaven and groomed for their celebration. As I watched those fortunate souls being reunited with their loved ones, and stirring music playing behind, it started to get to me, and soon tears were rolling down my face. Even Brutus admitted to feeling a little moisture in his baby blues.

The rescue was already being called a "miracle," and if ever the word was apt, it was here. However, those who called it an "act of Divine Providence" were begging a question like the one put to one of Voltaire's characters in *Candide*. "If God saved the thirty-three, why is it that, every year since 2000, an average of thirty-four other miners have died in Chilean mines?"

"Ah," goes the reply, "The *Devil* killed those ones . . ."

As Brutus and I worked our way closer to Buenos Aires, the four-lane highway was actually completed, so traffic was easier to handle (easier to pass). However, navigation became more difficult. As in any metropolitan area, you can't predict what information will help you make the correct turns—it might be a route number, it might be a town name (even one that's much farther away, and only coincidentally in the same direction you're aiming for), or you might get nothing at all. One set of ramps onto a major highway had no signs whatsoever, leaving us to compass and instinct. Both failed us a few times, but eventually we circled our way to a unique destination, the Resort Campo & Polo (always using the ampersand, rather than "y" or "and")—a polo club!

I knew from my friend Stewart Copeland's fine memoir, *Strange Things Happen*, when he was writing about being a keen polo player, that Argentina was the only place in the world to buy polo ponies. Near the town of Lujan, we started passing many vast horse farms and polo clubs, and arrived at our own destination, set amid wide green polo fields and lush gardens. Much like a country club hotel in the U.S. or Europe, it offered an elegant hotel and restaurant, but instead of golf courses, it was set amid polo fields.

And unlike most country club hotels in the U.S. or Europe, the Resort Campo & Polo ("campo" means "field," so I don't know why it's "field and polo") was unfazed by our wish to perform a couple of oil changes in their forecourt.

Brutus arranged for the perfectly sized drain buckets, and Michael came out early with the van and driver from Buenos Aires, bringing our toolbox and the fresh oil and filters we had packed with the band gear. I was glad to handle the mechanical part of the operation, having performed so many oil changes on my motorcycles over the years. (The service notes I keep in the back of my journal always tell an interesting story of where oil and tire changes have been done. For the *Time Machine* tour of summer and fall 2010, the list for one bike includes Los Angeles, Albuquerque, Chicago, Quebec City, Toronto, Nashville, Las Vegas, St. Louis, Columbus, New Jersey, and Lujan, Argentina. The second bike lists Toronto, Quebec,

Omaha, Tulsa, Atlanta, and—Lujan, Argentina. It was satisfying to add that name to the end of both lists—in the sense of a worthwhile job done, and in a *very* unusual location.

The driver of our van gave us a tour of Buenos Aires on our way to work, and though the cloudy day cast everything in a flat, gray light, the word that occurred to me was "monumental." French, Spanish, and Italian influences dominated the older buildings, while sleek modern skyscrapers were set off with artful metallic sculpture, like the stunning, giant polished-metal flower that opened and closed mechanically at morning and evening. The main boulevard, 9 de Julio, is said to be the widest in the world, and Brutus counted twenty-four lanes of traffic.

The venue, unfortunately, was far from "monumental"—a squalid old stadium with box-trailer dressing rooms and portable toilets. The audience, as in Brazil, was large and enthusiastic (32,000 people in São Paulo; 13,000 in Rio—where we had a "magic show" that echoed the one in 2002 that became our *Rush in Rio* DVD—and 10,000 in Buenos Aires). But the biggest show, in every way, awaited us in Santiago.

And it was one Brutus and I—and everybody else—were worried about getting ourselves to in time. We only had one day off to get there, and would have to ride 1,000 kilometers (600 miles) the first day, to Mendoza, Argentina, to be close enough to the Chilean border to be sure of getting to Santiago good and early.

Up in the dark and away by sunrise, we rode off across the Pampas again. . . .

In Buenos Aires, Brutus and I heard that "somebody" (probably the promoter) was sending a car to follow us across Argentina. Brutus passed the word back, "Just make sure we don't see the guy—at the hotel, or on the road." He and I agreed, "We don't want to be like Ewan and Charley," referring to actors Ewan McGregor and Charley Boorman, who have made a couple of amazing motorcycle journeys, around the world (as seen in *Long Way Round*) and from Scotland to South Africa (*Long Way Down*) but they traveled with a van carrying a film crew, medic, and security officer. Actually, of course we did want to be like Ewan and Charley (who wouldn't?), but without the "retinue."

Knowing we had a long way to go, we attacked the day that way. Brutus and I fell into the rhythm we had established on our first motorcycle tours together—changing the lead at every fuel stop, and hardly stopping otherwise. Several times on that long ride we had to use our spare gallons of gas to reach occasionally far-distant gas stations, but that was why we carried them.

At one stop I told Brutus that this ride reminded me of one earlier in that tour, across Western Kansas with Michael. At the time, I had described it to Michael as "flat, featureless, and fast," and Michael shot back, "Sounds like my ex-girlfriend."

I laughed and said, "Now *that's* why I keep you around!"

The goal was to arrive in Mendoza before dark, and we made it with an hour to spare. Brutus hadn't mentioned anything about the

Casitas among the vineyards–
Andes in the distance

accommodations there. (In previous weeks he had sent me a lot of websites to view, but being deep into the American tour at the time, I hadn't had time to look.) Along the way that day, he told me it was something called a "Wine Lodge," and the woman he had spoken to on the phone for directions had told him to look for "a dirty road."

Brutus cracked to me, "I'm *always* looking for that."

(Of course, she meant a "dirt road.")

After our longest day yet, over 633 miles, I was completely unprepared to be overwhelmed by the splendor of the Cavas Wine Lodge, a marvel of adobe-style architecture with fourteen separate casitas set apart, amid tidy vineyards, with the snow-streaked Andes to the west. Our casitas were perfectly appointed, organically shaped plaster, natural stone, and ultra-modern plumbing, lighting, and furniture.

I stood in the middle of the stone floor, gradually shedding my riding clothes among my scattered luggage, and thought, "This would be beautiful—if I wasn't too tired to enjoy it!" Though I did add in my journal, "Still—better than being tired in a *dump*!"

After a drowsy, but excellent meal and a short, nervous sleep, we were up at 5:00, packing the bikes, having some bread and coffee, and setting out at first light for the final ride.

(One postscript to the Cavas Wine Lodge, which had so impressed me that I was raving about it to people and recommending it to some friends who lived part-time in neighboring Chile. After Brutus and I returned home, he discovered some disturbing stories about armed gangs robbing guests at upscale hotels in that area, including the Cavas Wine Lodge. Apparently such robberies had occurred at least twenty-two times in recent years. Brutus said, "I'd say we dodged another bullet there—without even knowing it." So I'd better qualify my recommendation.)

Brutus and I expected that morning to be cold where we were headed—above 10,000 feet—so we basically wore everything we had: long underwear, sock liners, electric vests, thermal gloves, and plastic rainsuits over everything.

The grades started gently on the Argentinian side, with enough straight stretches to pass the few trucks we encountered on that Sunday morning. Soon enough we were above treeline, then into the nearly barren, snow-patched rocks of the highest peaks—glimpsing the white shoulder of Aconcagua, at 22,841 feet, the highest in the Americas, or anywhere outside the Himalayas.

The border crossing was near the summit of the pass, Los Libertaderos, at just over 10,000 feet. The promoter's representative at the border this time was a soft-spoken, bespectacled young man named Carlos, and he translated for the soldier, asking if I was the "*baterista*" (drummer). Carlos told me that the previous day's Santiago newspaper had reported that I was arriving to perform there in this unusual way, and a couple of fans showed up, too. I shook their hands and greeted them, but when they went on snapping photos with their handheld devices again and again, Brutus and I waved them away. Enough was enough, and we were plenty nervous already without any extra fuss.

Border crossings are always uncertain ordeals for anyone, even between Canada and the United States, and a lot was "riding" on this one. However, in contrast to the two-hour border crossing into Argentina, this time processing the paperwork for us and our motorcycles only took twenty minutes. Meanwhile, Carlos explained to me that the soldier was telling him we were to be escorted all the way into the city—just under 100 miles. Earlier, through Michael, we had asked if someone could meet us *just outside* the city, maybe, to help guide us to the stadium (the bikes were headed home from there, with the band gear, so this time we needed to deliver them right to the venue), but it seemed the officials had "overreacted."

I soon understood that there was no graceful way out of such a situation, and as we pulled away from the border, we followed a police 4x4 pickup. Brutus and I stopped for "action photographs" at the top of the steep switchbacks pictured at the beginning of this tale, then I swooped down ahead of the rest of them, leaning into those tight turns with the *commitment* they required, heart rate climbing. Where

It sure *looks* like trouble . . .

the road straightened, I let out a deep breath, parked my bike at the roadside, and waited for a shot of Brutus riding down. The pickup stopped beside me and one of the officers leaned out and waved his hand downward, saying, "*Piano! piano!*"

I guessed he wasn't suggesting that I should change instruments, but that I should slow down (the word actually means "softly, with slight force"), as he seemed to be explaining that our motorcycles were too fast for their truck.

Well, yes . . . but never mind. Accept the inevitable.

As the pass descended and opened up into scrubby woodlands and small towns, we were picked up by another set of escorts—two soldiers, *carabinieri*, on little dirt bikes—and the pickup turned around.

They led us to the city limits, pulling over by a tollbooth. The attendant leaned out and asked me, "*Baterista?*" I nodded as he pulled out his cell-phone camera to commemorate the event. A pair of Santiago officers on big BMW motorcycles took over from there, leading us through the nice-looking city, with the snow-frosted Andes still visible to the east.

Finally, we pulled into the stadium, and parked in a tunnel inside. Brutus and I stepped off the muddy motorcycles and shared a strong hug of relief. We had survived 3,000 miles—and made it to all of the shows. Our work was done.

Well—not mine, exactly, because now, at last, we come to the final show . . .

I had already decided that I wanted one more photograph to complete all the motorcycle and scenery shots I had taken: I wanted to take one *onstage*. In thirty-six years of touring, I had never *once* taken a photograph myself like that, and I thought it would make the perfect complement. Just before the show, I asked Michael to take my camera out to the stage and give it to my drum tech, Gump, with instructions for him to pass it up to me just before we played "Stick It Out." That was the fourth song, after "The Spirit of Radio," "Time Stand Still," and "Presto," and the point where Geddy talked to the audience for the first time—so they were lighted up for each of us to look at all of them.

When I talked with my bandmates at soundcheck, I learned that they had also been moved by watching the rescue of the Chilean miners. Geddy planned to dedicate that very song, "Stick It Out," to the miners, while a photo of them would appear on the giant screen behind us. Also, Alex's guitar would be decorated with the symbolic number of the rescue, 33.

So all of that is part of the "background" of this photo, the magic unseen but surely *felt*, in so many smiling faces among the 36,000 people, the flashing cameras, the Chilean flag in the middle, a *hilarious* sign to the right, and one to the left that I had Michael enlarge and enhance. It reads, touchingly, "All My Life/ For Rush."

("Me too, buddy—me too.")

At the end of forty-four shows for me, my bandmates, and our incredible crew, and at the end of 23,132 motorcycle miles for me and my riding partners, Michael and Brutus, Alex and Geddy and I stood (or sat, in my case) on that stage and looked out at that cheering, heaving, chanting crowd, and saw, heard, and felt . . . the power of magical thinking.

THE PRIZE

In rounding off this series of stories, I am irresistibly drawn to the next piece of writing I worked on after "The Power of Magical Thinking." It was a review for Bubba's Book Club of two novels, *The Amazing Adventures of Kavalier & Clay* by Michael Chabon and *The Lacuna* by Barbara Kingsolver. The review opens,

> "Be kind, for everyone you meet is fighting a hard battle."
>
> This beautiful truth is attributed to Philo of Alexandria, among others, but I favor Philo for the quote. Philo was a Jewish philosopher who lived in Egypt under the Romans at the time of Christ, which seems the right time and place to have offered such generous advice.
>
> That such deep wisdom is still rarely followed, after 2,000 years, is a shame, and you have to wonder, "Why didn't we ever *learn* anything from these ancient sages?" The easy answer is that humans are weak-willed and self-centered—yet it remains strange to me that we

often resist clear "goodness" (generosity to the unfortunate, say) so coldly, but devote ourselves unstintingly, selflessly, to following meaningless rituals and customs. Observe a holy holiday without fail, yes—but commit a random act of kindness? Not so likely.

Philo would agree; we've still got a lot of work to do when it comes to being kind and appreciating the hard battles others must fight every day.

I went on to discuss that spirit of generosity as expressed in literature, with particular reference to these two novels, and then got to my *real* point, the product of at least two years of thought. It is significant that much of that thought was engaged in while I was "far and away"—riding my motorcycle along an American back road, skiing through the snowy Quebec woods, or lying awake in a backwater motel. The theme I was grappling with was nothing less than the Meaning of Life, and I was pretty sure I had defined it: love and respect.

Love and respect, love and respect—I have been carrying those words around with me for two years, daring to consider that perhaps they convey the real meaning of life. Beyond basic survival needs, everybody wants to be loved and respected. And neither is any good without the other. Love without respect can be as cold as pity; respect without love can be as grim as fear.

Love and respect are the values in life that most contribute to "the pursuit of happiness"—and after, they are the greatest legacy we can leave behind. It's an elegy you'd like to hear with your own ears: "You were loved and respected."

If even one person can say that about you, it's a worthy achievement, and if you can multiply that many times—well, that is true success.

Among materialists, a certain bumper sticker is emblematic: "He who dies with the most toys wins!"

Well, no—he or she who dies with the most love and respect wins.

But why didn't anyone ever tell me this? No one—not Mom and Dad, not Reverend Chisholm at St. Andrew's United Church, not Miss Masters in grade six (she gave small prizes to students for memorizing bible verses in the early '60s—probably not allowed these days), not

Jesus, not Confucius, not Muhammad, not Krishna—no one ever seems to have imparted the simple idea that what we are supposed to do down here is go out into the world and earn love and respect.

Steve Martin once spoke of a life lesson he had learned: "No one will ever love you for working hard." That is true, but it doesn't stop many people from subconsciously living by that belief. (Guilty!) It is equally true that you will not earn anyone's respect *without* working hard—not only at pursuits that might be respected by strangers (writing great novels, hitting things with sticks), but by living each day with the kind of integrity and generosity that earns the respect and love of friends and family members.

Then there's love and respect for oneself—equally hard to achieve and maintain. Most of us, deep down, are not as proud of ourselves as we might pretend, and the goal of bettering ourselves—at least partly by earning the love and respect of others—is a lifelong struggle.

Philo of Alexandria gave us that generous principle that we have somehow succeeded in mostly ignoring for 2,000 years: "Be kind, for everyone you meet is fighting a hard battle."

Great literature takes us into that battle, and in every example I can think of—every celebrated novel of the past few hundred years—there is a quest for love and respect.

The stories in this collection are about . . . pretty much everything really, as stated upfront, but they certainly exemplify the same quest—for love and respect. The work and challenges I have undertaken, in music or words or shunpikers' trails, have an overall goal of continuing to earn my own self-respect, day by day—just as the way I try to live has the overall goal of earning love and respect from others, especially those close to me.

One facet of earning love and respect from others is illuminated by my observation, "Sometimes being 'good' means behaving better than we are."

Or, perhaps stated more clearly, "Sometimes being 'good' means behaving better than we *feel*."

We don't win that prize of love and respect every time, that's for sure, but it remains the ultimate treasure we seek, whether we know it or not.

I think of the lines I made up for Matt Scannell that morning described in "A Winter's Tale of Summers Past," driving together in my Aston Martin DB9 along the Pacific Coast Highway near Big Sur. We were talking about how fully we were *in* that moment—yet how it was equally true that we had *created* that moment, made it happen. Or at least, *allowed* it to happen. We had set the conditions under which something magic might happen, and were ready when it did.

In a major key, set to a fast, pounding rock tempo:

> Wake up every morning like you're gonna live forever
> Go to sleep at night like it's the last day of your life

I guess that's what all of these stories have been trying to say all along.

Someday I should make those lyrics into a song—a song called . . . "Far and Away."

Photo Credits

All photos by the author, except those contributions noted below:

Michael Mosbach: x, 24, 27, 64, 66, 67 (top), 68 (top), 73, 78 (bottom), 87 (top), 89, 239, 242, 245, 249 (top), 262, 271

Rob Shanahan: xi, 202, 203, 205, 206, 211, 220

Christian Stankee: xiv, 80 (top), 256, 258

Rick Foster: 1, 3, 7
To read Rick's tale of our travels, go to:
http://www.bmwbmw.org/forums/viewtopic.php?t=8693.

Greg Russell: 13, 14 (top), 15, 19, 71 (top), 158, 159, 293, 296

Brutus: 20, 28, 31, 32, 33, 36, 49 (both), 272, 279 (top), 280, 285, 286 (bottom), 287, 290

Mark Baddams: 44, 48

Andrew MacNaughtan: 50, 233, 238

Carrie Nuttall: 56 (top), 60, 141

Gino Ramacieri: 56 (bottom)

Matt Scannell: 59 (top), 137

David Burnette: 70 (top)

Dr. Richard Atkins: 84, 261

Brian Catterson: 77 (bottom)

Rebecca Truszkowski: 97, 98, 100, 101, 109

R. Andrew Lepley: 101

Lorne Wheaton: 104, 106

Charles de Serres: 153, 154

Craig M. Renwick: 155, 162, 163, 164, 167, 208 (enhancement), 212, 213, 215, 216, 218, 221, 223, 224, 225, 226, 230 (enhancement), 265

Jose Altonaga: 217, 221 (top)

Unknown: 227, 228

Courtesy Don Campbell: 229

Amanda Blake: 237

Arthur (Mac) McLear: 255

John Arrowsmith: 266

Kevin J. Anderson: 268

Also by Neil Peart

THE MASKED RIDER: Cycling in West Africa

GHOST RIDER: Travels on the Healing Road

TRAVELING MUSIC: The Soundtrack to My Life and Times

ROADSHOW: Landscape with Drums – A Concert Tour by Motorcycle